For my parents, Juan and Barbara

MEDIATED

*How the Media Shapes Your World
and the Way You Live in It*

THOMAS DE ZENGOTITA

BLOOMSBURY

NEW YORK · BERLIN · LONDON

Published by Bloomsbury Publishing, New York and London

All papers used by Bloomsbury Publishing are natural, recyclable products
made from wood grown in well-managed forests. The manufacturing
processes conform to the environmental regulations of the country of origin.

The Library of Congress has cataloged the hardcover edition as follows:

De Zengotita, Thomas.
Mediated : how the media shapes your world and the way you live in it /
Thomas de Zengotita.—1st U.S. ed.
p. cm.
ISBN 1-58234-357-8 (hardcover)
1. Mass media—Influence. I. Title.

P94.D393 2004
302.23—dc22
2004027564

Parts of this book first appeared in "Irony, Celebrity, and You," *The Nation*,
December 1996; "World World; or How I Learned to Stop Worrying and
Love the Blob," *Harper's Magazine*, July 2000; "The Numbing of the
American Mind," *Harper's Magazine*, April 2002; "The Romance of Empire,"
Harper's Magazine, July 2003.

Paperback ISBN-10: 1-59691-032-1
Paperback ISBN-13: 978-1-59691-032-4

First published in the United States by Bloomsbury Publishing in 2005
This paperback edition published in 2006

5 7 9 10 8 6

Typeset by Hewer Text Ltd, Edinburgh
Printed in the United States of America by Worldcolor Fairfield

CONTENTS

PREFACE

A CAVEAT TO all that follows, for the sake of simplicity and style, to save the text from endless qualifiers. The actual process of mediation is elaborate beyond imagining. It works differently for different people, in different places, at different times. I have tried to highlight some basic characteristics, but no generalization I make applies perfectly.

Most important, this acknowledgement: millions of human beings are trapped in realities so restrictive, so desperate, that the possibility of applying to them what I have to say in this book does not arise at all.

But the issue of the trend remains, for it is global. And so does the issue of mediated reality in relation to the immiseration of those millions, not as it is lived, but as it is experienced by the rest of us, by privileged citizens of the overdeveloped world who can choose to deal with it. Or not.

INTRODUCTION:
METHOD ACTING

ASK YOURSELF THIS: did members of the Greatest Generation spend a lot of time talking about where they were and what they did and how they felt when they first heard the news from Pearl Harbor? People certainly remembered the moment, and a few anecdotes got passed around—but did a whole folk genre spontaneously emerge? Did everyone feel compelled to craft a little narrative, starring me, an oft-repeated and inevitably embellished story-for-the-ages reporting on my personal experience of the Event? Or did they just assume that Pearl Harbor and its consequences were what mattered, and talk about *that*.

Well, where I was when JFK was assassinated was in the dance studio of an acting school in Manhattan. About thirty would-be actors and actresses were milling around the room in leotards, stretching, contemplating their mirror images, leaning against the walls, musing, chatting—waiting for our instructor to arrive. I was perched on a windowsill, looking out at the street. New York in autumn, when the world was young.

The studio door opened and, instead of the instructor, there appeared the assistant to the director of the school. She looked around, hesitating, groping for words, and finally just said, "President Kennedy has been shot. We don't yet know how serious it is." And then she left. There was some stirring and murmuring for a minute or so, a couple of people followed her out, and then someone, I couldn't tell who, said, "It's an improv."

1

Well. Ever hang out with really serious acting students? This was irresistible. We turned as one to consult our repertoire of methods, methods for accessing analogous memories, for identifying specific intentions, for sustaining internalized independent activities, for reacting rather than acting—we were all determined to "be in the moment," which was what one learned to do in those days, studying under Strasberg or Meisner or Adler, mentors to Geraldine Page and Robert Duvall, to Marlon Brando and James Dean, heirs to the prophet Stanislavsky, founder of modernist theater, who had scorned the external postures of "acting" and made inner truth, being real, the holy grail of his art. That was the point of all the strenuous psychological techniques known collectively as the Method, and we were devoted to them. So when, twenty minutes later, the assistant (who had been a talent in her day, we knew) returned to announce, her voice trembling, breaking, that the president was dead, well, at *that* point, the party really got started.

Acting students fall into two basic categories: the ones who love to do anger and the ones who love to do tears. I was the anger type, thank heaven, so there wasn't much in the way of overt emoting for me to do under this premise. I just lapsed into detached brooding, a fugue-state observing kind of thing. The situation didn't suit my talents; this was a moment for the impresarios of tears. And how they went at it. Within minutes, more than a third, almost half the people in the room were crying. Some were into silent weeping, sitting in a corner, maybe, uptilted face, the gaze averting now and then to rest at random on some stretch of ceiling where the pattern of the peeling paint signified the meaninglessness of it all. A couple of girls were crumpled to the floor, fallen to their knees, doing the helpless palms-turned-upward thing, keening like Electra over the corpse of Agamemnon. Still others linked up for communal shock and horror, for hugs and consolation and testimonials to Camelot. And so on.

Eventually one of the people who had left the room after the first announcement came back, caught on to what was happening, and began to set the record straight. The president was, in fact, dead. This was not an improvisation. Other people went to investigate. One came back with a transistor radio. Reality was reestablished.

I got out of there immediately. What I saw in those newly stricken faces, which had already looked about as stricken as faces can look, was more than I cared to see. Adjusting to this trick of fate, the actors were orders of magnitude more aware of themselves than usual—which is saying a lot—but aware also of a truth penetrating, looking for a virgin place to settle, looking for buttons to push that hadn't already been pushed. But to no avail. The embarrassment was excruciating, unique in my experience, before or since. It wasn't that we were exposed as phonies in the usual sense. Affectation and sincerity were not ultimately the issue. This went much deeper. It was the realization that there was nothing left, no level or nuance of feeling that hadn't become a resource for our enterprise of Method acting. It was the spiritual equivalent of the last step in the dark, the one that isn't there when you put your foot down. Coldhearted witness to the follies of humanity that I was, even then, I could not endure the spectacle. I felt sure we had all, in some subtle way, been damaged forever.

Okay, that's a special case—extreme, condensed, taut with ironic perfection. But it has stayed with me over the years, stimulated by more complicated cases that seemed somehow to echo that original. It was as if the day the actors mourned had established

3

a paradigm, as they (used to?) say, a pure standard to which messier manifestations of human reflexivity could only aspire. If you happen to be philosophically inclined, you might say those mourning actors exemplified a phenomenological essence, a perfect distillation of a defining quality.

I was reminded of them, for example, more recently, watching other mourners, assembled in their millions on the streets of London. Princess Diana's mourners, so many of them, so obviously exhibiting their grief, not even pretending that they weren't exhibiting it, understanding that this was their role, in both the sociological and theatrical sense, understanding that they were there for this purpose in service of the Global Show that their very presence was inciting, producing, and promoting in real time—a show about them "being in the moment" in what amounted to a worldwide improv. Celebrities all, celebrities at last.

And more than that. They also took control of the script, you recall, as they deployed their bouquets, batteries of floral cannon aimed at the gates of Buckingham Palace. This was, as one broadcaster (I think Jane Pauley) put it (not quite understanding the implications), a "people-driven story." The fact that stories usually aren't people driven suggests what was at stake. Those celebrity masses were, in effect, virtual revolutionaries. They were staking their claim to a new significance in public culture by means of a symbolic demand. They wanted Queen Elizabeth to step out from her antiquated privacy and away from her antiquated style of publicity too; they wanted her to join the New Britain in this new space, a space Di herself had done so much to cultivate, the way she fused premodern and postmodern forms of status, royalty and celebrity, so irresistibly into one figure, into one exalted, vulnerable, ruthlessly exposed life—yes, those InfoAge revolutionaries were forcing the queen into the kingdom that had been ruled by the "People's Princess," there to share with all and sundry, not her power or her wealth, but her feelings, like everybody else.

There is no direct parallel, obviously, no one-to-one correspondence, between the mourning actors and Di's funeral. But there's that common element, something like a hue, a tone. And I detect traces of that element, more elusively embedded, whenever I watch the bereaved on TV, the relatives and victims of every sort of mishap and disaster—I suppose I've seen, how many thousands over the years? Tens? Hundreds? But I always wonder, as I watch them in the glow—some for a passing moment, others turning grief into a worthy cause, taking up residence, launching a second life—I always wonder: what is this *doing* to you?

And it isn't just displays of grief that get enacted in this way. Take how athletes now celebrate themselves for scoring, for tackling, for making the play. And by extension, the way fans celebrate, not just the team or the victory, but themselves. There's that same element, that same quality, in the way those exhilarated men position themselves in front of each other, or the larger audience and the cameras, beefy faces alight with a peculiar blend of exultation and hostility, tendons bulging in their necks, fists pounding the air or curled tightly upward at the ends of crook-dangling arms, bodies thrust forward as if to bulldoze past all compromise, apparently frenzied, apparently berserk, bellowing in tones suggestive of profound vindication, bellowing, "Yeaauh! Yeaauh! Yeaauh!" And each "Yeauh" lifts above the preceding one, as if to reinforce it, but also to comment on it, even to parody it, and suddenly you realize, looking into their eyes, beaming out at friends and neighbors in the stands, you realize that this is also a performance, and a contest, a folk art—and oh so self-conscious after all.

And, by further extension, all the high-fiving and hissed-"Yes!"-pointing and thumbs-upping in the culture as a whole, in the continuous play of all the expressions and gestures that signify various degrees of, what shall we call it—triumphal intensity? The alchemy at work across that whole spectrum is, at bottom, just what we saw in grief over Di.

And that alchemy is today at work in every department of our experience.

This book traces modalities of that alchemy through the fabric of our lives, lives composed of an unprecedented fusion of the real and the represented, lives shaped by a culture of performance that constitutes a quality of being, a type of person—the mediated person.

So what made the difference? Why the emergence of that folk genre, the "where I was when the Event took place" story? Why *didn't* members of the Greatest Generation craft fables of their personal experiences of the Attack on America in 1941?

Because they weren't there, that's why. (There are other reasons too, but they are derivative, you'll see.) For starters, be assured that people who were physically at Pearl Harbor on the Day of Infamy *did* have stories of their personal experiences, and told them to each other, to reporters, in letters home—and repeated them as the years went by, be sure of that. Such stories are primal, anthropologically grounded. But people who just heard about Pearl Harbor on the radio and read about it in the papers didn't feel inclined to tell those stories because it didn't feel as if it had happened to them, personally, at all. At bottom, that's the difference. It's that simple.

One of the most popular public-service-type TV shows of the 1950s was *You Are There* (for reenactments of historical events).

The name sounds hokey now, because we take it for granted, but that was the original miracle of tele-vision. That's what blew the mind when it all began. Everyone became a participant/eyewitness to events on the world stage, past and present. And that's why people spontaneously told their stories about the Kennedy assassination, no matter where they were physically when it happened. They saw and heard it all unfold, not just on TV, of course—all the media were contributing, through every sensory channel—but TV was central, and Walter Cronkite was at the center of the center, and it was indeed as if you were there. Reams of coverage, endless coverage, amazing coverage—in a way *more* compelling than if you had been there physically, because virtually you were there from so many different perspectives. You weren't in one spot, the way you would have been if you were physically there, squashed behind a fat lady, looking in your purse for your sunglasses when the shots went off—you thought they were fireworks at first, until you heard the screaming. No, not like that: you were not there in one humble and limited spot; you were everywhere there, because that amazing coverage put you everywhere there, and more or less simultaneously to boot.

You had a sort of God's eye view.

This is a form of flattery so pervasive, so fundamental to the very nature of representation, that it has escaped notice, though it ultimately accounts for the much-remarked narcissism of our age. The flattered self is a mediated self, and the alchemy of mediation, the osmotic process through which reality and representation fuse, gets carried into our psyches by the irresistible flattery that goes with being incessantly addressed.

They say that the architecture and the landscaping at Versailles were originally designed to provide His Highness with various commanding vantage points, positions that made it seem as if the whole world were spread out before him, naked to his gaze.

That's peanuts compared to what mediation makes possible for all of us today.

At the most general conceptual level, *mediation* means dealing with reality *through* something else. Marshall McLuhan, God-father of Media Studies, thought of mechanical tools as media because, as artifacts that come between us and the given, they were "extensions of man," and so could be said to "mediate" in a certain sense. But this isn't an academic treatise. In this book, *mediation* refers to arts and artifacts that represent, that communicate—but also, and especially, to their effects on the way we experience the world, and ourselves in it.

Back to the JFK coverage, to those media resources that were devoted, to an unprecedented extent, to your personal experience of a historic event as it unfolded—some of that coverage became instantly iconic, you will recall. And it remained iconic through the decades, fodder for a lineage of Oliver Stones, recycled, recontextualized, reinterpreted endlessly, all those iconic images that had originally been so personally yours, brought to you (as they used to say) by the tube, brought to you in that atmosphere of special intimacy that binds you to the screen in your private space, when you are fully absorbed, when you are really into it. Those bovine Texas lawmen, sweating and squirming under their Stetsons—you could smell the fear and resentment, so out of their depth, ineptitude exposed, the dangerous, aimless anger. Jackie's bloody dress. Johnson's slab of a hand upheld to take the oath, chaos in the aisle behind him; were the Russians up to something? Was that why they were so frantic to swear him in? Johnson's eyelids drooping so—was he hiding something, or was he just exhausted? What did that expression mean exactly? Maybe nothing, maybe the camera just caught him in midblink. That happens sometimes; we all knew that because we were taking lots of pictures of ourselves by then. "Book depository," "grassy knoll"—you were there. You were there when Ruby shot Oswald, live, and if not live, you saw it over and over again afterward, and you knew it was live.

Knew it *was* live? Knew it was live over and over again? Reflect on grammar for a moment. And bear in mind: grammar goes deep, and grammar shapes conception, even perception.

You were there, everywhere there, over and over again, and you knew, over and over again, that it was live, except, of course, later on, when it was sometimes a scrupulously accurate fictional depiction of what was live or, in many cases, a splicing together of what was in fact live with a possibly really distorted fictional depiction of what was live.

The flattery implicit in representation may be irresistible, but it requires syntax torture, verging on logical contradiction, to describe the paradoxical conditions of life in a flood of imagery. The tangle of syntax gets so intricate it melts into a semantic blob (of which more anon). Saturation is partly responsible, but it only begins to tell the tale. It's not just our environment. Our minds are, as a matter of sheer quantitative fact, stocked with mediated entities too. Ask yourself: is there anything you do that remains essentially unmediated, anything you don't experience reflexively through some commodified representation of it? Birth? Marriage? Illness? Think of all the movies and memoirs, philosophies and techniques, self-help books, counselors, programs, presentations, workshops. Think of the fashionable vocabularies generated by those venues, and think of how all this conditions your experience. Ask yourself: if I were to strip away all those influences, could I conceive of my life?

Of course, for most of us there are still a few things that are just what they are. Maybe you still buy pencils or paper clips just to use, and not because of what they represent, what they say about you. Maybe you have a nice little relationship with your feet, rubbing them together under the blankets or picking at a callus on your toe. A few things. Precious few.

What it comes down to is this: Di's mourners were truly grieving *and* they were performing. Immersed in a world continuously represented from every angle, they understood Di's death as an opportunity to play a significant role in it, to represent themselves at levels of prominence usually reserved for the celebrated. But they already knew how to *be* representational.

That's because the same dynamic operates in anonymous daily lives. For example, let's say you've been in marital therapy. Let's say it was successful. Maybe group therapy, with role playing. Let's say you learned techniques in that therapy and from books, techniques for keeping channels of communication open, for owning your behavior, for constructive arguing. And you applied them, with your partner, and it saved your marriage, let's say, and that's a good thing, no question. But it is also a very mediated thing.

It's no accident that therapeutic techniques in general are so akin to the Method developed at the Actors Studio. Getting in touch with your feelings is the aim in both settings. And getting in touch with your feelings is a reflexive process that transforms the immediate into the mediated. You learn, through that process, how to have your feelings, how to express your feelings—which means: how to perform them.

So there is a self-consciousness, a reflexivity about you that makes your parents or grandparents look like automatons by comparison. Wonderful people they are, or may have been, but compared to you—utterly without perspective on themselves. And that puts you on the continuum with Di's mourners. We are all method actors now.

If the marital therapy example doesn't work for you, read on. The mediated world is capacious. Its middle names are Diverse and Inclusive. There's room for everybody and everything.

But remember. The issue is no longer representation versus reality, phony versus authentic, artificial versus natural. That was for nineteenth-century Romantics to worry about. A few existentialists and a bunch of hippies tried to revive those concerns in the twentieth century, but we know what happened to them. We've read the books, heard the music, seen the movies—and the remakes. But there is no going back to reality just as there is no going back to virginity. We have been consigned to a new plane of being engendered by mediating representations of fabulous quality and inescapable ubiquity, a place where everything is addressed to us, everything is for us, and nothing is beyond us anymore.

CHAPTER 1

Intimations of your real place in the great scheme of things. Whatever. It's all about options—and they are all about you. No limits. You are totally free to choose because it doesn't really matter what you choose. **Learning to love the Blob.** *Deconstruction and shopping (not buying, just shopping; maybe leasing).*

Recalling the Real

ALMOST NOTHING, anyway.

Say your car breaks down in the middle of nowhere—the middle of Saskatchewan, say. You have no radio, no cell phone, nothing to read, no gear to fiddle with. You just have to wait. Pretty soon you notice how everything around you just happens to be there. And it just happens to be there in this very precise but unfamiliar way. You are *so* not used to this. Every tuft of weed, the scattered pebbles, the lapsing fence, the cracks in the asphalt, the buzz of insects in the field, the flow of cloud against the sky, everything is very specifically exactly the way it is—and none of it is for you. Nothing here was designed to affect you. It isn't arranged so that you can experience it, you didn't plan to experience it, there isn't any screen, there isn't any display, there isn't any entrance, no brochure, nothing special to look at, no dramatic scenery or wildlife, no tour guide, no campsites, no benches, no paths, no viewing platforms with natural-historical information posted under slanted Plexiglas lectern things—whatever is there is just there, and so are you. And your options are limited. You begin to get a sense of your real place in the great scheme of things.

Very small.

Some people find this profoundly comforting. Wittgenstein, for example.

So that's a baseline for comparison. What it teaches us is this: in a mediated world, the opposite of real isn't phony or illusional or fictional—it's optional. Idiomatically, we recognize this when we say, "The reality is . . . ," meaning something that has to be dealt with, something that isn't an option. We are most free of mediation, we are most real, when we are at the disposal of accident and necessity. That's when we are not being addressed. That's when we go without the flattery intrinsic to representation.

Surfing the Options

But haven't things in people's lives always carried some message? Hasn't culture always filtered reality in some way and addressed people through representations of some kind—ranging from the categories built into a particular language to, say, symbolic insignia of rank and affiliation?

Sure. But *being aware of that* is new. This crucial point must be grasped and retained. Awareness of "culture" was once the prerogative of a very few reflective individuals. In the postmodern world it is common sense. In that awareness, the ethos of mediation is established. Academics express all this in a jargon about the social construction of race and gender—and of truth and value in general. But mediated people everywhere know that identity and lifestyle are constructs, something to *have*. The objects and places and mannerisms that constitute our life-world are *intentionally* representational. What cultures traditionally provided was taken-for-granted custom, a form of necessity—hence of reality. Options are profoundly, if subtly, different, and so are the people who live among and through them.

And this holds even if you never exercise those options, even if you cling to some tradition. You know you *could* be different, and so, perhaps, you cling more desperately. Fanaticisms flourish in an atmosphere of unlimited choice.

But most people are cool with it. At least in the blue states. And Europe.

The slang expression "whatever" distills the essential situation into a single gesture. It arose and caught on because it captures so precisely, yet so flexibly, the Janus-faced attitude we assume as we negotiate the field of options that so incessantly solicit our attention and allegiance.

On the one hand, it's a party, a feast, an array of possible experiences more fabulous than monarchs of the past could even dream of—it's "whatever," as in yippee!, as in *whatever* you want, whatever you can imagine; you can eat whatever, see whatever, hear whatever, read whatever, even *be* whatever. "No limits," as the SUV and Internet ads all promise.

On the other hand, an environment of representations yields an aura of surface—as in "surf." *It is a world of effects.* This is another existential consequence of the fact that representations address us by design. We are at the center of all the attention, but there is a thinness to things, a smoothness, a muffled quality—it's all insulational, as if the deities of Dreamworks were laboring invisibly around us, touching up the canvas of reality with digital airbrushes. Everything has the edgeless flowing feel of computer graphics, like the lobby of a high-end Marriott/Ramada/Shera-ton—the sculptured flower arrangements, that glowy, woody, marbly, purply, cushioned-air quality. Every gadget aspires to that iPod look—even automobiles. The feel of the virtual is over-flowing the screens, as if the plasma were leaking into the physical world. Whole neighborhoods feel like that now, even when you're standing in the street.

Especially "historic" neighborhoods. It's as if the famous ones—like Baltimore's Inner Harbor and Quincy Market, parts of York and Canterbury—have all been subjected to the renovating ministrations of the same giant company with one idea, the Red Brick, Gray Stone, and Iron Filigree Restoration Corporation. And as for little towns and villages with some claim—*any* claim—on our attention, well, I wish I had the copyright for those signs, painted in Ralph Lauren green or blue with the gold trim and the gold inlay of Gothic script. I mean, how did so many people in so many places decide to hang those out at the same time? Was that Martha Stewart's fault too?

Even what's left of the wilderness can have this virtual feel (see chapter 6). It's as if nature were succumbing to all the times it has been depicted in travel tales and adventure movies and nature shows, to all the times it has been toured and photographed and otherwise used—not, in this case, for raw material, but to provide an experience.

Here's a measure of how far into the natural realm virtualization has penetrated—one of my favorites, cross-indexed under Subtle. At the little zoo in Prospect Park, Brooklyn, one building is given over to a sequence of exhibits that illustrate the concept of an ecological niche—you know, flora and fauna from a rain forest, an Alpine meadow, a desert, a wetland, etc. Very educational. Perfect place for bio students on a field trip. And guess what the Prospect Park Zoo calls the building that houses this exhibit?

"The Hall of Animal Lifestyles."

I just love that one. Options everywhere—even animals have options.

And that's why, like so many expressions of mediation, the "whatever" gesture is a dialectic. As reality and representation fuse into a field of options, opposing tendencies arise like shadows. Haunting the moment of "I can experience whatever I want" is the moment of "What difference does it make," because this moment, the moment of the shrug, is essential to our mobility among the options.

We need mobility among the options because they are only representations.

And that means they are no more than they appear to be.

And so they are never enough.

And that's why more is on the way. Always. That's why trailers are better than movies. That's why you are always already ready for the next show, even before this one is over. That's why, in the midst of a fabulous array of historically unprecedented and utterly mind-boggling stimuli—whatever.

So mobility among the options in a virtualized environment gives to human freedom a new and ironic character. You are completely free to choose because it doesn't matter what you choose. That's why you are so free. Because it doesn't matter. How cool is that?

This is another source of virtualization's edgeless quality. It's as if you live in a nested set of consoles, each with its own Undo and Rewind buttons. The notorious disposability of commodities is an aspect of this, of course, but, in a mediated world, disposability goes way beyond the physical. This isn't just about paper cups and plastic bottles and Pampers. Take relationships (see chapter 5). The word "committed" now means something like "throw your whole self into it and hope it works out." As opposed to "for better or worse, no matter what," which is what it used to mean.

So the real world, dissolving into optionality, is reconstituting itself on a plane that transcends ancient solidities of nature and custom, craft and industry. The whole process, of which we have just afforded glimpses, has been accelerating since the invention of modern communication technologies (telegraph, photograph, telephone), and it crossed a qualitative threshold in the past couple of decades, with the rise of the new media. At the same time, there has been a convergence of the digital and the biogenetic that will lead eventually to a full-blown merger between the real and the representational in every department of our lives.

Here's the basic situation: On the one hand, there's the World Wide Web, satellite-cable TV, Palm Pilots, DVD, Ethernet—virtual environments everywhere. On the other hand, cloning, genetic engineering, biotech, and also AI, robotics, nanotech—and that adds up to virtual beings everywhere.

Optional environments, optional creatures. Made for each other (see chapter 7).

When people (or whatever they are) look back on our time, all this will appear as a single development. It will be called something like the "Information Revolution," and the lesson of that revolution will be this: what counts is the code. Digital or DNA, they are both susceptible to mediation, to human control of what the code expresses. It doesn't matter what the platform is made of, as long as the program runs. Silicon or carbon based. Artifact or animate. The difference between them is disappearing. This is not science fiction. This is happening. Right now, for example, in an Atlanta hospital, there is a quadriplegic with his brain directly wired up to a computer. He can move the cursor with his thoughts.

I don't know if he can click.

Yet.

In Denial

Some people refuse to accept the fact that reality is becoming indistinguishable from representation in a qualitatively new way. They find permanent refuge in the belief that nothing is new under the sun. They already understand what they need to understand in order to understand everything else. These same people tend to think it's deep to talk about historical pendulums swinging back and forth. Anyway, they never fail to remind us at some point, in that special perhaps-I'm-missing-something tone, as if reluctant to spoil the speculative fun, they never fail to remind us that there have always been representations and choices and etc., etc., and isn't what's going on now just more of the same?

Beliefs like that are crude denials of the psychological processes that actually determine how we function. Really fat people believe they are on the stocky side. Abject drunks believe they are poetical free spirits. Malicious prudes believe they are selfless do-gooders. And a lot of people still believe that, with some obvious exceptions involving hoaxes and errors, we know what's real and what's not. We can tell the difference between the loss of the *Kursk*, that Russian sub, and *Titanic* (meaning, the movie, of course), for example.

And maybe we can—when specifically focused on the issue. We can comb through daily experience, identifying and quantifying degrees of fabrication and orders of representation quite easily. It might take awhile, of course, because there *are* so many gradations when you stop to think about it. For example:

> **Real real**: You fall down the stairs. Stuff in your life that's so familiar you've forgotten the statement it makes.
> **Observed real**: You drive by a car wreck. Stuff in your life where the image-statement is as salient as the function.
> **In-between real real and observed real**: Stuff that oscillates between the first two categories depending on the situation. Like, you're wearing something you usually take for granted, but then you are introduced to someone attractive.
> **Edited real real**: Shtick you have down so pat you don't know it's shtick anymore, but you definitely only use it in certain

situations. Documentaries and videos of all kinds where people are unaware of the camera, although that's not easy to detect, actually. Candid photographs.

Edited observed real: Other people's down-pat shtick. Shtick of your own when you are still working on it. Documentaries and videos where people are accommodating the camera, which is a lot of the time, probably.

Staged real: Events like weddings and formal parties. Retail clerk patter. Politicians on talk shows.

Edited staged real: Pictures of the above. Homemade porn.

Staged observed real unique: Al kisses Tipper. *Survivor*.

Staged observed real repeated: Al kisses Tipper again and again. Anchor desk and talk show intros and segues. Weather channel behavior.

In the interest of time, we can skip the subtler middle range of distinctions and go to the other end of the spectrum:

Staged realistic: Movies and TV shows like *The English Patient* and *NYPD*.

Staged hyperreal: Oliver Stone movies and *Malcolm in the Middle*.

Overtly unreal realistic: SUVs climbing up the sides of buildings. Digitized special effects in general, except when they are more or less undetectable.

Covertly unreal realistic: The models' hair in shampoo ads. More or less undetectable digital effects, of which there are more and more every day.

In-between overtly and covertly unreal realistic: John Wayne in a contemporary beer ad (because you have to know he's dead in order to know he isn't "really" in the ad, whatever that means).

Real unreal: Robo-pets.

Unreal real: Strawberries that won't freeze because they have fish genes in them.

See? No problem. The differences are perfectly clear.

But the issue isn't *can* we do it; it's *do* we do it—and the answer is, of course not. How could we? The perceptual and cognitive categories and rhythms of action we live by are determined by a daily experience completely saturated with these entities.

Take the new Times Square, everybody's favorite icon for the virtualization process, because that's where what is happening in the culture as a whole is so effectively distilled and intensified. All the usual observations apply—and each observation contributes its iota to muffling what it was intended to expose, including this one, my little contribution, which consists of noticing how everything in that place is *aimed*. Everything is firing message modules, straight for your gonads, your taste buds, your vanities, your fears. But it's okay; these modules seek to penetrate, but in a passing way; it's all in fun. A second of your attention is all they ask. Nothing real is firing, nothing that rends or cuts. It's a massage, if you just relax and go with it. And why not? Some of the most talented people on the planet have devoted their lives to creating this psychic sauna, just for you.

And it's not just the screens and billboards, the literal signs; it's absolutely everything you encounter. Except for the eyes of the people, shuffling along, and the poignant imperfections of their bodies; they are so manifestly unequal to the solicitations lavished upon them. No wonder they stuff themselves with junk—or, trying to live up to it all, enslave themselves to regimes of improvement. The flattery of representation has a downside, as we shall see—for the flattered self is spoiled. It never gets enough. It feels unappreciated. It whines a lot. It wants attention.

Yes, there were ersatz environments and image-driven commodities and glitzy ads back in the 1950s, say, but this is something else entirely. Saying that it's just more of what we had before is like saying a hurricane is just more breeze. So you need to ask yourself this: do you parse the real from the fabricated in that mélange? Not *can* you, but *do* you? The Fox screen is showing an Afghan woman learning to read—real or not? Posed? Candid? Some glorious babe in her underwear is sprawled across 35 percent of your visual field. She's looking you right in the eye. You get that old feeling—real or not? A fabulous man, sculpted to perfection by more time in the health club than most parents have for their kids, is gliding by on Day-Glo roller blades eight inches high. He's wearing Tex-Tex gear so tight it looks like it's under his skin, and the logos festooning his figure emit meaning-beeps from every angle—real or not? What about the pumped-up biceps? If he uses steroids? But, once again, the issue isn't what you *can* do when I call your attention to it. Then you can be reassured—you can say, "Hey, okay, cool. I see what you mean but I still know the difference." Not the point. The real issue is *do* you make the distinction as a matter of routine processing? Or do you rely instead on a generalized immunity that puts the whole flood in brackets and transforms it all into a play of surfaces—over which you hover and glide like a little god, dipping in here and there for the experience of your choice, the ultimate reaches of your soul on permanent remote.

The Moreness of Everything

For small groups of privileged people there have always been style choices, entertainment choices, experience choices, of course. But slower to change—and fewer, far fewer. In kind and number. And this matters, because here we collide with a real limit, one of the only ones that remain, a limit to which even today's modes of cultural production must submit—namely, how much the screen of human consciousness can register at a given moment. No innovation in techno-access or sensationalism can overcome this bottleneck. It determines the fundamental dynamic of our public culture: the battle for your attention.

Compare, say, the cereal and juice sections of a supermarket today with one of thirty years or so ago. For you youngsters out there, take it from Dad: it used to be Wheaties, Corn Flakes, Cheerios (oats), Rice Krispies—and that was about it. One for each grain, see? Ditto, fruit juice. But now? Would you prefer pineapple-banana-grape or strawberry-orange-kiwi? And that's just a sample of the mixes from Tropicana—check out Nantucket Nectars'. Makes of cars? Types of sunglasses? Sneaker species? Pasta possibilities? On and on.

The business types understand all this. Umbrella brand names toss off diverse and evolving lines of market-researched products for targeted niches of self-inventing customers who have continual access to every representational fabrication ever produced in the whole of human history. That's "the environment," as they say. Vedic ankle tattoos anyone? Nineteen thirties cockney caps? Safari jackets? Inca ponchos? Victorian lace-up high-heel booties? Anything you can think of, you can have. If you can afford it.

The moreness of everything ascends inevitably to a threshold in psychic life. A change of state takes place. The discrete display of options melts into a pudding—and what I will call the Blob, usually a metaphorical entity, shimmers into visibility at this moment, the moment when you stand a-mazed before the vast display at the MegaStore.

Under these conditions, the mind is forced to certain adaptations, if it is to cohere at all. So, for example, when you hear statistics about AIDS in Africa for the 349th time, or see your 927th picture of a weeping fireman or an oil-drenched seabird, you can't help but become fundamentally indifferent—unless it happens to be "your issue," of course, one you "identify with," a social responsibility option you have chosen. Otherwise, you glide on, you have to, because you are exposed to things like this all the time. *All the time.* Over breakfast. In the waiting room. Driving to work. At the checkout counter. All the time.

I know you know this already. I'm just reminding you.

Which is not to say you are never moved. On the contrary, you are moved, often deeply, very frequently. You are entirely accustomed, actually, to being moved—by footage, by stories, by representations of all kinds. That's the point. Often you glide by, but sometimes you weep. You weep at movies, you weep at live coverage of 9/11 ceremonies, you weep when you hear "The Star-Spangled Banner" or when you hear Martin Luther King invoking his dream in a PBS documentary. I once found myself, alone in a motel room (admittedly at a vulnerable moment in my life), weeping over the "like a rock" lyric in a Chevy truck commercial.

It's not your fault that you are so used to being so moved; you just are. You spend a great deal of money and time accessing what moves you. You are a connoisseur of what moves you. So it's not surprising that you learn to move on to the next, sometimes moving, moment. As a mediated person, you know that your relations with the moving will pass, and the stuffed screen accommodates your adaptation to it by providing moving surfaces that assume you are mobile enough to accommodate them. And so on, back and forth, back and forth, everywhere at once, all day, all night, innumerable vibrations, back and forth, myriad capillaries of individuated mediational transactions engulfing the planet.

One might say, "Well, people didn't respond deeply to every

dramatic development in the world two hundred years ago either." And that's true, but it isn't an objection; it's a confirmation. To begin with, until these media came along, people didn't even *know* about such developments, or not as quickly, and above all, not as dramatically or frequently. Also, there weren't as many developments, period. This is a crucial factor, another aspect of just plain moreness that gets overlooked. *Less was happening.* And what was happening was happening slower, and most of it didn't reach beyond those immediately involved.

The contrast is stark with, say, the Middle Ages. By the industrial era, a lot more was happening, obviously, and the possibility of overload became an issue then. Think of Baudelaire, adrift in the city crowd, celebrating the artist for maintaining vulnerability in that chaos of stimulation, setting the standard for the genius of modernism. But a qualitative threshold has been breached since then. Cities no longer belong to the soulful flaneur, but to the wired-up voyeur in his soundproof Lexus. Behind his tinted windows, with his cell phone and CDs, he gets more input, with less static, from more channels, than Baudelaire ever dreamed of.

The Blob

Okay, for those of you who find the term "postmodern" really annoying because you still can't figure out what the hell it means—it basically means the whole situation I've been describing. The term is frustrating because it seems to depend on what it isn't for its meaning, but the expression won't go away because, in fact, it means much more—too much more. A historical development as vast and various as this one is just plain hard to characterize positively, hard to imagine as a whole. For years I've been looking for the phrase that gets it right, the high-concept expression so dear to the heart of the pitchmeister. I've never quite managed it, but for a revealing reason. The problem with trying to comprehend the process of mediation is that you can't get outside it. It is like a shadow that expends no energy and makes no effort, yet never falters. Perpetual reflexivity is a haunting.

So I've taken to filing it all under the Blob, just informally, for casual reference purposes. The heck with trying to name the incomprehensible, so fall back on a pop culture joke, right? How familiar is that move?

(*The Blob*, 1958, Steve McQueen's breakout flick. Several sequels, plus, of course, on *Comedy Central*'s *Mystery Science Theater 3000* you can watch the witty host and his robo-companions watching the movie. And if you want, you can tape yourself and a witty companion watching them watching the movie and then watch that. Not that you would, but you could.)

After a while I began to see virtue in the name. It isn't much of a metaphor because it's so inexact, and that began to seem like the point. Anything more specific couldn't possibly do justice to mediation precisely because it proceeds so variously. It works on a case-by-case-by-case basis. It comes from all directions and no direction. Nothing is too great or too small for its textured ministrations. Its elasticity is without limit, its osmotic processes calibrated to enfold the tiniest, most private gestures of your secret life and contain your sense of the universe and the meaning of love and death as well.

Perhaps you bridle. Perhaps you believe that you have retained sharpness and edge? I doubt it. The Blob will not tolerate edges—though "edgy" is fine; perhaps you are edgy, that's very possible. The Blob invented edgy. Edgy is one of the Blob's most active digestive enzymes.

Once in a while, in the public realm, some eruption of fate or evil—9/11, obviously, but also, say, a school shooting, the abuse at

Abu Ghraib, the hostage beheadings, something like that—will feel as if it might be sharp enough, as if it might pierce the membrane and slice the pulp, as if it might at least *interrupt* the Blob's progress through the universe.

But no. Watch as the media antibodies swarm to the scene of those nascent interruptions. These are the junctures that require the most coverage—and the latent meaning, the ironic dialectic implicit in that word emerges. What must be *covered* is any event or person or deed that might challenge the Blob with something like a limit, something the Blob cannot absorb, something that could, in resistance or escape, become the one thing the omnitolerant Blob cannot allow, something outside it, something unmediated—something real.

But not to worry. The Blob may have to devote some extra time and energy to these challenges, but in the end it prevails. And how is the moment of its victory marked? By your indifference. That's the signal to move on, the signal for the Next Thing to appear. That's when the original being of the real thing has been fully mediated. It becomes representational, and that means optional. You can turn it off, or on. It's up to you again. The Blob is sated. The thing-that-would-be-real has been digested and incorporated. It no longer threatens to be anything *else*.

The Hard Part

The basic themes and concepts have been given, along with a general sense of how they work. The central notions representational flattery and optionality's role in the virtualization process— are, so far as I know, original, but they synthesize ideas that have been out there for a long time, in the work of McLuhan, and in Ong, Lasch, Boorstin, Postman, Harvey, Sennett, Lapham, Gitlin,

Rifkin, Rushkof, Gabler, not to mention Baudrillard and Eco and DeBord and all of them. If this were an academic treatise, I would have to parcel out a lot of credit.

These ideas are not difficult, taken individually. The trick is bearing them in mind together. This "bearing in mind" of aspects has been essential to phenomenology since Husserl, and it takes some practice. But the truly hard part, in this case, is evaluation, the ethical-political judgment piece.

On balance, is pervasive mediation a good thing or a bad thing?

One reason it is so important to get over the issue of real versus artificial/phony and focus on real versus optional is that if we don't get clear on that, we'll never see the problem of evaluation for what it is. We are coming up to a chapter on childhood, so here's an illustration that anticipates that topic.

Nowadays, when I watch little kids (in certain neighborhoods) at play, I have to laugh. Bike helmets that could deflect a bazooka shell. Knee pads. Elbow pads. The playgrounds are padded too. Big rubber tiles carpet the whole space and all the equipment is rounded wood or plastic—nary an edge or a point to be found. Sometimes I think, yikes, where does this end? Why not just live in a bubble and be done with it?

Nostalgia for the real, they call it—in this case, nostalgia for the days when kids (especially boys) over the age of, say, eight, pretty much ran free. No one ever heard of a bike helmet, and injuries of all kinds were the assumed risks of childhood. In a way, you were supposed to get hurt, practically expected to break your arm at least once. The general idea was that this was part of learning to make your way in the world.

I get that nostalgia, but when it comes down to what I would *do* if I were the parent of a young child today—well, that's a horse of another color, as my mother used to say. Now that I know about bike helmets, now that they are an option, it would be downright irresponsible not to strap one on little Justin's head before he takes off along the (very uneven, quite treacherous, actually, I never noticed before) sidewalk on his razor scooter, wouldn't it? Imagine the guilt if he suffered a serious but avoidable injury. No, no, it looks sort of silly, a bit too precious; no doubt it's boomer narcissism run amok, all these kids being treated like hemophiliac heirs to the throne of the Hapsburgs—and we haven't even begun with educational mobiles from Baby Einstein dangling over *Consumer Reports*—approved cribs and self-esteem camps and Ritalin and all the rest. Easy to mock, but the point is—and this is how it works across the board—you end up opting for these options because, on balance, it's better than not opting for them.

I remember when health clubs began to appear. The first few times I saw rows of people on those cardio machines, pumping and peddling so furiously, sweat dripping, faces etched with determination, all working so intently—*and going absolutely nowhere*—I thought, this sums it up, this is the most ridiculous display of . . . of . . . something, hard to say exactly what, but something very definite and symptomatic. Imagine what it would look like to people who put out this kind of energy doing necessary things, like getting in the crop, hauling in the catch, reaching winter pasture. On the cardio machines, you're not even trying to score points or goals, it's not even a game. You are just pushing and puffing and straining on a machine very specifically and expensively designed for you to push and puff and strain on, and for nothing else. How weird is that? So ingrown. A sculpture of reflexivity.

Of course, what eventually happened is that I became one of those people, and now I barely give it a thought. Three or four days a week, there I am on the StairMaster, climbing, climbing—climbing nowhere. Because it is so convenient, after all, and it's a good workout, you can't deny that, and I get some reading done at the same time, and the truth is my legs can't take jogging on cement anymore, and bike riding in the city, with all the traffic and the fumes, is very unpleasant—to me at least, obviously some people are into it, and more power to them; that's *their* choice.

And so on, across the whole spectrum of options. Call it the Justin's Helmet Principle. The dynamic of evaluation goes like this: to begin with, an aesthetic sense that something is amiss; then the realization that you can't pin down exactly what the problem is, while the advantages are obvious—and that queasy feeling will subside in time.

Take a more extreme example, same dynamic, just more intense. This is an option the biotech folks are anticipating you will have in the not-too-distant future: you can have a clone of yourself—minus the brain, just the body—kept alive in a vat. The idea is that you will be able to harvest the organs from it as your own wear out. No more rejection issues in transplants. No more agonized waiting for that kidney.

Now, this is an unsettling prospect for most people to contemplate, at least at first. But scrutinize it. Why not? We already do transplants routinely. We've tried pig organs in humans. We froze Ted Williams whole. We supported partial-birth abortions where the brain gets vacuumed out of the skull. So what's wrong with this clone organ-farm idea, given what we already do? No one's forcing it on anyone, don't forget. It's just an option. And once they start doing it, you'll get used to it. It's just that first image of this brainless living body that looks exactly like you floating in a vat, that's what got to you for a minute—but people used to feel the same way about using cadavers to teach anatomy. Just superstition, when you think about it. Right?

And what applies to these particulars applies to the entire

process as well. Evaluation of the whole is slippery in the same way. Because the fact of the matter is that Disneyfication and diversity, say, are indissoluble aspects of the same gigantic phenomenon. It makes no sense, in the end, to be "for" one and "against" the other in any sort of an ideological way. You can't have those inspiring CD-ROMs on the civil rights movement without Jerry Bruckheimer war movies. You can't expect to accommodate Latino culture without a talking Chihuahua in a Che beret. Kermit the Frog gives college commencement addresses *because* no dominant discourse now determines value—*and* vice versa.

And so on. The key fact is this: *you* can pick and choose among the options—*you* can refuse to own a TV and spend all your time reading Proust (not that you would, but you could)—because *all* the options are out there. At some level, you accept this, and that is why evaluation of the whole is ultimately swamped with ambivalence as well.

Or would be, if people were clear about the issue. But many are able to avoid this ultimate ambivalence because of the fact that millions of people in this world live in utter misery, with little or no media and very few options, and the corporate interests that propel economic globalization are responsible for much of that misery—and are *also* the producers of mediated culture (see chapter 4). So it can seem to make sense to reject Big Macs and Jerry Springer, but not sushi and Salman Rushdie, on something like aesthetic grounds, while still holding the huge conglomerates to account politically. You can blame them for the vulgar options *and* for the misery of those left out of, or damaged by, the whole process.

But the truth is that sushi and Salman Rushdie are also brought to us by globalization, and the *ultimate* evaluational question about pervasive mediation doesn't arise *unless you assume that economic globalization has made room for everyone, and media culture is universal.*

Pretend this is a forced-choice exercise in a values' clarification workshop. Nietzsche was willing to judge history aesthetically, willing to sacrifice the herd and all its works to higher specimens and their lofty enterprises, but are you? Suppose the "objective conditions of history" (remember them?) are forcing this choice upon you: not socialism versus capitalism or civilized versus vulgar, but mediated options for all versus continuing human misery on a massive scale. Suppose, in other words, that universal material well-being could be achieved and the environment protected, but only at the cost of having everything virtualized and everybody mediated—every person on earth immersed in the flattering field of commodified options that only some of us enjoy today. Just suppose. What would you decide?

Of course. It's just like the bike helmet for Justin.

Incidentally, now you can see why destabilizing fixed categories and opening up multiple readings was all the rage at the university. Deconstruction was the academic equivalent of shopping. Perpetually entertaining options among undecidables, exercising them provisionally, in accordance with a context and the needs of the moment—that's intellectual shopping. One may lease, as it were, a reading, but one never buys, for interpretations are bound to multiply, and no definitive documentation, no historical condition or authorial intent, will ever secure a settled meaning and resolve the play of language—any more than the purpose of soap or shoes can restrain the way commodities are packaged and marketed as representations of something or other, or the way you construct yourself over time by choosing among all these options—soap, shoes, health practices, readings, relationships, careers, whatever.

CHAPTER 2

Ironic Parenting. **The cult of the child.** *From Peter Pan to Harry Potter. Goodnight Moon, Hello Holden. From* Leave It to Beaver *to* The Simpsons. *Where the Wild Things Were. Learning to be yourself. Why you have to learn that, because it's a weird concept when you think about it. Anyway, whoever you are, you are very special and, hopefully, very nice and, if so, you deserve to live in MeWorld.*

A Collective Memoir

REMEMBER THE 1950s? I literally remember the 1950s, but you remember them too, even if you're only, say, twenty-nine. And that's interesting, because there is no way I remember the decades when my parents grew up, no way I remember that era the way my kids remember the 1950s, even though they were born in the late 1970s and early 1980s.

Sure, I heard stories from my parents about their childhood experiences; more stories, and more elaborately and frequently told, than those I've told my kids, who had so much more to attend to than I ever did. After all, when I was a boy and the family went on car trips, I didn't get to snuggle down in Walkman privacy in order to escape the exquisitely specific tortures of parental companionship—the way they address you so earnestly when it's family time, the lame attempts at humor, the habitual affectations and maddening intonations. The agony of it. I used to ask for stories, just to get away from them.

The thing about stories being that, when they told them, they *weren't* addressing me directly; they would get lost in the telling, musing on their lives—much more comfortable all around. Looking back, I now realize that the stories they told could have happened anytime, that the focus was always on people and events, never on atmosphere, style, cultural texture. There was no period feeling. Once in a while, they would say something like "Of course, in those days, not that many people had a car . . ." or "In those days, refrigerators weren't electric. There was an iceman who . . ." and that certainly had an impact. But it didn't come close to reruns of fifties sitcoms for capturing an ambience. Or all those movies they make nowadays that so scrupulously reconstruct the furnishings of those years. Not to mention old news footage and documentaries.

I mean, if you are over fifty, consider how little you know of popular culture in your parents' day. Rudy Vallee? Was he somebody? Something about "Mairsy Doats" and "Dozy Doats"? Charlie Chaplin and W. C. Fields?—but they seem to exist in their own timeless universe. Really jerky black-and-white film showing flappers dancing and Woodrow Wilson in a top hat (and a pince-nez?) riding in a big square car? Packard? Roadster?—are those car types? Duesenberg?

Fragments like that is what you have, and arrayed at random, a little heap of them, no context.

But my nineteen-year-old son knows more about the Beatles and Bob Dylan than I do, and not only their music but their lives too. Youth culture is representational through and through, and it has been moving in that direction since the 1950s, and so the whole cultural trajectory has been preserved and is continuously recycled. It is perpetual. Elvis lives. My daughter gives me mix tapes for my birthday and she'll include something by the Drifters, maybe, or the Indigo Girls (with their 1960s style) but also a Spanish (!)

version of Roy Orbison's "Crying," recycled courtesy of David Lynch in his ethnographically meticulous *Mulholland Drive*. And so on.

"Mix" is the word! Make your own—anything. Out of anything.

But she doesn't make these choices just because she wants to get old music for Dad. It's all part of *her* cache. My kids can distinguish instantly between 1970s movies and 1960s movies; they have a feel for the hairstyles, the outfits, the manners and settings, all the little conventions that marked those decades as they came and went. They can even feel nostalgia for the 1950s.

They can feel nostalgia for times they never lived through.

That's how much a part of the contemporary environment representations have become. And that's why it is possible to have a media memoir of the past few decades that is collective, that works in various ways for people of all ages, whether or not they lived through those decades physically. We've all lived through them virtually.

How long can that continuity go on? Probably not indefinitely; it will likely turn out to be an effect that could only attach to the dawn of this age. A hundred years from now, presumably, people will not have a gut feeling for the way the 1960s emerged from the 1950s, for the moment captured in a movie like *American Graffiti*. By then there will be too much on the representational record, too much to process genealogically. Already, there are signs of collapse into synchronic pastiche (see chapter 7).

Ironic Parenting

The philosopher Richard Rorty is widely admired among academics for his understanding of the transition from modern to postmodern. He distinguishes between a "liberal metaphysic" (e.g., the modern belief in natural rights) and a "liberal ironism" (e.g., the postmodern defense of such rights, minus the belief that they are natural). He thinks high-culture types can uphold such values while ironizing them in the general sense—putting them in quotes, as it were, understanding that they are social constructions. But Rorty doubts that the masses can handle this—and the reason he gives has to do with parenting. He says he can't imagine "a culture whose public rhetoric is ironist . . . a culture which socialized its children in such a way as to make them constantly dubious about their own process of socialization."

Where has Professor Rorty *been*?

I guess he never saw T-shirts that read BECAUSE I'M THE MOMMY, THAT'S WHY or bumper stickers on the Winnebagos that proclaim AVENGE YOURSELF; LIVE LONG ENOUGH TO BE A BURDEN ON YOUR CHILDREN or watched *Beavis and Butt-head*, *Married with Children*, *My So-Called Life*, *Clarissa Explains It All*, *Rugrats*, *South Park*, *Malcolm in the Middle*—the list goes on and on. I guess he never saw the Chevy Chase *Vacation* movies, and he must have missed the entire oeuvre of *Nick at Nite* retro television, which, while nurturing nostalgia for the 1950s in ten-year-olds, is inculcating ironic reflexivity about the whole idea of "being a dad" and "being a kid"—a reflexivity that returns to dominate what has to be the single most ironic (and long-running, and widely disseminated) account of family life in history: *The Simpsons*.

In fact, of course, the whole of popular culture is drenched in an ironism only a professor could miss—and a primary target is precisely the child-viewer's "process of socialization."

But this should come as no surprise. How else could children of the sixties raise children? They couldn't just move, unreflexively, into adult roles they had thrown so radically into question when they were young. They couldn't pretend that they took such roles for granted, saw them as natural, accepted traditional definitions of them—because they didn't and were proud of it. What has the whole story of parenting since the 1960s been, if not the story of how our self-consciousness about this most basic of all social functions got intensified to a degree without precedent in all of human history. The very word "parenting," for God's sake—try to imagine your grandfather saying it.

It's the options thing, again, of course. And it starts even before the kid is born.

The question arises: now that you've made this momentous choice, much more irrevocable and transformative than getting married after you've been living together for years—now that you've made the decision to do it, *how* are you going to do it? Dad in the delivery room? Dad to cut the umbilical cord and bond with Junior? Dad to videotape the whole thing? Lamaze classes, breathing routines (the drugs'll be there if you really need them)? Midwife or doctor? Or maybe compromise with a female obstetrician who has a midwifey persona? Or, hey, why not go all the way: how about home birthing? Or is that just *too* hippie-dippy?

And, of course, if you go with the traditional scenario—Dad pacing the floor in the waiting room while old-fashioned medicos treat the whole thing as a clinical procedure—well, that's a choice too.

And, of course, even though I am sort of making fun of all this, we are back to the Justin's Helmet Principle, no question. All this choice is mostly a good thing.

I remember how it was when we had our first, back in 1978. We read some books and articles, got a lot of input from friends and relatives—and I mean a *lot*. We shopped around, visiting various doctors and clinics and institutes. The most radical place we went to was *very* serious about home birthing. For these folks, this was religion. I think we both knew right away that it was too out-there for us, but we joined the group of prospects—all of us in a circle on the floor, cross-legged, no shoes—and more or less immediately the discussion turned into one of those who's-the-hippest-in-the-land contests barely disguised as a sharing session. The guiding principle, of course, was the naturaler the betterer. Finally, after some woman finished describing her previous home birthing experience—one in which she was out in her organic garden, tilling the soil, infant on her hip in a sling, three hours after giving birth and eating the placenta, or some damn thing—my wife chimes in, a bit plaintively (mask for exasperation), and says something like:

"I don't know, sometimes I think it would be nice to be in a hospital where there are all these people around who know what they're doing, and all that special equipment in case I need it? I mean, sometimes I wonder how I'm going to feel when I have to deal with this completely strange foreign little being who is all of a sudden just *there* . . ."

Not the Earth Mother note. Pretty good stuff, on the merits, but not the right setting. Things got very cold around us very fast. We slipped away from there.

Eventually we made our choice—and we made all the choices that came after that as well. Books, doctors, magazines, relatives, friends, shrinks, counselors, workshops, support groups—they were all there, enriching the field of options. Not that we made use of every one, but we could have, we knew they were there, we had some sense of what they offered, we had to choose *not* to look into this one or that one, and we had to wonder if we should have, but it was literally impossible to do them all, there were so many, and they dealt with every issue imaginable—thus making them all, willy-nilly, into "issues." Breast feeding, toilet training, diet, vitamins, pacifier weaning, feeding on demand, sleeping through the night, stimulating toys, nannies, babysitters, play dates, gifted-child tracking tests, on and on—and all of them involving choices, choices that might bring benefit or harm to this precious dependent creature (so desperately precious; like nothing else could possibly be).

But not only that. They were also all choices that said so much about us, about who we were. Self-defining choices.

But getting back to Rorty—here's the thing. As soon as our children were old enough to understand any of this, we began to include them. We did it automatically. We let them know that we were making choices. We invited them to share in our self-consciousness about our roles in innumerable implicit and explicit ways, some light and humorous, some more serious. And that inevitably meant we invited them to be self-conscious about themselves and their roles, as well.

So it wasn't just TV and movies pumping reflexivity into their little brains. It was us, living it.

How many times did I have conversations like this one, for example:

After some potentially traumatic event in our lives, I made a point of taking my son for a ride so I could ask him if he wanted to talk about things. I was wondering if he was sitting on some feelings it would be better for him to express—only to have him say something like this (he was maybe eleven at the time):

"Look, Dad, I know you're trying to help, you want me to 'have my feelings.' Well, I've had enough of my feelings. I don't *want* to talk about it anymore, it will just make me cry again, and I don't want to. I don't even want to think about it anymore."

Well, I mean to say—hard to argue with that.

Then there was the time my ten-year-old daughter was under some social pressure in school and I tried to get her to unload a bit so maybe Dad could give some sage advice—no doubt I approached her like that, by the way, sincerely offering, but letting her know at the same time that I knew this was a bit of a scene, making the offer in slightly self-mocking tones—giving her room to decide what she wanted; that was the point of it, using phrases like "sage advice from Dad" and so on. So she pats me on the arm and declines, obviously not wanting me to feel rejected, but not about to confide in me on this one. Instead she tells me she's having a "little identity crisis," which is "perfectly normal at her age."

Well, I mean to say—hard to argue with that.

Of course, that doesn't mean that my kids had everything worked out and didn't suffer and feel confused and so on—of course they did. Having access to psychotalk doesn't guarantee mental health. But it does reflect an inner distance, a mediational relationship within the self, an ironic self-awareness in the broad sense, which often translates into ironic self-description in the narrow sense as well.

As we all know.

Take another example, subtler but perhaps even more telling. How many times did I think to myself "I can't believe I'm saying this," as I admonished my children in terms like these:

"I don't care what the other kids do, I'm not going to let you . . ."

"I'm not mad, I'm just disappointed . . ."

"Because you're part of this household, that's why. Everybody has to pitch in and do their share . . ."

But I didn't just think "I can't believe I'm saying this." I would often say that I couldn't believe it. Right after the parental line itself, I would add the commentary—in a completely different tone, an include-the-kid-in-the-joke tone. Maybe I would laugh and clutch my brow in mock exasperation and say, "I can't believe I'm saying this," letting my child know that I could remember being on the receiving end of just these admonitions. I think I intended it mostly as a reflection on the passage of time, an effort to give us both a little distance from the spat, a little perspective— one pitfall of family life being how out of proportion little annoyances can become. Maybe not just a little perspective, now that I think about it, maybe offering a reflection on how strange it is that this is now and that was then and someday you (the kid) will be saying this to *your* kid—but this last would not be said in the first-order tone of "Just wait until you have children, then you'll understand" but in a second-order tone that said, "Let's you and me take a break for a moment from this stupid hassle and count our blessings against the coming of the end of days . . ."

Maybe my kids couldn't quite hear the echo of the end of days, but they definitely picked up on the idea that the petty dispute didn't matter that much, all things considered. It was a way that we had to relate to each other sometimes, but not the kind of thing that matters when the chips are down—when all that really matters, more than anything, is the miracle of our inexplicable being in the first place.

The Cult of the Child

No society in history has ever sanctified children the way we do. That may seem to sit strangely alongside all that ironic parenting—but mediation is nothing if not a fount of paradox. No need to make the factual case. Just think of the specific resources in time, energy, and material that we collectively invest in children, real and imagined. Think of the political rhetoric about families, of the way kids get sentimentalized in journalism, in movies and TV shows and commercials. Children are icons of the media age.

But why? Why the cult?

Because what we, in our time, find in children goes way beyond innocence, in the sense of absence of corruption. What we see in children, through children, is all things given for the first time.

No doubt adults have always had the chance to see the world anew through the eyes of children. That was always the gift they offered to anyone who enjoyed their company—the philosophical pleasure of their naïve questions, the way they set ordinary matters in profound relief. "Why do I have to shake hands?"—the kid is just asking, but you find your mind suddenly propelled across eons, a glance at primate ethology, an acknowledgment of the fragility of trust, the meaning of an open palm. But maybe, savoring the unintended depth of the question privately, you only say, "Oh, that's just what people do."

And then there's the poetic magic in a child's linguistic innovations. "You very do it," "We very hurry," my daughter used to say, misled by phonological similarity, extending the reach of "very" into semantic zones belonging to "better," creating, in effect, an all-purpose adverbial intensifier. The effect was irresistible; a possibility of meaning hidden in the language, brought so suddenly, so charmingly, to light. It became part of our family slang, of course. Most families owe a little tradition of such expressions to their children.

But, though children have always offered such moments to their elders, entrenched in routines, it is unclear to me whether adults in traditional societies would want to grasp the opportunities. Wouldn't "that's just what people do" seem like an entirely adequate reply? Wouldn't a myth about the origin of the handshake be ready to hand? In any case, the gift of such a moment could not have been as precious in a traditional society as it is to us now, when everything is presented and re-presented, when the routines we follow are *less* entrenched than at any time in human history (think of all the ways there are to shake hands—or bump fists). Because we are so deeply and constantly, if half-consciously, aware of the arbitrariness of the ways of our lives, because we are haunted by the knowledge that everything could be otherwise, because this is our framing state of mind—that's why we have become the child's ideal audience. The "out-of-the-mouths-of-babes" effect has its revelatory character for us because we are perpetually on the brink of realizations they accomplish and complete.

But why is this revelation—coming from a child, as opposed to a lecture in cultural anthropology, say— so very poignant? Another ironic doubling is at work; get used to it. This is the way of the Blob. The child's-eye view of this mediated world is the view of one *who has no choice but to live in it*. That is, for the child, there is no difference *in kind* between our world, saturated with representations and options, and an African savannah in the Paleolithic. To a child, thrown into an individual existence, they are equally given.

Through the eyes of a child, the world we know as a construct becomes a mysterious necessity once again.

In this way, children connect us to the real. They are the affirmative complement to illness and death on the other horizon of our lives. For a very young child, everything is like those things by the road where your car broke down—and, for that reason, so are children themselves. They are just what they are, for reasons utterly beyond us.

Yet, in the case of children, we are the instruments and vessels of their becoming. They are the beyond *in* us, the given *in* us, and so, by irresistible implication, the givenness of our lives as well. They signify the ultimate limit to our options—*the fact that we exist at all*.

Children are what is left to us of metaphysics.

That is why it can still be enough just to be with your child, not doing anything in particular. That is why your child's attention— the gaze upon your face, the concentration on your words, the thoughtful response—feels like the light of heaven, and a tiny bereavement follows each withdrawal of her interest from you.

And that is also why some parents shy away from their children, or cover them over with expectations. They don't want to be reminded of being and time.

Surely you have had this experience. You are in the middle of an average everyday moment, perhaps engaged in some domestic task with your mother. Suddenly you are struck by the fact that *this* is you and *that* is her, the one who bore you. It is as if someone pushed a Mute button, froze the video, as if you could "see" through some undocumentable sixth sense, through some kind of astral projection, yourself in this room, in this building, on this street, in this town, in this state, on this continent, on this planet—you are struck by how totally unlikely your existence is and, at the same time, by the fact that you undeniably are. And somehow that realization depends on the unwitting presence of a person known so intimately, your mother's figure at the table, the particularities of her skin and hair, the tilt of her head, the way her shoulders slump at the end of the day. That's my mother and this is me. So familiar, so strange.

If you say your own name to yourself at such a moment, it will seem utterly alien. You will then understand the sacrament of baptism.

*   *   *

So the mediated world appears to children as if it were real. That is why we especially venerate them.

But they soon learn. Enormous resources are devoted to educating them, and—irony of ironies—the whole aim of that education is to teach these beings, whom we cherish because they are given, how to make themselves into anything they want.

But ironies aside for the moment. This much is straightforward. A child born into contemporary culture is in a perfect position to learn what she needs to know about life in a field of options and representations before her education gets under way. The cult of the child could have been intentionally designed to prepare a baby for the entitlements a mediated world confers. Even before the flattery inherent in representation takes hold, even before the options multiply—over and above the egoism that is natural to the undifferentiated psyche—in our culture, the child is the center.

A Brief History of "Child-Centeredness"

One thing is for sure. *Anything* a modern adult produces for children is going to teach a lesson of some kind—and intentionally, not just because it assumes some framework of values. We left the Middle Ages behind, and good riddance, because we wanted more leverage on the kind of world we live in and the kind of people we wanted to be—that was the whole idea of progress, the whole idea of modernity. And children were made to order for the project, obviously. They were the raw material. It's no accident that John Locke—he of tabula rasa fame in philosophy—was so psyched about education. It has been thus all along, generation after generation, in revolutionary France and Lenin's Russia and the postwar United States, right up to and including postmodern educators jettisoning traditional three Rs instruction and deconstructing the canonical curriculum for the sake of multicultural reforms.

Scratch an educational philosophy and you'll uncover a political scheme. Every time.

This has been true of even our Romantic/bohemian/hippie moments, when moods of rebellion against all plans and schemes hold sway. At those moments, the message adults send to kids is, in effect, the logical limit to the idea of teaching them something. "Hey, just be a kid!" is also a teaching. And you can bet that the details of the curriculum, the literature, the movies, and the shows that peddle *that* message, are laced with more specific subversive messages directed at restrictions and pretensions—wait 'til we take a second look at *Winnie the Pooh*.

The point? In a broad sense, you could say educational visions have always been "child-centered," necessarily so. But that means very different things in different times. Leafing through a little volume called *Children's Books from Long Ago*, I come across samples from the sixteenth century and early Victorian period. You could call them "child-centered"—if what you meant were something like "targeted." Zero empathy, zero understanding, zero "identification with," as we know it today. Really harsh stuff, enhanced by scary little pictures of Master Tommy suffering the consequences of pride, declarations that "Hop Scotch is a silly game; it is calculated to wear out the shoes and is played by the lowest kind of children." Most revealing is a lesson urging "my pretty Miss and Master" to make regular entries in a "memorandum of the benefits you receive from others and always to set down the faults and failings which at different times you discover in yourselves."

Why is that last one so revealing? It's the reference to writing in relation to self-awareness. Writing is the medium through which the modern enterprise was launched, after all. Literacy is associated, not just with puritanical guilt-tripping, but with the very idea of self-knowledge and self-government. Think of Robinson Crusoe totting up his credits and debits as he takes control of "his island," or old Descartes himself, for that matter, realizing that the only thing he could be sure of was his own existence as the subject of his own experiences—his "self" in the matrix—and then telling us about it, in tones of personal intimacy unprecedented in philosophical writing, tones that so obviously address the inner life of the anonymous reader, that address *you*, the subject of all addresses.

Acres of academic prose are devoted to such icons of modernity because they represent the emergence of the modern individual. But we don't need to plod across those acres; it's the media piece we're after. The idea is that reading and writing, by their nature, turn the mind inward, cultivate habits of rational reflection, encourage the imagination, the inner life in general—thus giving birth to a self in the modern sense. A self that didn't need the intervention of priests and rituals to connect him to God because his soul had direct access, by way of scripture—call him a Protestant. A self informed by a free press, enabled to make up his own mind about political issues—call him a citizen in a representative democracy. A self that could decide on a career and choose among commodities—call him a participant in a capitalist economy.

That's the basic idea.

And, later, *she* and *her* as well, of course.

The point? What we are calling the flattery of representation goes *way* back, back to the printing press. We've been undergoing mediation for centuries. In recent decades there's been a quantum leap in the variety and intensity of mediation, and that has had profound consequences, but the basic process has a long history.

And, every step of the way, children have been educated into it.

Pan and Pooh

If you pick up the original 1911 *Peter and Wendy* and read it cold— you will be surprised, I promise you. No whiff of Disney in J. M. Barrie's text, that's for sure; no Mary Martin panto-musical either. You realize immediately why it's Peter *Pan*—as in, goat-boy god with horns and seductive pipes.

Here's our first encounter with him, at the end of the first chapter, when Mrs. Darling, alerted to his visits by various clues, finally catches him in the children's bedroom: "He was a lovely boy, clad in skeleton leaves and the juices that ooze out of trees; but the most entrancing thing about him was that he had all his first teeth. When he saw she was a grown-up, he gnashed the little pearls at her."

Just mull that image over for a while.

Peter Pan's principal trait, we soon learn—and we are reminded of it over and over again—is his "cockiness." I don't know if "cocky" had the same connotations then as it does now, but even if it didn't, it's impossible not to see that Peter Pan is all about instinct, imagination, and, above all, utter selfishness, the selfishness of children whose animal energies are intact, undiluted, uncompromised. Peter Pan is that selfishness personified, impenetrable as a cat. He forgets everything he doesn't enjoy. For example, he promises Wendy to return to her every year, to take her back to Neverland for "spring cleaning." He shows up the first year but misses the next one. Wendy pines like a lover abandoned, and when Peter, to her surprise, shows up again the following spring, he doesn't even realize he missed a year. He was involved in some adventure. He just forgot. Completely.

As children do.

It is a powerful moment, one of many, providing insight into what it would be like never to grow up. We are told again and again—in the very last sentence of the book as well, lest we somehow miss the point—that children are "gay and innocent *and heartless* [italics mine]." When you come across it the first time, the "heartless" is a shock, a slap in the face that interrupts a comfortable anticipation of further cliché. And the force of that interruption is not diminished by repetition, because the story constantly reinforces the truth of it, subtly and subversively.

Barrie also plays games with form, breaking down the fourth wall in a way calculated to amuse the adult without alienating the child. So, as the Darlings, warned by Nana of their children's impending departure, race up the stairs to restrain them, Barrie writes, "Will they reach the nursery in time? If so, how delightful for them, and we shall all breathe a sigh of relief, but there will be no story."

Even Wendy is not exempt from subversion. Mother to the Lost Boys, and to Peter, she may be; but we find out that she (like Tiger Lily and Tinker Bell) would rather be something quite different to him, if only he would *grow up!* Oh yes, lots of possibilities are hinted at for Wendy—as for example, when a "frightfully *distingué*" Captain Hook (he has aristocratic origins, we learn), having bound and gagged the boys after invading their underground home, undertakes to escort Wendy out of her little house upon his arm. We are told that she is "too fascinated to cry out," and Barrie, tongue bulging in his cheek, apologizes for being "tell tale to divulge that for a moment Hook entranced her," though it turned out to be a lucky thing because "had she haughtily unhanded him (and we should have loved to write it of her)," then she would have been tied up like the boys, unable to aid in the escape as she later did.

Well.

What we have here is Edwardian decadence. It is as if Virginia Woolf and Lytton Strachey had decided to mock Eminent Victorians for an audience of kiddies—but also for grown-ups presumed to be reading the story to them. Barrie's ideal reader is bifurcated. A loving but jaded adult—someone who has come to terms with Darwin and Freud—reading aloud in the drawing room to an eight-year-old in a pinafore, reading repeated indictments of the little listener's heartlessness, and observing that the child is indifferent to the slight because the only thing that matters is the pleasure of the story. A mainstay myth of the Victorian age is crumbling before the adult reader's knowing eyes, but the child just enjoys—or perhaps does not, and demands another story—and Barrie is confirmed.

"It is only the gay and innocent and heartless who can fly" is the way he sums it up somewhere, and adults get the point immediately. But only adults get the point. They are being invited to indulge in a bit of harmless and undetectable revenge—against the young, who hurt us so and take so much for granted—to indulge a sense of sly superiority at the expense of the child who, while entranced with the tale, doesn't get the message. *Peter Pan* is about mortality, about the inevitable limitations of earthbound maturity as against the freedom of amoral and unbounded phantasy, an authentically tragic vision only an adult could understand.

That's why when Wendy, long grown up and a real mother, encounters Peter once again, in her own daughter's bedroom, she stays "huddled by the fire not daring to move, helpless and guilty, a big woman." But Peter, "not noticing any difference, for he was thinking chiefly of himself," greets her cheerfully, out of his (by now) quite terrifying innocence, and proceeds to ask after John and Michael, as if they might be tucked in their little beds in the next room. When things finally sink in, and Peter is sobbing as he realizes that Wendy has grown up and can no longer fly away with him, she "lets her hands play in the hair of the tragic boy" to comfort him and then gives him permission to take Jane, her daughter, instead. Peter brightens up immediately and does just that. He turns at once to Jane, quite satisfied, nary a pang, crowing and cavorting again, forever young, forever gay and innocent and heartless.

Only an adult—and a sophisticated one at that—can feel the chill evoked by the spectacle of so abrupt a recovery.

Let's take a peek at *Winnie the Pooh*. It's the same deal. Much gentler, of course, this is an altogether tender enterprise. The motives of children and their animal projections never extend to darker regions of the psyche. But they are extended, charmingly, in ways that children can enjoy—but once again in ways only adults can fully understand. The whole thing is satire, a send-up of pretenses of all kinds, the pretenses of children included.

Most obvious? Mangling words, in cute ways, as children do. "Heffalump," "Jagular," "Haycorn." That sort of thing.

But isn't it a stretch to call that satire? Well, maybe, until you notice that word-mangling goes on in areas where satiric intent is more obvious. An expedition becomes an "expotition," an introduction becomes a "contradiction," "instigate" and "interrogate" fuse into "instigorate," and so on.

At first glance you might think, okay, more cute Heffalumps— but no, not in these cases. Like Pooh's habit of treating himself to "a little something" at eleven A.M. (by his broken clock, which always says eleven, the mangling of these words—and the ludicrously inconclusive conduct of the enterprises they refer to—makes mock of our human inclination to self-deception and self-regard. We are being invited to smile at the whiff of pomposity that attaches to all adult enterprises, especially imperial and governmental and intellectual enterprises of Great Moment and Grave Consequence, you know the ones. The Bold Expeditions. The Weighty Investigations. The Solemn Introductions.

My, my, yes, how very, very serious it all is and how very important we all are, to be sure.

That's the satirical tone that runs constant throughout.

And the way Pooh and his cohort lapse inevitably into whimsical irrelevance in all their undertakings—they wander off, forget what they came for, mistake this for that—it all serves to set off the pomposity that the capital letters signaled in the first place.

But it's not just grown-ups who come in for a ribbing on this score. Capital letters mark much more colloquial expressions that children adopt from adult language because they inflate the child's sense of self. Piglet keeps walking in the snow, though he really wants to stop, because he doesn't want Pooh to think he is Giving In. All the creatures do this sort of thing. They consider that some suggestion is a Grand Idea and that so-and-so is a Great Help, and they wonder if some news will Get About, and they even notice that someone has failed to Think and, as a result, will surely be Sorry.

It's all about affectation, in this case the affectations of children who adopt adult clichés because of the way they sound, and use them, mostly correctly but without quite understanding what they mean. The effect, so precisely and simply accomplished in the stories, is hard to define. It's like when a precocious child latches on to some adult expression—for example, "actually"—and then overuses it: "Actually, I want to go" and "You can have your own, actually" and "Actually, I do like strawberry."

Once you realize what's going on in Pooh's world, satirical intent becomes more and more apparent. Piglet, ever fearful, struggles to achieve denial of his fear in the most transparent ways. Owl, the wise, can read, of course. Not. Rabbit always has important missions like—er, well, Organizing Something or Writing a Notice or Seeing What Everybody Else Thought About It. Tigger can do anything you care to name—except, he's not in the mood to do *that* at the moment.

A. A. Milne is, in effect, teasing the children he is writing for, even though most of them won't know it—that part of the fun is for adults only, as it were, just as with Barrie. And if some of the kids begin to catch on, to realize that the foibles of these creatures are their own, no harm done, for there is such forgiveness in Milne, it is all so gentle.

In both Barrie's and Milne's books, then, a deep appreciation of children opens up a continuum of possibilities for responding and understanding that ranges from the sophisticated adult, for whom the whole apparatus is laid bare, to the very youngest listener, innocently involved with the story, as if there were no more to it than the idyll that E. H. Shepard evokes in his illustrations.

The point? *Peter Pan* and *Winnie the Pooh* are child-centered, but in a particular way. They sit somewhere between Victorian children's literature and the identificational kind of child-centeredness that emerged with the proliferation of mass media and the explosion of reflexive popular culture in the 1960s. Victorian instructional literature targeted children and many classics of Victorian entertainment literature were nominally about children—but neither made any concession to what it is like to *be* a child. The heroes of *Treasure Island* and *David Copperfield* were placeholders for the omniscient author, protagonists with a transparency that suited his descriptive gifts.

In *Peter Pan* and *Winnie the Pooh*, we still find the adult in charge, but empathy and understanding are at work. An appreciation of children informs a marvelous art, an art that tells two stories at once. The adult is the knowing, anonymous observer and purveyor and the child is beneficiary, potentially a protégé. This kind of child-centeredness is also to be found in John Dewey and Jean Piaget. It is the child-centeredness of progressive adults in the first half of the twentieth century.

The tell-tale criterion is this: adult authority is no longer imposed, but it is retained. No matter how skillfully the child's thoughts and feelings are accessed, the adult still presides.

For Kids of All Ages

The child-centeredness we have come to know since the 1960s is something else. In TV shows and books—and in classrooms—the adult point of view is radically transformed. In paradigm cases, it is effaced. Adults no longer wished to observe kids from above, no longer cared to instruct them by rote or preside, all knowing, over their independent quests. Adults wanted instead to see things through children's eyes, to share their point of view—as in the essays teachers began to ask children to write, essays in which they learned to describe not just what happened but how they felt about it.

Consider the source of it all, apocryphally speaking: the infinitely consoling *Goodnight Moon*.

That little book dates from the late 1940s, and evokes the 1950s prelude to the 1960s—think beatniks, Jackson Pollack, white jazz musicians. Margaret Wise Brown wrote it, and others too, though none so enduring. "Brownie" was her nickname. A cutting-edge lady, a society beauty, sexually out-there, companion to the likes of

John Barrymore and the prince of Spain (Katharine Hepburn in the movie version?). She worked out of the Bank Street Experimental School in New York City—where it was all happening in those days, in the city and the school, yes, cutting edges everywhere, and Brownie was ahead of the curve.

And to what did she attribute her success as a writer for children? To an ability to "reach down into the soul of the child that still lived within her."

Which puts it all in a nutshell. Long before the multitudes lined up to get in touch with their inner child, Brownie had been there. She pioneered the whole thing.

That's why, reading *Goodnight Moon* to a two-year-old at bedtime (so loaded a moment, inexorable passages), the adult finds comfort.

In the same way as the child.

That's the criterion for identificational child-centeredness.

You just know, as you read that book, you just know that your thoughts and feelings echo the child's—the whole rhetorical structure guarantees it. The minutely varied repetitions and illustrations are designed so that you can console your inner child too. "Good night to this," "good night to that," and with every page that turns, the room darkens so slowly, by such tender degrees—the antithesis of the abrupt brutality of a light switch—by insensible shifts, rather, in just the way that sleep itself comes, when it comes gently. And so it's good night to each thing in the great green room, and beyond— which means all things, the very world, will be there in the morning, and so will you.

"Now I lay me down to sleep . . ."

But we would never suggest that prayer to a child today. The way it ends, I mean—gruesome. Like those old fairy tales that the brothers Grimm collected before we cleaned them up, made them more age-appropriate. Even for a grown-up, that prayer is a bit much. Why tempt morbid obsessions?

Think of it this way. *Goodnight Moon* does not expect you to identify with the reassuring presence of Granny Bunny in her rocker—it expects you to be comforted *by* her.

That's the key, that's what makes this little book representative of the shift to a more intensely mediated childhood. The talent and attention of the adult is now focused on making a mirror for the child, on representing the child's world as the child sees it, on representing the child to herself. As this focus takes hold in the culture—and, boy, does it take hold—it leads to a more elaborate self-consciousness in children, and that self-consciousness comes earlier and earlier in their lives. Inevitably, also, it means more picking and choosing between proffered versions—so many possibilities to identify with or against, to mix and match, to try on and discard, so many options among these representations of young selves.

Goodnight Moon is to toddlers what *Catcher in the Rye* is to adolescents. Do I need to spell out how completely Holden-centered that book is, how saturated with adolescenthood? I believe it was Norman Mailer who called J. D. Salinger the best writer who never left prep school. By implication, he was telling adults who like *Catcher* that they are identifying with Holden still—because that's the only way to enjoy the book. You have to basically agree with Holden, see the world as he does, see adults as phonies, their authority exposed as hypocrisy. There isn't any other way to read it.

Both books date from the same period, the same ultrahip postwar New York milieu. And you can feel it—especially in *Catcher*, of course—you can feel the 1960s coming. These books were harbingers of that era, a significant aspect of which is the mediation of childhood—and that will in turn condition the emergence of the most fully mediated type of human being in the history of the world.

The Teenager.

But that's the next chapter. What a mediated childhood essentially entails is this: as kids learn to be Jonah or Jenny, they also learn to be "kids." They assume a status that stands on its own, that is self-conscious and self-validating because it exists in a representational world that reflects back on itself.

If adults want to enter that world they can, of course, but they have to become kids again to do it.

And, as it turns out, a lot of us have been so inclined.

For a while, it was nostalgic improvisation, rereading *Anne of Green Gables* when you came across an old edition, pleasantly yellowed and just a bit mildewed—the very smell of time—on a shelf in the place you stayed one summer.

But the producers of culture caught on and they began to aim at this emerging market.

Take *Harry Potter*. The books come in two different bindings, one for adults and the other for kids, and the movies attract a lot of adults without children in tow. *Harry Potter* may be the most successful generational crossover brand of all time.

It's instructive to contrast J. K. Rowling's world with Barrie's. Dark forces again, that's for sure—but they are not hinted at, they abound, they flourish in manifold varieties, elaborately described. They do terrible things, awful things—they kill Harry's parents and other people close to him. But, terrifying though they may be, especially in the last book, they don't reflect the psychology of evil as we know it in everyday life—so much smaller, so much uglier, and above all, so very self-deluding.

If *Peter Pan* has a story for adults hidden in a story for kids, then

Harry Potter is a story for kids that adults can enjoy, if they want to be kids again. Harry's grown-up fans are adults on vacation, as it were—and, Lord knows, we can use it (see chapter 5). One of the many benefits of having optional selves is that you get to be a kid again if you feel like it. And adults enjoying Rowling's world can do so without fear of interruption. Their is no thematic subtext, no "second book" accessible to adults only, lurking beneath the one the kids are enjoying. You never wonder what Dumbledore and Madam Pomfrey might be up to in the dungeons, for example, or anything along those lines.

Of course, one reason for this is that a lot of kids today would catch on to such innuendos, if they were there. These kids are not surrounded by adults who talk delicately about "the facts of life" and "the birds and the bees"; such euphemisms would be ludicrous in today's environment. Your average eight-year-old knows about Clinton's blow jobs and sees Madonna tongue-kiss Britney, understands the gay-friendly message, and probably knows what a publicity stunt is to boot.

So one ironic effect of fully mediated child-centeredness is that, as soon as it gets under way, the distinction between child and adult begins to blur, and the overlap runs both ways. And more and more of our cultural productions aim for this fusion of sensibilities.

The Blob is all about fusion.

The basic mood of the *Harry Potter* movies, as opposed to the books—especially the first two movies—goes back to *Star Wars*. It is the mood of a quintessentially postmodern genre. Call it the family action-fantasy-adventure. As contrasted with the macho action-fantasy-adventure. Brendan Fraser in *The Mummy*, not Bruce Willis in *Die Hard 6*. In this genre, everything, no matter how scary, is leavened with a very specific kind of humor, the kind that includes the audience in metacommentary, that sets off the frightful against a reassuring backdrop of deadpan whimsy. When Hagrid, in spite of all the evidence, insists on treating his pet dragon as if it were cuddly, explaining to Harry that he's packed the dragon's teddy bear in case he gets lonely, you hear ripping noises from inside the crate as teddy is being torn apart—and Harry has that blank, eyes-slightly-widened expression, the one actors use to signal incredulity restrained by consideration for the feelings of an idiot companion, the one that says, "Uh, okay, whatever (I can't believe I'm even *in* this situation)."

That look is everywhere nowadays, have you noticed?

The dynamic that propels this type of movie is a perpetual play-off between the horrific and the comic. Some over-the-top huge, vile, loud, sudden Something accosts the hero whose response must be—though it seems impossible—a match for the magnitude of that Something, an even more incredible sequence of action heroics that teeter on the brink of slapstick. And so he finally, *just barely*, conquers or escapes, in a way that nobody could have anticipated, let alone planned for, through a sudden stroke that saves his sorry ass and leaves him dazed and blinking, as incredulous as we are.

Notice that none of this would work if the producers couldn't count on us to recognize the genres from which this genre lifts and mixes.

Harry Potter is a perfect embodiment of more substantive aspects of our mediated age as well. The books especially serve as allegory for our politics, for "identity politics" (see chapter 4). As with the *X-Men*, so with these apprentice wizards and witches. They are outsiders *and* they are special. They are, in general, subject to Muggle prejudice and indifference—and Harry himself in victimized by the ultra-conventional Muggles who raise him.

There's a strong undercurrent of 1960s rebellion against middle-class conformity in *Harry Potter*, and that appeals to parents who grew up in those years and want to pass the legacy (minus the excesses) on to their children and celebrate it for themselves at the same time.

Harry and his kindred function as a perfect projection site for anyone, adult or child, who understands what it means to go through life feeling *different*.

That's the real magic word in Rowling's lexicon. And that's the word that, more than any other, unites the concerns of people who worry about stereotyping in grammer schools and those who meditate upon the impossibility of fixed meaning in discourse systems. That's the single word that best evokes the social aspirations of postmodernity—and *Harry Potter* is a long trope on the theme of difference, and the play of marginalization and vindication that attaches to it.

In the case of the wizards and witches, the vindicating transition from different to special comes easy, as befits a fantasy. Empowerment is automatic if you can walk through walls and turn a mouse into a snuffbox. On the other hand, Rowling's world manages to provide all its different and special people with their own sort of normalcy as well—and this is the ultimate key to her success. Spells can go awry, you see, just like gadgets do in our everyday lives. If magic cars and doors and wands don't always work the way they should, and if your rival has a better brand of broomstick than you do, and if classes on the dark arts get boring because too much memorizing is required—well then, we can all feel pretty much at home.

The immediate effect, each time Rowling rings this bell, is comic. But the cumulative effect is profoundly reassuring. Like Harry and his motley crew, the fans aren't just being recognized for being different, or celebrated for being special; they get to belong as well.

The Blob is all about having it both ways. Or more.

From *Leave It to Beaver* to *The Simpsons*

The same shift is evident in other media, in television shows that deal with family life, for example. In the archetypal *Leave It to Beaver* (but it could be *Father Knows Best* or *The Donna Reed Show*), the assumed audience watches the children from an adult point of view. That's the fun of it. The kids appear on-screen in medium close-up, absurdly well groomed, reciting their lines with only a few of the broadest sorts of mood indicators in their performances—"Aww, Ma, do I *have* to?" and "Gee Dad, *why* can't I have a bike like Timmy's?" and so on. The expectations that surround them in the script, the settings, the direction, everything, is closer to Shirley Temple than to Lindsay Lohan. Method acting it wasn't.

The basic plotline hinges on how kids deal with a given world, which is just there, something that will someday make sense, something that has to be faced, understood, and finally managed with the help of knowing, kindly adults. The humor typically involves the various ways in which children misunderstand that world and the way adults can be, though only temporarily, sweetly baffled by the children.

So, for example, a typical episode: The Beav has a falling out with his best friend and Dad tells him the story of Damon and Pythias, underlining and endorsing the lesson that friendship, no matter what, is an absolute value, etc., etc. The Beav makes up with his friend the next day and retells the tale of Damon and Pythias, at which point the friend leans on a reluctant Beaver to help him cheat in math class. The teacher catches on, but only to the Beaver's role, and he, observing the letter of his new principle, takes the rap alone. Mom finds out and suggests to Dad that the friend's parents should be in on this, but Dad, in his presiding wisdom, decides to give it some time. And sure enough, the friend has been feeling guilty and the next day he turns himself in, and the teacher, in her wisdom, lets them both off. This time.

Adults writing and watching such a show are indulging in a nostalgic appreciation of childhood, of how the world looks to someone learning to navigate it. There's a kind of identification, enough to guarantee understanding and empathy. The basic joke is always "Oh, how cute. See how charmingly skewed are the perceptions of the innocent." And there is a lesson too. It's "See how children can be brought to maturity with the help of enlightened adults." That last theme is characteristic of media productions about children after World War II and through the 1950s.

Neither Barrie nor Milne would have corrupted their art (for art's sake) with such moralizing—too reminiscent of Victorian preaching. But, while it is moralizing, it is not in the Victorian style at all. The model is not the minister lecturing but, once again, the psychologist presiding. The long march toward a therapeutic society has begun, but during the 1950s, when doctors in white coats endorsed everything, it was still in the hands of experts. Authority hadn't yet shifted to the flattered self. The democratization of therapy, the explosion of varying modalities of self-improvement through self-discovery, was still on the horizon.

Now glance at *The Simpsons*. The contrast says so much about how we got from the 1950s to the new millennium, and why the 1960s was the great divide. We are no longer watching kids from a knowing distance. The assumed audience for *The Simpsons* identifies with kids entirely. Above all, we are no longer charmed as children slowly learn to make sense of a world that does, in fact, make sense. Because it doesn't. The world of *The Simpsons* is chaos. No one is in charge. It is absurd in small ways, teetering on the brink of catastrophe in larger ways—in the world of *The Simpsons* there is nothing to learn.

Bart has only to survive to prevail.

And we with him.

Adults in this show are weak, conniving, hypocritical, vain, confused, deluded—at best, they are well-meaning but inept. Political and cultural figures and ideas are constantly invoked, only to be relentlessly mocked. There is no guidance to be had, no meaningful future, nothing to aspire to, nothing to make you better than you were. The only reliable touchstone is the family—but this is family as refuge, not as nursery or social-building block. At least here the craziness is familiar and resolution guaranteed. We know the Simpsons will gather again on their couch, bathed in the glow of their giant television, passive, unblinking, sucking figuratively on their collective pacifier while Maggie sucks on a literal one as well. If we are meant to feel a bit superior to this family of couch potatoes, it is only because our awareness of their state entails an ironic reflection on our own. We understand why they immerse themselves in representations to shelter themselves from whatever reality there is out there—may the saints preserve us from it.

We do the same thing.

Where the Wild Things Were

But *The Simpsons* is comedy. Its success derives from an underlying sense that people have about our world these days—namely, that it's going off the rails (see chapter 7). But that's underlying. In the trenches of daily living we don't typically give in to nihilist apprehensions. On the contrary, we stuff our lives with schemes and projects.

And no project feels more essential than the well-being of our children. To that end we supply them with everything we can, take every option into account, in an effort to provide for their happiness in every department of life—from the careers they might consider in the distant future to the emotional distress they might suffer tomorrow.

I don't remember ever being expected to "share my feelings" as a child. No adults ever asked me how I felt. Maybe my mother, patting my knee—"What's the matter, Tommy?"—trying to nudge me out of a mood. But my feelings were mostly my own business. If anything, adults assumed that my feelings were obvious—often too obvious—and if they had any interest in them at all, it was directed at getting me to restrain or reform them. The point was never how I felt; the point was what I did or didn't do.

Correcting behavior is still the ultimate aim of a lot of adult intervention in the lives of children, I suppose. But somewhere along the line the circuitry got so elaborate you could make a case that the inner life of the child became an end in itself, at least in some settings.

Take those now-customary expressions of ethical judgment "appropriate/inappropriate" and "acceptable/unacceptable." People who grew up in the 1960s and 1970s adopted them because they served a manifold of purposes so smoothly. For a generation that defined itself in opposition to authority, this language helped to justify the authority they assumed as they moved into positions of responsibility in institutions and families. It did that by limiting authority to a context and renouncing more extended claims. To call some behavior inappropriate is to distinguish with exquisite precision between behavior and the inner life. It implies that no one has a right to judge a person—especially a child—absolutely. At the same time, the implication gives an institution room to enforce certain standards of behavior as a condition of participation. The harried mother addressing the darling dawdler on the sidewalk thusly, "I need you to walk faster now" or "You really need to walk faster now," is a mother intent on persuading her child, not to be obedient to adult authority for its own sake, perish the thought, but, over the whole course of his upbringing, to play an appropriate part in a social configuration.

Of course things don't always work out. If inappropriate behavior is habitual or particularly outrageous then it becomes unacceptable and sanctions are necessary—and therapy and medication too. Sanctions are only justified because they are functional. No moral fundamentalism is suggested, no question of the child *being* bad or good, no question of *deserving* punishment in itself. No, punishment is justified because it teaches children that, in society, actions have consequences. It teaches children to "take ownership" of their deeds—a telling phrase, for, with ownership, presumably, comes self control, and that is the aim.

Because it is understood that anyone who behaves inappropriately is "acting out."

The directional preposition in this once clinical expression points the way back to the source. The flip side of even the most severe judgments of behavior does in fact call attention to one's inner being—in this case, to the child's inner life, which is beyond moral judgment, in the realm of psychology or even neurobiology. The clear implication is that the thoughts and feelings that get expressed by inappropriate behavior are not themselves to be condemned, though they are presumed to be tumultuous, intense, conflicted, maybe painfully so, even frighteningly so. Hence, the term "acting out"; it marks an inner distress too intense to control.

And so our attention is directed at the internal landscape, at the psyches of the young. And, again, ambivalence abounds. Paradox prevails. On the one hand, here is the source of everything that is powerful, everything that flows and rises, everything that fulfills and transcends. On the other hand, here is the source of everything vicious, dangerous, and cruel. Creativity, passion, commitment— we want them for our children, and we know that will only come to pass if powerful emotional forces propel them through life. At the same time, we want them to be at peace, to be comfortable and safe, not to hurt others, and never to suffer at all.

Oh, the ids of our kids! What a dilemma for a generation suspended between images of Woodstock and Altamont, the Beatles and Charles Manson.

And the answer is?

Maurice Sendak.

Did any grownup in my childhood ever say to me, "It's okay to be mad, but you mustn't hit. Or curse. Or break stuff." I don't think so; I may not remember it, but, as I said, I don't recollect a distinction between my feelings and my actions. They were both understood to be in or out of control together. But as a parent, I made the distinction all the time. And Maurice Sendak was there to help.

So where are the Wild Things?

Well, we grown-ups know where they are, don't we? Inside us. But that is the only thing in this book that the grown-up understands that the kid doesn't, at least not in so many words. In fact, the whole point is to help the kid get a grip on the wild things within by externalizing them in the story. What myth and fairy tale once did without conscious design, Sendak does on purpose.

Clinical psychology is the obvious source for this archetypal therapeutic book, and the adult reader gets that right away. So there is a layer of old-fashioned presiding in this otherwise very 1960s tale.

That psychology aside, the kid and the grownup are simultaneously addressed in Sendak's story. We are all subject to extreme feelings that burst upon us when we get angry or upset, that explode, that assault us from within, and this is a very scary fact of life for all of us—for grown-ups too. It is particularly frightful to see your child in the grip of these forces—it's like demonic possession or something, although of course you know better than that—but your child having a tantrum can be very alarming; you have to keep a grip on the kid just to keep a grip on the panic and anger that starts up in you, and vice versa. And if it's that scary for you, imagine what it's like for the child.

Your spontaneous inclination, no matter how many years you spent in therapy, is to blame children when they throw a tantrum, to resent the bratty way they seem willfully to collaborate with it—but psychology and Sendak are there to assure us that the wild things within are just too much for the child to handle. And help is on the way.

Remember how it goes? Sendak's little Max has been acting out. He's dressed in a wolf costume and his mom (reacting angrily) sends him to his room without any supper and his room morphs into a forest world and a boat (named Max) comes by and he sails to an island where the wild things are and they threaten him, but he quells them all just by looking them right in the eye and so they make him their king and *then* he lets them all bust loose in a wild rumpus, led by him, and then he sends them all to sleep and then he gets lonely and sails back to his room—where supper is waiting on a tray. And it's still hot.

An expedition into the interior jungle then—both Freud and Descartes applied that metaphor to their introspective ventures, by the way, and Max is following their lead on behalf of all his little readers, all of whom must learn to *manage* their most primal desires. Not crush, not deny, not project—but manage, tame.

The little touches in this lovely book point to the same moral. So, for example, we see pictures of Max being bad. In one, he's hung his teddy bear by a string from a coat hanger—but the noose is around teddy's arm, not his neck. In another, Max is chasing the family bowwow down the stairs with a . . . fork. A fork? Hmmm. Well, I suppose lynching teddy by the neck and attacking a pet with a knife would make Max badder than we want him to be, wouldn't it? You might start thinking future serial killer as opposed to normal naughty boy.

And the wild things themselves, what is it about them exactly? In the illustrations, I mean. They are huge and they do indeed have, as we are told, "terrible teeth" and "terrible eyes" and "terrible claws," and no doubt, "terrible roars" as well. But they are actually kind of goofy monsters when you examine them more closely, definitely not smart, not even malicious—they look pretty confused in most of the pictures. They are literally all mixed up too, like there is one that has bird feet and a furry body and another that has scaly legs and a furry body and another that has a rooster head and a furry body, but this somehow doesn't add to monstrousness, as you might expect; it gives an effect like that of a person wearing socks that don't match. Most of all it's their eyes, though—they're just not that fierce. The one picture in which the eyes do look a bit fierce depicts the wild rumpus, but it is also the picture in which crowned king Max is riding one of the monsters, looking proud and serene, wielding his scepter above them all like a parade master's baton.

So, yes, you see, we *can* have it both ways. Sort of. Even in the darkness of the id. We can have the power without the terror, real terror, the kind that comes when control is truly lost. We can have the power without the terror if we transform that inner wilderness into a mediated conservatory, contained in reflexivity. The trick is to do this without loss of the essential wildness, and, of course, that's always going to be a problem, and we just have to acculturate accordingly, on a case-by-case basis. Max is only the beginning; this manifestation of mediation's dialectic is especially fertile, and resolutions, in all their variety, are necessarily a balancing act.

That's why the term "domestication" is important—it points us toward the virtuous middle way, the synthesis, somewhere between repression, on the one hand, and license on the other.

There are various strategies—just to pursue the same paradox into other regions for a moment, to provide a glimpse of its extent. There's the venue strategy, for example. Vast swathes of the entertainment industry, from Hollywood blockbusters to professional wrestling to scary rides at theme parks, are dedicated to this mode of domestication. But the same can be said at the opposing end of the commercial spectrum —three-day raves in the Mojave Desert, for example. Likewise, extreme sports and extreme vacations (see chapter 6). They all have to reckon with the fact that they are optional, that they are designed—that they involve nooses around arms rather than necks, as it were. To compensate, they have to take up the slack that undermines enterprises of domesticated wildness by definition. They have to make up for an essential unreality with artistry, skillful manipulation, enhanced repetition. They have to find ways to do the same thing differently, over and over again, but bigger and faster, endless variations on the theme of arousal and resolution—endlessly varied, but controlled, encounters with the primal, the apocalyptic, the ecstatic, the Dionysian.

When we are older and more accustomed to the show, when we understand that it *is* a show, the sensational possibilities are much greater, of course. Necks and knives are fine. It doesn't matter how many people are slaughtered, it doesn't matter how brutally and cruelly, as long as we know that the book has only so many pages, that the movie will end, that some protagonist will walk away safe, safe as Max in his bedroom, safe as you will be when you emerge from the theater or close the book.

Because this is the lesson that all these representations teach. Over and above the specific stimulations—*you* are the one they are *for*, you are the one who chooses this one rather than that one, you are the one who can change your mind at any time, put down the book, walk out of the movie before the end.

And Maurice and Max teach you how to treat your own psychic depths in the same way.

Talk about options.

Mediated people in a world of effects aspire to elude all genuinely tragic visions of the human condition—for example Freud's, for whom the *necessary* discontents of civilization depended unavoidably on the frustration of instinct and the dilution of Eros.

But tragic visions are out these days. Especially around kids. They aren't nice.

MeWorld and The Nice Agenda

> I like you just the way you are.
>
> —Mr. Rogers

They couldn't come any nicer than Fred Rogers. He was the unchallenged master host of enlightened children's television in the United States during the last half of the twentieth century because he understood in his bones what it took to become the very best sort of mediated person. He liked us just the way we were, and he assured us of it daily, and convincingly, and that message is at the very heart of postmodern child-centeredness. It is meant as an antidote to the unenlightened parenting we are refusing—the kind that oppresses children with judgments and stereotypical expectations. Mr. Rogers liked us just the way we were so we could accept ourselves.

But he was not encouraging complacency, oh my, no. His neighborhood was all about constructive projects. To put it in a nutshell, you could say that Mr. Rogers was spiritual father to a form of parental commendation you hear everywhere these days, "Good job! Good job!"—rapt parents salute the smallest accomplishments in this way. Did little Emily, adorable embodiment of toddler concentration, finally manage to retrieve the toy or mount the step or open the box? Then it's "good job, good job"—how she beams in response!—and a particular vision of her future is evoked, one in which Emily will master an ever-expanding horizon of undertakings and stand securely at the helm of the unfolding enterprise of being herself.

Mr. Rogers's message tells us not to be driven to anorexia by fashion magazines but to realize, at the same time, that the flip side of self-acceptance is a spur to accomplishment, a realization that *now* you can follow your dream and be what you want to be.

As long as you're nice and make space for others to do the same.

That's pretty much what they teach kids in school nowadays, at least in the more progressive precincts of our land. That's the basic lesson.

I remember a conversation I had with my daughter when she was, oh, nine or ten maybe? Somehow, we were on the subject of admiring people, and she asked who I admired most and I said this philosopher Ludwig Wittgenstein and she asked why and I was trying to explain in suitable terms, making a royal hash of it, I'm sure, although she was (with typical perspicacity) picking up on a theme, realizing that there was something rather stern and forbidding about my hero. I could see her getting a little worried as that impression took hold, and finally she got impatient and asked, in her patented exasperated-with-Dad tone, she asked—"But was he *nice*?"

I had to admit that he wasn't very nice, and she *really* didn't like that, really didn't want her father admiring someone who wasn't nice.

The rise of niceness as a core value, how is that revealing, what's it got to do with mediation? Well, the first thing to notice is how different niceness is from civility, from politeness, from which it took over after the 1960s. *Niceness* implies an inward inclination, a quality of character. It is, in effect, evidence of a domesticated id. A nice person is automatically sensitive to the feelings of others; indeed, niceness morphs officially into sensitivity when we move down the political track (see chapter 4). It leads us—especially in educational settings—to reject tolerance of difference in favor of embracing difference. Tolerance is condescending, it hurts my feelings to be merely tolerated, and niceness is all about feelings.

The older we get—and especially in hold-out masculinized sectors of our culture—the more backlash against niceness we encounter, and we'll consider that later (it's just as mediated). But in the female-dominated world of early childhood education in progressive settings, niceness rules. Sensitized parents and teachers are constantly drawing the attention of children to feelings, their own and others. That is how kids are taught to behave—to show respect, to take turns, to pay attention, to share—all sorts of behavioral goals are envisioned, but the prevailing mode of access is through reference to the feelings of others by way of your own. The classic question is "How would *you* feel if so and so did such and such to you?"

If you believe, with Carol Gilligan, that, by and large and on the whole, girls bring a "different voice" to social life, that they are inherently inclined to negotiate social issues in terms of feeling and personal connection, then the emphasis on niceness will give at least some girls a social advantage from the get-go. They are already oriented toward people's inner lives. If you don't buy that, you still have to concede that the niceness trend leads to enhanced awareness of self and others and leads away from modes of masculinity we once took for granted—when boys weren't supposed to cry and so on.

When I was growing up, for example, it was accepted practice in one of my schools for male teachers to organize fights (boxing gloves in the gym) between boys who fell into spontaneous combat in the hall or on the playground. In another school I went to, the unwritten rule was "take it outside," which meant off school property and after school hours. There was a customary place for these encounters in a nearby field, cut off from public view by a stand of trees. A fight took place there every week or so. Crowds of kids would gather round, in numbers large or small, depending on the reputations of the combatants. This was just what boys were expected to do. What it was doing to the boys, psychologically, wasn't really an adult concern. Becoming a man meant handling such things yourself.

Put it this way: in general, most of what we now recognize in school curricula as "social-emotional learning" was expected to take place naturally. Teachers and administrators stayed away from our feelings and relationships unless our *behavior* crossed whatever the lines were, and then they intervened to enforce rules. Rules of etiquette or, in serious cases, rules of law—but behavior was the focus. The inner life of a child before the 1960s was, by today's standards, a remarkably private place.

It is revealing to notice how much of what goes on at the university level, things you wouldn't normally associate with niceness—gender theory and African-American studies, say—boils down to niceness when the seeds are planted in the early years. There just isn't any other way to introduce the complexities of diversity—modalities of gender and race construction, and so on—to seven-year-olds. The best you can do is get across the idea that everybody is entitled to be whatever they happen to be, or want to become, that no stereotypes should restrict the possibilities, and that we are all in this boat together.

That comes down to being nice to others and expecting niceness in return.

In fact, a lot of educational issues that may not seem at first glance to entail niceness orbit obviously around that value when educators first address them.

You are an eight-year-old student in a progressive school somewhere in the United States. Your class is doing art, drawing a plant on the windowsill. You look at what you did and compare it to what the kid next to you did. His looks like the plant and yours doesn't. You exclaim, "I suck at art!" Your teacher hears you and comes over. She studies both pictures closely. With your self-esteem in mind, she silently invokes modernist principles of abstract expressionism recalled from graduate school, hands back your picture, and says, "It's not better or worse, it's just different."

For the teacher this little lie is vaguely justified by high-culture aesthetics, but what really matters is that she thinks it will be empowering. She wants you to feel good about yourself. She is nice. She may be more or less conscious of her comment as a lie. She may talk about it later with a colleague and say, "I have to remember not to sit Jordan next to students with confidence problems; he's so talented, it's intimidating," thus conceding a straight-out lie in a good cause. Or she may believe it more deeply; perhaps she turned to abstract art herself because she couldn't draw, perhaps this is a lie of larger convenience. In either case, for the teacher, it flat-out works. It serves the purpose of making the child feel good about herself.

But for the student, who knows the truth because she was trying to draw the damn plant in the first place, the empowerment that little fibs like this confer requires some pretty Blobby adjustments. The most resonant implication is that the value of what she does is somehow unrelated to her abilities, or even her intentions, that the worth of her work springs from the mere fact that she did it.

Especially if she tried really hard.

This species of empowerment will be constantly and continuously enhanced by a curriculum loaded with inherently flattering assignments that ask her to represent herself (her pets, her family, her ethnicity, her religion, her dreams, her fantasies, her preferences, her favorite this, her favorite that) and to represent them in every possible way (in words, in pictures, in presentations and performances) and probably in portfolios of these representations, accumulated over time, and maybe augmented by computer graphics and digitized photographs of herself and whomever and whatever she chooses to include in this world she is building, this little MeWorld that she shows to teachers and doting relatives and friends.

For the latter she will also act as audience, taking turns, for, though she is at the center of her MeWorld, she is also learning that others are at the center of theirs.

Now consider this, drawn from research done by a seventeen-year-old senior on the origins of ethical relativism in lower grades: he gives a precocious ten-year-old Lawrence Kohlberg's famous "you find a lot of money in a paper bag on the sidewalk what do you do?" dilemma. The fifth grader decides (completely predictably, though he sees himself as defying convention) that it would be right for him to keep it, but, for another person, it might be right to take it to the police, for another, to donate it to charity—and, in general, that there are different rights and wrongs for different people and who can say more? In an inspired moment, the interviewing senior suggests maybe God? The fifth grader asserts his (again, completely predictable) agnosticism in magnanimous tones. He knows that weak and ignorant folk somewhere out in the boondocks might find his enlightened views unbearable. But he is willing to entertain the hypothesis that God exists and acknowledges that, if He does, "God could have a different opinion from mine."

Now *that's* empowerment. This is a kid who definitely feels good about himself. This is a kid to whom a lot of people have been very nice. This is a flattered self if there ever was one.

By the time that fifth grader is finishing high school, he will get the joke, but his sense of entitlement will be just as absolute; indeed, it will have merged completely with his sense of personal autonomy. The scope of this entitlement will extend even to logic. Confronted with "It is impossible to conceive of a square circle, given our definitions of those terms," he will want to say that it ain't so. He will want to believe that he can, or at least could in principle. When, after much discussion, he realizes that he cannot, he will likely insist on this position: "I may not be able to do it now, but they laughed at Columbus and who knows what some future scientist might conceive, I mean haven't they proved that there's, like, twenty-six dimensions at the subatomic level or something?"

He wants to believe that *anything* is possible for him, as long as it doesn't hurt anyone else—for others enjoy the same entitlement, we are talking about the decent majority here, kids with domesticated ids. Nietzsche's searing nihilism, in due course democratized, turns out to be nice (see chapter 7). Thus insured against mayhem, we experience any limit, even a purely logical limit, on what might be possible as an unjustified imposition on our freedom. What the flattered self enjoys by way of options in the mediated world in general gets expressed philosophically as that notorious "relativism" that conservative critics—ever suspicious of theory, glued always to the surface of phenomena—blame for everything they don't like and/or can't understand about contemporary culture.

Which is a lot.

I once had a senior in a philosophy class who declared that he was, at that very moment, conceiving of a square circle. After some questioning, and good-natured teasing, he finally admitted his concept was "a little vague." Other students were skeptical, but they would not categorically deny that he was thinking of what he said he was thinking of. They weren't entitled to tell him what was in his own mind. They wouldn't want anyone telling them what they were thinking

Which leads to how ready most kids are to assent to solipsism, the ultimate form of relativism, in philosophical discussion. The idea that everyone has their own reality, constituted by their own experiences and perceptions, comes almost automatically. It feels like common sense. And for good reason. The everyday MeWorld they are constructing out of all the representational options that surround them reflects their own tastes and judgments back at them constantly—think of a teenager's bedroom—that MeWorld they have been taught they are entitled to, morphs quite naturally into solipsism when they come to talk philosophy; they don't miss a beat. I can't count the times I've been struck by how spontaneously students come to agreement on the essential idea that we create our own realities—how the discussion becomes general when the topic arises, how they look at each other and nod and smile together, how they complete each other's sentences, how their eyes and tones of voice express reciprocal affirmation of their separate sovereignties.

They are acknowledging a tacit social contract.

Niceness, then, becomes a central value for well-adjusted mediated people. It animates a certain kind of very flexible self-awareness that depends on habitual reflexivity about emotions and relationships. It enables a mediated self to negotiate a social topography of unprecedented complexity and fluidity. In order to be the author of your being and becoming in a virtualized environment, you need to know yourself within the context of your possibilities, your optional selves—some of which are open to you, like career, procreation, sexual habits, hobbies, friends, etc., and some of which are not, like being gay or being Asian.

It is essential to these latter options, however, that they be virtually open to you.

That is what enables you to embrace difference.

And, of course, in accordance with the Justin's Helmet Principle, this is mostly a good thing. Maybe a bit *small*, some of you might be thinking, to have niceness as a core value? Compared to the lofty aspirations of more heroic ages, I mean? Well, maybe.

Still.

Conclusion

In a book published in 1962, Philippe Aries persuaded a generation of academics that what we think of as "childhood" is an invention, a category that emerged in early modern times to reflect changing social conditions. The basic idea was that, in the dominant classes, kids no longer went to work as soon as they were physically able, but lingered on the threshold of adult activity—going to school, learning to read and write, learning manners, and so on. According to Aries, this all got started in the sixteenth and seventeenth centuries, and went on from there.

An analogous argument, of more recent vintage, could no doubt be made for adolescence. Whence the "teenager"?

Well, it's bound to be a complicated story, no doubt, but one thing is clear—the teenager is the creature and creator of pop culture, a citizen of a separate society (actually, many of them). There just wasn't anything remotely like this in 1823 or even 1923. If "childhood" emerged as a category because people needed time to learn to be modern adults, "adolescence" emerged because, the more elaborate popular culture became, the longer that process took. With the rise of recorded music, film, then TV and all the rest, the field of representations got so dense and extended that you had to, in effect, learn to learn to be an adult—that is, you had to learn to be an adolescent first.

That correlation seems plausible on the face of it, because there's no doubt that adolescence has been getting longer and longer over the course of the twentieth century. Any veteran lower school teacher will tell you that "teenage" behavior is starting earlier and earlier, especially among socially dominant girls—as early as fourth and even third grade, when they are only eight or nine years old. And there is no question that the way the media exposes these children to the prospect of adolescence—to the prospect of sex, most of all—drives this process. On the other end of the spectrum, if you're in your mid-twenties, even pushing thirty and you're not married, or coupled up in a serious way, and you're still hanging with your crew, and you still spend serious time playing video games—then I don't have to tell you how long adolescence can last.

People used to get married in their teens and became grandparents at forty.

So what's taking us so long to grow up? Well, there is so much more to absorb—that's just a brute fact, as noted—but there are also so many different *ways* to be, so many different lifestyles, so many different versions of the world. Haunted by the possibility of buyer's remorse, we dawdle on the brink, trying this, trying that.

Options.

CHAPTER 3

*Who thought up this whole teenager thing, anyway? We don't know exactly, but I bet it was, like, a bunch of girls. **Twilight of the Heroes**. From George Washington to Martin Luther King. From Lindbergh and Churchill to, uh—why there's no name I can put here. So we'll just say New York City firefighters on 9/11. Performers and fans. Virtual revolution. You, again.*

Music has the power to form character.

—Aristotle

Like,

SEVENTH GRADE. Who can forget it? Repress, yes, forget, no, forgive, *never*. Posttraumatic stress disorder anyone? I still get flashbacks.

I see three supremely confident twelve-year-old girls confronting two boys in a school stairwell. The conduct of a third boy in relation to yet another girl has them riled up, big time. And they love it. They specialize in righteous indignation and withering contempt.

It seems a breach of confidence has occurred. The two boys fumble for explanations, trying to get a friend off the hook before the three furies catch up with him. Alas, they are having difficulty comprehending the offense. "But everybody knows she likes him," one boy keeps repeating hopefully. He does not grasp the vital distinction between general knowledge and a specific revelation that the girl in question *said* so.

Well, *duh*.

A fourth girl approaches the group and chimes in, trying a little too hard to merge with the tone of exasperation and outrage. One of the original three turns to her and says, with a special emphasis, "Excuse me? Are you even Amy's friend?"—then, turning away, followed by the other two, she flounces up the stairs.

Enough of these *losers*.

The boys, a bit shell-shocked, are as uncomprehending as before. But the overreaching girl has been pinned precisely in her place. Fifteen years later, she will still feel the needle. Like it was yesterday. Three o'clock in the morning, maybe, she'll think of it again, for no particular reason, and feel herself blushing in the dark.

Has there ever been a moment in human history when females ruled so completely over a mixed-gender group as does the central clique of girls in the more progressive middle schools in the United States today? It seems unlikely. Their power is nearly absolute, ferociously acquired, disputed, and defended. Even teachers feel their spell and curry favor or, more hopelessly, attempt reform. But the phenomenon runs too deep for adults to influence very much.

What gives these girls such a hold on their society, and why do they eventually lose it? Adults chalk it up to differences in maturational rates; boys enter puberty later than girls—adults love to say that, it makes them feel like they know what's going on. It is true, of course, and even relevant—if you're far enough removed to (pretend to?) be Super-Objective Clinical Person about it all. But the actual mechanisms of control escape all top-down health-ed-type explanations. The reality is so much richer. Girls, certain girls, dominate these settings because they are impresarios of an evolving social art. Propelled by incipient sexuality, yes, but across the whole range of its sublimations, they devote enormous energy to mastering an array of symbols and cues, an interplay of appearance, clothes, accessories, music, slang—a totality of customs that constitute their emerging world. And when they understand it well enough to play with it, improvise with it, innovate and disseminate, they take up their positions in that ruling clique and their authority will be recognized by all who know them. It will be their privilege to control the tones and terms that catch on and shape the flow of days, and the long weekends. This clique of girls dominates because it presides over a Wittgensteinian language game—meaning, not just a language, not just the slang, but also the whole form of life that goes with it. Everybody who wants to be anybody must live by it, and they are the gatekeepers.

They are media queens. They are familiar with everything it has to offer by way of example, insight, and reflection. They become who they are through that media, gazing out its windows and into its mirrors, determining expenditures of billions of dollars as they steer vast industries this way and that—great, clumsy cart horses responding to the flick of their whims. They know *every-thing*. Every lyric, every gesture, every band, every brand name, every novel expression of approval or disdain. But they know much more than that. They are not mere scholars. They are not pedants. They are not just an audience of passive consumers. They are not even merely judges—though, Lord knows, they are that too.

They can do it themselves. They are performers.

That means obvious things, like being a really good dancer, but it also means subtler things, things that are as pervasive as the media windows and mirrors themselves, things that escape our notice for that very reason.

Take, for example, the notorious "like"—as in, "I'm, like, *so* not ready for this whole, like, *gym* thing." Disapproving adults, dense as posts, blind as bats, think this is a verbal tic, akin to finishing sentences with "you know?" They discourage it the way liberal-minded adults used to discourage swearing when I was growing up—as if limiting one's vocabulary were the issue. Please.

Today's "like" has a long history that parallels the rise of mediation and expresses a cultural transvaluation that took place along the way. The expression derives from the beatnik-hippie usage, which was itself a popular manifestation of a high-culture crisis in linguistic philosophy concerning the limits of what can be said as opposed to shown. In that original usage, the phrase "Like, man" or "Like, wow" preceded an attempt to describe some idea or experience, and it implied that you just couldn't squeeze something so deep into phonic containers, man, like, this is too far out to be brought back to mere words, man, this is really, like—*heavy*.

What was suggested was not limited vocabulary but the inadequacy of language in principle. It conveyed the futility of trying to put into words what could only be known directly, and the constant implication was that one would "get it" only if one were "where it's at" already—that is, as a function of one's level of enlightenment, and that was a constant issue in those days, believe me; a lot of harsh judgments were rendered along with all that talk of peace and love, a constant jockeying for position in a hierarchy of relative hipness. It was so important to be *down*, to be the source of gestures and remarks that blew the mind.

"Like" still connotes the inadequacy of language in principle and it still operates in a competitive social field, but now—thanks to the queens of middle school—it is performatively integrated with conventions of that media. Adeptly employed (and only the queens can do it just right), "like" acts as a kind of quotation mark in conversations that no longer work discursively, but work more like TV commercials or movie trailers. The word introduces a tiny performance rather than a description, a "clip" displaying a message in highly condensed gestural and intonational form. It all depends on the way language is coupled with the ongoing flicker of imitative visuals, as in this girl's report on an encounter with an ex-friend:

"She was, like, 'I'm *so* happy for you . . .?' but she didn't know that, like, I already *knew* what she said to him . . .? So I just played it, like, we *are* the sync sisters . . .? Because I wanted her to find out later that she, like, had this booger hanging out of her nose the whole time . . .?"

Each "like" is followed by a fleeting pose, held for just an instant—the whole performance is a string of "takes"—and the ends of key phrases curl up into questions, seeking audience indications that the visuals have been received: a silent and subliminal call-and-response sort of thing, and woe betide the clunky wannabe who can't follow the nuances, who can't improvise a version of her own, and make it seem effortless and natural when her turn comes. Among such girls, the interrogatory incantation takes on a tentative tone, a tone that reaches perpetually for reassurance and permission to go on.

Painful to behold.

Life is one long improv, and only the method-ready thrive. You gotta keep it real, but you gotta be good at it too.

Adults who have been playing themselves for so long they've almost forgotten it's an act often underestimate what kids face during this, the most intense phase of their induction into a mediated existence. It takes talent, application, and sheer courage to compete in this environment. If the central group of girls in seventh grade launch a project in which, say, every boy in the grade is to be classified as a flavor of ice cream, it represents a challenge and an opportunity for any girl who dares to participate. Her personality and intelligence will come under intense scrutiny as the enterprise gains momentum, and the social savvy of the strivers gets put to the test. Every exchange in the hall or cafeteria is a gamble. The pitch and timing of every expression and gesture goes to make or break one's presence in the dance of the moment, all the more so if one dares to innovate in some way, to claim, for example, to detect some hitherto unnoticed quality in some boy everyone else has pegged in a certain way. And, once again, it all has to unfold effortlessly. Nothing is more pathetic than trying too hard. That's what the overreaching girl in the stairwell did.

The ice-cream project (a real-life example) pretty much says it all about boys, by the way. They are mostly pawns in the struggle for power during early adolescence, though they often deny this in later years. They *still* don't know how much they didn't know. There are exceptions, of course. There are some boys who become intensely interested in social and psychological nuance—boys who like gossip, in effect. But most boys have only a generic sense of the subtle arrangements of indicators that determine the social hierarchy. They know what it is generally, but they don't get the finer points. The dominant girls not only get them, but define them. The society they have mastered is dependent, above all, on the torrent of judgments that issues from the heights they occupy. No one else can match the wit, the insight, and the sheer speed with which these judgments are rendered. That's how they rule.

But a lot of boys—and some girls too—can and do exercise the option of flight. They abandon the struggle entirely and retreat into their own little worlds, other little worlds, niches that turn out to be just as mediated, but defined by "alternative" (the actual word comes a bit later) codes and modes. They can immerse themselves in computers, sports, skateboarding, fantasy/quest games, and a whole lot of other things I've never heard of, no doubt. In this way, they contrive a defense against the social judgments levied upon them by the clique, though in their hearts they know they are running and hiding, and many suffer humiliations under that regime of scorn from which they never fully recover. But there is one thing the queens introduce them to, one thing they can't escape, no matter how desperately they invest themselves in the intricacies of game worlds—and that's postmodern self-consciousness, mediated reflexivity. From now on they will know themselves *as* this or that. From now on they will be constructing themselves and performing the constructions. They will never again just be.

Other boys, a few boys, *achieve* popularity, of course. That's because they meet the basic physical requirements and have sufficient poise to converse with a powerful girl without dissolving into weird wriggles and gross jokes. But it is the clique of girls that *allocates* popularity, the most valuable of all commodities. It is they who anoint the suitable boys because they are needed, temporarily, to serve as props for what is really going on here.

An extended rehearsal for the real thing— high school.

Summing up. There is a structure to it all, even though there is no conscious design; it is a classic ethnological case study. In fact, I did research on clique formation using second-semester seniors in an anthropology course I used to teach. At seventeen or eighteen, they made ideal field workers, still close enough to the situation to remember the details, recognizing earlier versions of themselves in the kids they were observing and talking to, but halfway out the door themselves, the college process mercifully concluded, differences between them that once loomed so large diminished by the common prospect of the most significant life rupture they had yet faced. What my crew of participant-observers discovered was a trajectory of development with deeper roots than any of us had expected to find. It turns out that, as early as kindergarten, an informed observer can predict which girls will come to power in middle schools like the one we were working in. There are two criteria:

1) They fuss with their hair a lot, patting it down, fluffing it up, gathering it in their hands, letting it fall across their eyes, tossing it aside with a particular shake of the head.
2) They insist on picking out their own clothes, rather than letting Mom dress them.

In other words, they have already noticed that style exists—and matters. I don't want to claim it's hardwired, but it goes deep. It also has to do with social class, of course, with a sense of entitlement, access to commodities and sophisticated opinion. In any case, these are the girls who will eventually rule.

By the time they are eight or nine, they are becoming aware of themselves in relation to style. They have learned to look for themselves—various possibilities of self—through media. This is when they begin to assert control over the customs of their peers. Who hangs out with whom becomes *the* social issue, and the accidental play-date friendships of the past come under intense pressure. By fifth and sixth grades, the powerful girls are systematically deploying their store of performative knowledge, gained through exhaustive and collaborative studies of media, especially music. Over the next two years, competition intensifies as individuals and subgroups jockey for position, or retreat to the relative safety of the margins. Seventh grade is usually climactic;

tactics for purging and excluding reach the outer limits of duplicity and cruelty. Membership in the core group varies from two or three to seven or eight, and extends to a porous periphery of ten to thirty girls who are drawn to the center of power, and enjoy many of its benefits, but lack sufficient fire in the belly to sustain an all-out assault on centrality. That's because, as a member of this latter group remarked to one of our researchers, "You know what's funny about really popular girls like Meredith? Nobody likes them."

It's lonely at the top.

The tension often slackens in eighth grade, for a common future now looms on the horizon for all these thirteen-year-olds—it's like a mini-senior-year. As high school freshmen, they will be uniformly insignificant by definition. No one knows it yet, but the dynamic of clique formation, building on its middle school foundations, is about to diversify into the more elaborate high school pattern (jocks, preppies, alternative, etc.) and that variety will leave room for a lot more individual initiative, for people who can straddle categories, and so on. This looser structure emerges because, as if by some predetermined alchemy, the dominant clique of girls in middle school begins to dissolve once they get into high school. Its central figures remain popular, and their combined judgment still counts for a lot, but they do not maintain the intense solidarity of yore. They begin to go their separate, sometimes competing, ways—seeking the attention of prominent boys among the eleventh and twelfth graders. And many of those sixteen- and seventeen-year-old boys are, in turn, trolling ninth and tenth grade waters, looking for girls like the ones who treated them so blithely in days gone by. The balance of power between the sexes begins to even out and—until recently, at least—to reverse itself.

Adult educators, motivated by gender politics to prepare girls for more institutionalized forms of power later in their lives, have devalued and even opposed the power they in fact hold—partly because it involves such stereotypically feminine concerns, partly because of the ruthless tactics involved. But no matter how hard they try, they can't prevent that clique of girls from coalescing when it does, the way it does. On the other hand, the postmodern educational agenda—not just in schools, but in the media too (*Bend It Like Beckham*, *Buffy the Vampire Slayer*)—has succeeded in expanding the subsequent possibilities, not just for girls in cliques, but for everyone.

Small example, but quite telling: a couple of senior girls in my anthropology research project—they had been clique queens in their day—were trying to remember when they started wearing frayed jeans instead of Benetton, and why they had switched. "I don't know exactly when it was," one said, at last, "but I decided at some point that I didn't want to be an airhead." Her friend nodded appreciatively, yes, that was it, that was the reason.

And a back-assed, lightweight reason it was too, at least in the opinion of one very smart, slightly nerdy kid on the other side of the room, who was rolling his eyes discreetly at his friend to convey his disdain. But discreetly. He had been severely mauled by these two girls back when they ruled the only roost there was and, though he was much respected now (superb musician, Harvard-bound), he still wasn't about to take them on directly, no way.

But here's the point. One of those girls went on to become a serious writer, the other a successful lawyer. That would have been a very unlikely outcome forty years ago. No, there's no question, the core dynamic of the middle school clique may not have changed much in the last few decades, but—at least in progressive schools in the United States—the universe of possibilities around that clique and its victims has expanded. Girl athletes are cool. In the last decade—and in the face of considerable backlash in the last few years—gay students have formed clubs and begun to attend proms as couples. Have they been harassed? They have, but a lot of them are *out*, and they get powerful institutional support. I can remember when the word most commonly used for gay was "pervert"—and it meant something absolute, drew a line you couldn't question. That's a *huge* change.

And, speaking of proms, these days you don't need a date at all, you can just go with a bunch of friends—what a relief! And, at least in schools of the kind I am describing, African-American kids may hang out at their own tables in the cafeteria, and those tables may be off to the side, and some people may wish it were otherwise, but, by and large, it's a choice—and they take center stage for assembly on Martin Luther King Day and receive a mostly respectful hearing.

This is not perfect, far from it, and the psychological costs can sometimes be weirdly high precisely because discriminations are more muted. But just think how things were only fifty years ago.

Perhaps most revealing of all is the way people socialize in multigender groups in later adolescence. How many parents of seventeen-year-olds walk into how many living rooms at nine o'clock on a Saturday morning to find an indiscriminate mass of lunky and nubile bodies sprawled out across the floors and furniture like so many exhausted seals on a convenient rock? Boyfriends, girlfriends? Going steady? Breaking up? Dating? Well, maybe, sort of—but it's mostly about hooking up now and then, or being with someone for a while, someone who's been a friend for years and will still be a friend when it doesn't last.

Then there's "friends with benefits"—you've heard that expression? There's also hooking up with people you meet on the Internet, not like you get lured into it, but Web sites that sit there in the ether like virtual beaches during an endless spring break.

I just don't get the whole scene, I'm the first to admit it. It's riddled with gradations and nuances that I couldn't possibly fix in an analysis. I doubt if anyone could.

Because they aren't fixed, that's the whole point—and here we are again, in a field of indefinitely many, always evolving options to be negotiated by reflexive individuals performing their lives according to improvised scripts they cobble together as they go along.

More power to them. I couldn't do it. I remember *panty raids*, for God's sake. I remember when boys and girls in high school and college looked at each other across a great divide, two different societies, almost two different species, each with its own store of secrets, its own values and manners. Co-ed dorms? Unthinkable. I remember when the minds of females seemed to be as different from mine as their bodies were, and both were veiled in ways that lent a mythic charge to what was hidden and glimpsed and accidentally-on-purpose brushed up against in crowded hallways. Awesome in the true sense of the word, frightening as well as alluring, and vastly more powerful than such things could ever be today, I'm sure of that. And reciprocally for girls, no doubt, and probably for gays too.

I remember taboo, that's the point. Real mystery. I remember when sluts were sluts and good girls didn't go all the way, even if they *were* going steady—except, then, sometimes they did.

It was serious stuff, back then.

But who knew exactly what "it" even was? I mean, in any detail, with a clear idea of ways and means and preferences within a visible and expanding horizon of kinky possibilities. You had to go it alone in those days, you had to deal with the most primordial aspect of human existence with almost no representation to keep you company, to help you see beyond your own experience or reflect upon it. I remember being taught how to masturbate by some older—or at least bigger and more confident—boy when I was twelve or so. He told me to hold my dick in one hand and rub the palm of my other hand vigorously back and forth across the head.

I applied myself diligently to this formula for I don't know how long before I figured out a better way.

But now, yikes, what don't kids know, and how early do they find out, and how graphically and frequently is it all portrayed, and how openly is it all discussed, and with how many people? From sex-ed classes to HBO and MTV, and Victoria's Secret is right there at the mall, and explicit porn and sex toys everywhere, and on the Web and cable too.

But don't mistake this for a Lynne (Mrs. Dick) Cheney decency complaint. Au contraire. Leaving aside the tiny population of psychos who are roused to action by all this stuff, mediated openness about sex is (here we go again) mostly a good thing. Better than the fear and ignorance and embarrassment that surrounded all things sexual in my day, better than traumatic misunderstandings and missteps that could, and often did, taint and distort and, above all, restrict and inhibit a person's sexuality for a lifetime—borne along in memory, as such things had to be, in secret and in shame forever. Better than vicious sexual stereotyping that applied so automatically it was bound to be internalized to some degree, even by its victims.

It's just like where the wild things were, isn't it, just like little Justin's bulbous bike helmet. It's all for the best, but something is lost, a dimension of meaning and power that we can only encounter at the point where our comprehension and capacity to manage end. At the edge of the real.

Which accounts for the fact that we have so many public exhibitions of sex that aspire to be transgressive. But—the dialectic of mediation again—in reaching for the real in that way, they succeed only in extending the reach of the virtual. That's the way of the Blob.

Back now to "like," our introduction to mediated teenhood: it turns out to be a bit of folk art, postmodern folk art, invented and disseminated across a continent by cliques of powerful girls who never meet, but keep virtually in tune by way of media throughout those crucial years, collectively choreographing a legacy—a never-ending ballet of fashionable expressions and tempos that shapes the flood of mediation engulfing us all. For those who fall short of mastery at the center and construct alternative worlds at the margins—they too must learn to become who they are in some niche of representation. This is the critical period in that process, no matter who you are. This is when you realize your optionality. This is when you really start *deciding* who you are.

This is when you choose a look. This is when you start saying "dude" all the time, and without scare quotes, or only sometimes and heavily ironized, or maybe not at all. This is when you get your first tattoo and stud, or go for the cords and the blue oxford shirt. This is when you decide to study hard, to get top marks, even though it takes a lot of time—or you decide to blow it off and cruise for Bs, or drop out entirely and fuck 'em all. This is when you decide that you are the kind of person who really cares about the environment or gender equity or you decide that taking political positions is just so affected. If you're more or less embedded in a minority niche, ethnic or economic, or both, this is when you decide to negotiate the dominant culture or, because the very idea of that is humiliating, you commit to enterprises that belong to you already. This is when you get invested in team sports, or attach yourself to a skateboard and join the crew down at the financial center plaza. This is when you dabble in a bit of both, or several, because you've got other ideas, you're not sure exactly what, sort of a loner-artist-type thing developing—but there's examples of *that* in every third thing you read and see as well, so you've got the company of reflection even when you "go your own way," because that's such a category too, there's no escaping it, this side of madness anyway, and even then, half the school shooters in the heartland saw themselves as Neo in *The Matrix*, or something along those lines, didn't they?

Above all, this is when you choose the music you will live by, a soundtrack to accompany the performance of your life.

Attitude

Why are musical preferences so intensely important to kids? You can disagree with friends about movie stars (do we still call them that? If it's beginning to sound quaint, see "Virtual Revolution," below) and about TV shows and even humor (though this last is a close call, for essentially musical reasons) and you can still be friends. But you can't be friends with someone who loves the latest boy band, in a totally unironic way, if you are into Ani DiFranco or Gillian Welch. It's not that there's a rule that says you can't. It just wouldn't happen. Tastes in popular music go deep.

Why music especially?

Well, it's no accident that certain ancient Greeks, suspicious of representation, linked music and morals so closely, no accident at all. They were already thinking about the psychological consequences of mediation, even back when media were pretty basic, long before the fabulous representations we take for granted today could even be imagined. Given their interest (not to mention genius), it was only natural for them to ask which among the forms of media was most powerful. Unlike McLuhan, they did not conflate practical tools with media; they drew the line around arts and artifacts whose essential purpose was to communicate through representations of some kind. So it was that, when they asked their question, they found one modality that obviously belonged with communicating arts like writing and painting—yet could not quite be contained by the representational criterion.

Music.

Because music doesn't represent anything else, does it? It's there, humanly crafted, yet given, more like the wind itself than a description of the wind or a picture of trees swaying? It moves out of us and into us im-mediately. It blends with emotion, it *becomes* emotion—or "passion," as they used to say.

Well, this leads into a thicket of distinctions: We could wonder about modern art, abstract art, which doesn't represent anything either—or ancient decorative arts, for that matter, designs on porticos and pottery, designs that flow and twine, sort of like music, and they don't represent anything; they're more like the ripples in the stream than a description of the stream. On the other hand, such patterns are static, whereas music, like the stream, like time, like life itself, will not stand still no matter what, no matter how artfully the silent beat is held aloft to seem to last forever before the final crescendo brings our sweet suspense to its conclusion—it will not last, it cannot last, it is music, it is mortal.

No need to press for conceptual perfection. The consensus of the wise has been that music is unique among the arts because it operates on the same plane as the unmediated, the given. It belongs to sensation itself, to bodily existence and, for that very reason, it elevates that existence in a way no other art can match. Music takes hold of you on levels of your being that precede intentional articulation, levels of being that *contain* what you can put into words.

And that is why words, when they are sustained by the immediacy of music, have a unique power. They represent, they articulate—*and* they penetrate, they fill dumb bodies with meaning.

There is nothing like a song.

And that is why no committee of commissars or mullahs can compete with pop music. It shapes way-of-life values at levels that transcend any ideology. The commissars and mullahs know this, so they ban the music, just as Plato proposed to ban dramatic poetry (think Homeric rap) in *The Republic*.

That's where the morals part comes in. Those ancient Greeks—and Romantics like Rousseau, most ardent of their modern heirs—thought of music and morals as inseparable because they understood that values adhere first of all in postures, in rhythms of speech and gesture, prior to semantics, deeper than any code. That's why a code that is anchored in music has the power to "form character," as Aristotle put it. And mediated teenagers understand this too, precisely because they are engaged in constructing themselves from the ground up. They are deciding on more than fashion accessories. They are learning the fundamentals—how to stand, how to sit, how to wave, how to look eager, how to register perplexity, how to high-five and bump chests, how to intone sorrow, how to say "like"—in a nutshell, how to perform the fine-grained details of being a self over time, from moment to moment, which is, as just noted, the way music works too.

Ah, those iPods. Plato would have *flipped out*.

Which brings us to attitude. Attitude names what the fundamentals of posture and gesture and rhythm come together to engender—the gestalt of a personality, the form that makes details of expression and deportment into a coherent identity. Attitude is the very nexus of music and morals.

Take the most striking example since the rise of rock and roll: hip-hop. Hip-hop nation, they called it, and with good reason, for this has been what a "nation" looks like in a world of post-territorial communal entities. Hip-hop's stars have been heroes to millions all over the world. Their influence reaches to Serbia and Indonesia, Zimbabwe and Korea, everywhere you see those shoulders rolling to propel arcane finger signs on high, proclaiming—well, the content varies, of course; if you think this is just about bling and gangstas, then you're like people who thought the Beatles were just about long hair. Iraqi insurgents in Sadr City, for example, make hip-hop CDs to recruit for the cause of militant Islam. Yes, the content varies greatly, clothes, tags, techniques—the messages, above all, are varied, but the overall form is uniform, an identifiable style, and it says me, me, me, in your face, me.

That's the essential attitude. That's what those heroes model, that's what they teach, because attitude is what the fans crave, it's what gets them through the day, through the barrage of fragmented stimuli in this ocean of representation we all have to navigate, in something like one piece. Attitude comes as close to authenticity as the ethos of reflexivity allows. Attitude is all surface. It hides nothing. It governs a perpetually improvised unfolding. It leaves no room for perspective to take up a position within it. It eludes the internal contradictions of depth. It is self-reference without division. It is preadapted to inhabit a virtualized world, to move on always, to glide over moments, to sustain itself across engagements, to be just what it is and nothing else.

Many virtualized subcultures, whatever the differences between them, thrive on this basic attitude—call it "defiant self-celebration." Skateboarders have attitude, in this sense. So do U.S. troops on the ground in Iraq, with their shaved heads and their wraparound shades. So do models strutting their stuff at fashion shows. And trash talking athletes, of course—and professional wrestling is devoted to the thrill of attitude, carried to extremes that border on parody. Winners of almost anything, celebrated or otherwise, display attitude—like James Cameron accepting the academy award for *Titanic*, proclaiming, "I'm king of the world!"

Sometimes it seems as if half the commercials on TV are structured around attitude.

The word "attitude," used by itself, takes the meaning beyond defiant self-celebration toward sheer defiance, bordering on contempt. There's a fine line.

Contrast that, for just a moment, with the way heroes were expected to comport themselves in the old days, with the way Lou Gehrig ran the bases after a home run, the way Charles Lindbergh clasped his hands together and shuffled uneasily as he listened to praises heaped upon him, the way RAF pilots shrugged off their deeds.

Why the shift in expectations? Why have so many people come to identify so deeply with defiant self-celebration?

No doubt you've already realized that attitude is about the flattered self coming into its own?

But we'll take that up in the next section.

First let's register the fact that, although there are many other kinds of attitude out there, they play the same essential role as the prototype. They sustain the bearer in the flood, they unify the improvised performance of a life. Attitude is the ethic of a society of surfaces. Like Dubya's simplicity. Like Blair's sincerity. Like Cheney's in-chargeness and Rumsfeld's directness. Like Bill Clinton's empathy. Like Hillary Clinton's pluck, Kerry's gravity, Edwards's optimism. Attitude is real—as in keepin' it real—because it cannot be false. There is nothing else to it.

That is what accounts for the absence of shame that everyone has been remarking on lately, especially since Clinton, but elsewhere too—Rush Limbaugh and Dick Morris and Governor John G. Rowland, the corporate bandits, and the whole reality-TV, Jerry Springer world for that matter. You wouldn't expect actors to feel shame on behalf of their characters, would you? Mediated people who identify themselves with attitude are similarly immune. They have transcended the old-fashioned keeping-up-appearances thing, which, when it crumbles, crumbles into shame. People who identify with attitude have nothing to hide that could be exposed in any crumbling. They may lie, but they can't get caught. Even when they're caught, *they* aren't caught.

They just move on. Sustained by attitude.

Twilight of the Heroes

When historians look back on the twentieth century, will the rise of rock and roll and TV—pop culture generally—take on a significance comparable to the Reformation? Will the emergence of "teen/youth" appear as analog to the rise of the bourgeoisie in the seventeenth century and the proletariat in the nineteenth? If so, the great performers of this culture will have to be regarded as the heroes of this age. They were the founders and propagators of its ethos.

Maybe we should just forget the whole statesman, warrior,

scientist, artist, thinker business—idols of that type are dead or dying, surely? People who cling to such figures—are they just slaves to nostalgia, nostalgia for the real, for the heights and depths to which earlier ages aspired? Are they epochal snobs, so to speak, anachronisms clinging to the judgment that pop culture is just too *pop* to be taken seriously? Are they just refusing to believe that the place of real heroes could be usurped by mere performers—when, in fact, that is exactly what has happened?

Ask yourself this, if you are under forty: who are your heroes? No, not counting people you know personally, we'll get to them later, I mean public figures? And if you are too old for that test, if you can honestly answer Malcolm X or Barry Goldwater or Bobby Kennedy or Ludwig Wittgenstein or Virginia Woolf, then try this one: who do the kids you know idolize, if anyone?

Let's go to an anecdote.

A few years ago, a headmaster of my acquaintance sent me an article lamenting the loss of heroes for today's youth. The article concluded, as all such articles must, with a solution to the problem, in this case a strategy for presenting George Washington, of all people, in some way that was guaranteed to secure the admiration of students. I barely glanced at it. There is no such strategy. Just talking about "how to present" is already hopeless capitulation.

At about the same time, the *New York Times* ran a story that showed exactly why any such attempt is bound to fail. It was about a new team of curators of Washington's estate at Mount Vernon, where attendance-trend lines had been dismal lately, especially when compared with the numbers that Thomas Jefferson's Monticello was racking up. What with a couple of popular bios on the stands, scientific and architectural projects on display, a Nick Nolte movie, and, best of all, the hi-tech DNA sex scandal over Jefferson's relationship with his slave, Sally Hemmings—well, there was buzz out there for Tom. He was hot. The folks at Mount Vernon were determined to liven up the stodgy image of their founding father, show evidence of cool hobbies, make those wooden teeth a plus, and generally put their hero back on top of the charts.

The centerpiece of their plan was a tour of the grounds and mansion, culminating in a visit to the "death scene."

"Death scene" meant the room where the real George Washington really died, furnished with all the real things that were really there at the time. But the folks (re)creating this death chamber understood that real wasn't real enough. More was required. So they tried piping deathbed smells into the room. They didn't follow through with this, but linger over the implications of the fact that they even had that idea. Presumably sane and sincere people were driven to overreach so ludicrously because, in their hearts they understood that the real George Washington could never compete with performers like Oprah or David Beckham. It was as if they felt they had to grab visitors by the lapels and shout, "This is real! It really happened! Right here! Goddamit, smell it if you don't believe me!"

Real isn't real enough. That's the tell-tale sign of an otherwise invisible tipping point in the historical balance between representation and represented. It marks a threshold of saturation, the point beyond which no real entity can survive in public culture. We crossed that threshold long ago, and that is why no real person can be a public hero anymore.

We will get to some details, but first be assured that the phenomenon is universal. Lamenting the absence of heroes is endemic. It cuts across all the political and cultural categories. The National Organization of Women, the Gay and Lesbian Alliance

Against Defamation, and the National Association for the Advancement of Colored People all worry about it as much as stodgy defenders of the Western canon like Lynne Cheney and good old William Bennett—you remember, he's the one who managed to parley a stint as Reagan's Secretary of Education into an ongoing (and very lucrative) gig as America's voice of righteousness until he got caught at the slots in a hotel room in Atlantic City. Yes, everyone agrees that kids today need heroes, they just don't agree on *which* heroes.

Take, for example, the flap over the Martin Luther King Center in Atlanta. It differs in a lot of significant specifics from the Mount Vernon case—but, at bottom, the same paradox framed events as they unfolded. When Dexter King took his cue from the designers of Elvis's Graceland in an effort to bring the King Center into the digital age, he outraged a lot of the old guard who thought of it as part of a process of commercialization—using Dr. King's voice and image in commercials for Internet connectivity and so on. But such interests merely fuel the process. The process itself has its own specific characteristics. Dexter King rightly understood that if you were going to reach the next generation at all, you were going to have to do things like surround-sound and stream-video experiences of assaults on the freedom marchers, the hoses, the dogs, the hate-twisted faces spitting out epithets. And what the old guard understood, if only unconsciously, was that the price for such virtual engagement would be high. Moved emotionally the customers would certainly be, as they so regularly are—but moved to action? That's a different matter.

Here's a thought experiment to crystallize the issue. It shows what you would have to do if you really wanted to convey the significance of some iconic reality to succeeding generations in the context of ubiquitous representation. A "way to present," if you like—but at the logical limit. That's why it would work and also why it couldn't be done.

Hence, "thought experiment."

Say you wanted to ensure that the Holocaust would never be forgotten, the full horror of it, the original meaning, the reality. The only way you could do it, at this point, would be to ban all graphic representations and extended descriptions. No photographs or documentaries, no depictions of skeletal survivors being rescued, no ovens, no piles of shoes and bones. And no memoirs, no Anne Frank, no museums, no memorials, no movies, no *Shoah*, certainly no *Schindler's List* or *Sophie's Choice*, definitely no *Life Is Beautiful*, nothing even in the textbooks, beyond the stark fact that it happened.

A taboo, in other words.

But all the documentaries and photographs and oral histories would still exist. They would be preserved in a single archive, displayed in one place and one place only. And the educational requirement would be this: at a certain age, thirteen or so, every child in the land spends a week in that archive.

And that's it.

They would never forget, believe me.

But, you might protest, it would traumatize those kids; it would scar them for life. Exactly. That's why they would never forget. But look, we want them to remember and understand the full horror, the reality, but we don't want to do psychic damage, that's not right.

Ah, well then—you're stuck. The reality, the full horror of the Holocaust, *can't* be grasped without causing psychic damage. So we'll have to settle for some middle ground, we'll have to do our best to have it both ways, find some Blobby form of never-forgetting that won't be *too* burdensome but, at the same time, hopefully, not too trivializing either; there will be some controversy about that going forward, no doubt.

Which is just to say that we'll end up with—just what we've got.

And we are back to the core evaluational paradox, back to the Justin's Helmet Principle on a more serious plane.

The real heroes issue is more complex than the Holocaust thought experiment, of course, but shaped by the same contending pressures. Having a real hero means devoting yourself to someone, subordinating yourself, shaping your life in accordance with another's.

And that's asking a bit too much of a flattered self, a self that exists in its very own field of representations, that constructs its own identity, chooses what it wants to be. A self like that doesn't want to be devoted.

Devotion isn't trauma, of course. But it does seem a bit severe, shall we say, a bit medieval, if you know what I mean? Cult whackos come to mind. Jim Jones and David Koresh and so on.

Devoted followers are anachronistic in a world that's made for devoted fans. That's why patriotism is becoming a species of fanhood.

People who believe everything can be fixed don't want to consider the possibility that some things can't be, so they are attracted to more contingent explanations for the decline of heroes, explanations that might point the way to remedy. There are several possibilities.

One of the favourites rested on the absence of national crisis over recent decades—no great challenge to unite us in urgency and allow heroic figures to rise up before us. But that one lost its purchase after 9/11. Nobody would call Bush and Blair heroes in the old-fashioned sense, though they tried gamely to fill the position. They just couldn't. Forget the political hassles, it was deeper than that. They were just, somehow, too *small*. Even New York mayor Rudy Giuliani—more lionized than anyone since, I don't know, Alexander the Great?—even he had sense enough not to try to make a speech at the ground zero services.

He knew he wasn't big enough for that.

The flip side of this impossibility was all the media hyperbole during the Iraq invasion—when not just maintenance specialist Jessica Lynch, but every GI on the ground was ludicrously christened "hero." On that side of the equation, runaway inflation sucked the meaning out of the concept almost overnight.

Another favorite account of the hero vacuum, especially in the postmodern academy, welcomes the loss as a triumph for critical theory. Good riddance to monumentalist delusions, the reign of Dead White Males, etc. This high-culture response mirrors a pop culture development that high-culture critics, overlooking what makes their critique of monumentalism viable, typically disdain: the obsession with personality, with scandal, the gossip explosion ("We should be talking about *issues*"). Scrutiny of the private lives of contemporary public figures is understood to account for the decline of real heroes, but it has in fact characterized high-culture scholarship as well. In learned biographies, as in the tabloids, debunking personal scrutiny intensifies, and feet of clay are found where pedestals once stood.

But the explanation that comes closest to the one I'm proposing is the most favored of all, and it says that real heroes have been replaced by sports and entertainment stars. And that's exactly right, as far as it goes. But the tone that goes with this most favored explanation shows how short it falls from understanding the phenomenon it only identifies. The tone is typically critical—as in scolding. It laments the loss and calls for reform. It implies that we can *fix* the situation. It suggests that if we somehow got our act together and did a better job of presenting, we would have real heroes again.

But the situation is better understood if we rephrase the favored explanation. Put it this way instead: real heroes must become stars if they are to exist in public culture at all.

That is, they must perform. But as soon as they do that, they can't compete with the real stars—who *are* performers.

How neat is that?

True enough, then, each favored explanation to its own world-view sufficient—but the threshold effect that frames the whole cultural shift goes unremarked. Once again, a Blobby law of paradox determines a whole panoply of specific transitions, camouflaging the workings of reflexivity. The conventional wisdom comes in pieces. How to fit them together?

The key to synthesis lies in this fact: the essence of real heroes in the good old days—Newton and Napoleon and Goethe, say—was that they were, as heroes, essentially *un*real. They were not known as people at all. They *were* their works and deeds, they *were* their myths. Nelson and Byron and Lincoln were basically fictional constructs, even in their own lifetimes. They were the inventions of the people who idolized them, on the basis of a few stories and images—so very few, and so infrequent. That is what must be understood: the whole dynamic is a function of representational quantity and quality.

Real heroes of the past were represented with a frugality that is almost impossible to credit today. Texts of speeches or essays or poems, committed to memory by devoted followers; a few dozen images known to everyone; places he stood, things he touched; and, most important, a store of anecdotes, circulating informally, the way Polish jokes and elephant jokes used to before the Internet substituted itself for what was left to us of oral culture.

Anthropologists and social historians know the special power that infuses stories of this type. They come alive with each retelling because they are subject to constant editing, enhancement, and local variation. Unlike printed accounts, such anecdotes are undetectably adaptable. There is no official version, no dictionary or encyclopedia to set a standard. Unadulterated perfection and immediate relevance are guaranteed by these means. Paucity of representation makes it possible for the imagination of followers to supply their hero with just the right attributes, and their identification is correspondingly intense and intimate.

At the same time, such inventions were anchored to flesh. People knew that, unlike Paul Bunyan and Old Saint Nick, their heroes were in fact real people. Robert E. Lee led Confederate troops into battle on a horse named Traveler. Florence Nightingale took care of sick people. Goethe wrote *Faust*. That is why minimally represented real heroes of that world could inspire millions to life-transforming action. They were perfect *and* real— perhaps someone you knew personally, your uncle or your brother, was there on that glorious day, and saw, with his own eyes, Napoleon take his stand upon the bridge at Lodi, and he has been telling the story with irresistible fervor and pathos ever since.

Here's another way to look at it. Right after 9/11, but before the representations multiplied to the point of pointlessness, New York City firemen attained authentic heroic status. That sense of them lasted longer for some people than for others—the last straw for me was the marketing of that "Calendar of Heroes" showing real firemen, handsome fellows all, decked out in their gear but stripped to the waist and invitingly posed for their admirers. That's when the bubble popped for me.

But there was a period early on when, no matter what your politics, if you lived in New York City and you saw them on their trucks, flags anchored to the fenders and streaming in the wind, and you knew what they had done, what their comrades had done, you couldn't resist, didn't want to resist—your heart lifted out to them, to the heroes riding by.

There's a confluence of reasons why that was possible, and it's revealing to sort them out. During that period, firefighters were represented as a group; there was a generality, a Rorschach indeterminacy about them. One or another would get photographed or interviewed, but no one personality became emblematic, no one got covered in detail—what came across in the media were "firemen" in general. There were a few iconic shots, to be sure, but they were of otherwise unknown men, smothered in uniforms, this one kneeling, weeping in the rubble, that one comforting a wounded woman in a doorway. Then there were the facts we did know, the number who responded, the number missing and injured, the number who died. Then there were the real individuals, in the passing trucks, or at entrances to firehouses, receiving flowers and candles from neighbors who once took them for granted.

In other words, we saw real people in glimpses, but glimpses of great potency, concrete reminders of the fact that, though we didn't know details, they really did run up those stairs while everybody else—ordinary people like you and me —ran down. And we could imagine, fully, gratefully, in wonder, just what it took to do that.

And so, for a while, because of the way those vectors converged, the generic "FDNY" secured a position in public culture analogous to the one individual heroes used to occupy.

As recently as Einstein and Lindbergh, Churchill and FDR, the essential representational conditions held—though such figures have suffered a loss of mystique recently because of the way they have been representationally resurrected in personal biographies, with the echo-chamber publicity and the psychosexual exposure.

But back in their day, it was different.

Just think how utterly impossible it would be now for a president to be paralyzed from the waist down, as Franklin Roosevelt was—and the public in ignorance of it. Take that as a measure.

Okay, summing up: it's like the way special-effects movies about outer space made coverage of real space adventures boring for most people. The pathetic production values and shapeless plot, flickering videos of people you can barely identify doing lame things with vials and tubes? Please. No wonder NASA fell into decline, clinging to life-support hype about spin-off applications and educational benefits while equipment and procedures atrophied and contractors robbed the store.

In the same way, as soon as real heroes are represented publicly, repeatedly, they are doomed. In effect, the virtual heroes—the real performers, the stars (what a word!), the Madonnas and the Maradonnas—present themselves fabulously and consistently across decades and make it impossible for hero candidates from reality to succeed. The central irony is that we don't have real heroes anymore because they are *too real*, representations of them are too rich and detailed. There is no space for our imaginations to occupy, no room for us to supply them with mythic life.

Heroes we do have, however, of a kind, and plenty of them—in venues where performance is the raison d'être to begin with.

Real Performers

No domain of endeavor in our culture is more relentlessly mediated than sport. The contest is well-nigh smothered in coverage, promotion, technological enhancement, Nintendo versions—representations of all kinds. And nowhere is the profit motive more transparently at work. If the media age is best understood as a process through which experiences—as well as material goods—are being commodified under "late capitalism," then sport should be high on the list of things succumbing to virtualization. But it isn't. Why?

Now, my view of postmodern media overlaps significantly with such neo-Marxist views; I don't disagree with them, as far as they go, but they don't go far enough. Suppose you had a child who was obsessed with animals, doting on specifics like what speeds the falcon and cheetah can attain, would a lion beat a tiger in a fight, how big are the teeth of the great white shark, and so on. And you came along and said, "Look kid, whatever, with animals it all comes down to ingestion, locomotion, and reproduction, and that's it." Would you be doing justice to his interest?

Accounts of modern media that reduce it all to economics are like that. Not wrong, just much too broad. They overlook the internally significant aspects of the phenomenon—like why sports, in spite of all the commodification, has not succumbed to virtualization. Sports heroes still exist. Why is that?

For years I tried to convince myself that real sport was somehow coming to an end. I wanted to believe that when Rosewall played Laver at Forest Hills it was somehow realer than Venus playing Serena at Flushing Meadows. But that was the curmudgeon effect, that longing for the good old days that is always such a risk for a social critic. My students, usually so open to my overall analysis as I worked it out with them, always balked at the sports example.

And I could see it in their eyes; Derek Jeter means as much to baseball fans today as Ted Williams once meant to me, and in more or less the same way; and the same goes for Zidane as compared to, say, Péle—in spite of all the marketing contrivances. So I was stuck with this question: if ubiquitous representation can virtualize politics and religion and family life, why should sports be exempt?

My students were supplying the answer all along, but my politically motivated inclination to blame commodification for everything prevented me from taking it in. In effect, they kept saying, "Yeah, okay, Jordan looks like a digitized special effect in all the slow-mo replays and commercials, but, during the game itself, he has to make the shot. He really did make that buzzer-beating shot to win against the Jazz in the NBA finals of 1997. That was an incredible performance, a historic moment in the history of the game, and it was *real*."

One day, the word "game" jumped out at me. Suddenly I understood why, in spite of unprecedented excesses of commodification and representation, sports could retain their peculiar authenticity.

They were already games.

Sports were thus inoculated against the virtualizing effects of mediation. Athletes perform, by definition, but when it comes down to it, they are also doing something real—hitting the mark, sinking the putt, catching the ball, crossing the line. Real within the boundaries of the game, of course, *but that was always understood.*

For the same reason that sports, no matter how hyped, resist virtualization, entertainment performers who stand for something across their appearances come as close as our culture allows to heroic stature. That means pop music stars especially. Movie stars too, but they do not perform live—except on the Leno and Letterman shows maybe, but that's not them, somehow, not what we know on-screen; they have a way of muting themselves when they appear in person like that. Movie stars are insulated by the arts of film construction from the actual event, the living moment that confers that special blessing. And movie stars are, at least on the surface, playing characters, being someone else. This provides another layer of insulation.

Movie stars are not heroes in the way that pop music stars and athletes are—their land is too distant, too fictional, a realm of dreams, not of this world at the end of the day. But Bob Dylan, Bruce Springsteen—such artists, and their songs, directly express and define actual lives as they are lived. They instill and reinforce values and condition the life choices people make, especially the *ways* they make them, the style—the attitude, as we noted before.

These stars can be heroes because their performances fuse the real and representational on a new plane. They are, in effect, leading us into a new reality—the reality of *being* mediated.

And this applies to Barbra Streisand and to Luther Vandross, to Frank Sinatra and Garth Brooks and Selena—to the whole range of types we know so well. And others we don't know so well. There are so many now.

And all these types represent the selves their fans have chosen to be. That's how it works, that's how the circle closes.

Maybe you're thinking, so what if adolescence is a modern construct, people have always had to learn styles— mannerisms, accents, slang, rhythms of conduct, and so on, right? What's the big deal? That would be the "hurricane is just more breeze" fallacy again. In traditional contexts, style was picked up auto matically, from older siblings or charismatic friends. With modernity things get much more self-conscious, much less automatic, as represented options multiply. With postmodernity, there's a quantum leap.

Back to the influence of the performer at the center of the stage. In shaping the event of the song, the performer leaves sane fans with only one choice: if they want to follow their hero, they must expand the stage. Undeniably, fans have become part of the show while it is being performed. At games, they flaunt their painted faces, crafted signs, elaborate chants and cheers. At concerts, they do the wave, they dance, they mosh, they hold lighters in the air. But these obvious forms of participation only suggest the more profound developments.

In concert, especially, these new heroes provide fans with the only experiences of transcendent social belonging most of them will ever know. Hence the undeniably religious quality of these events, when they go well, when the heroes meet the awesome expectations. Then they offer, in song and persona, the only cultural vehicle we have left that can penetrate lives, that can make people feel collectively recognized and acknowledged in their otherwise irreducible individual complexity, understood and somehow redeemed in the moment of the chord that seems to reach forever and the lyric that brings it all back home. These heroes discover us, tell us who we are, and who we aspire to be— which is what real heroes used to do.

But consider what that means in this new context. It means that, in the end, these new heroes, these performer-heroes, are all about us. Because now there is no cause they are summoning us to serve—other than the cause of being whoever we are.

That's big-time flattery. It has to have consequences.

Virtual Revolution

The stars may be on the stage, being adored, being pursued, they may be—they are—the ones most obviously at the center of it all while we, the fans, are individually invisible. But there's another side to this relation, the ironic dialectic of mediation is at work here too. Consider the totality of the relationship, not just between you and your particular performer-hero, but between you and all of them, all of those celebrities, vying for your attention.

Is it not ultimately we, in our very hiddenness, who hold sway, who have the last word? Great power attaches to the anonymous spectator. All the gratifications of voyeurism accrue to a judge nobody knows, passing sentence upon the celebrated, the mighty and the fallen, from that central position in the panopticon of representation. She can love this one and admire that one and condemn the other one, and she and her friends can indulge themselves at length in these ongoing assessments and comparisons, and they do, they gossip about celebrities as if they were coworkers—and it's all risk free, no matter how cruel, no matter how arbitrary. And those celebrities, competing for the judge's attention and approval, are in effect inviting the treatment they get. They are so needy, actually—dressing up, dieting, touring, posing, exposing privacies, cavorting desperately, endlessly, before us. In a way, at a certain level, celebrities are pathetic, undignified, utterly dependent.

No, don't underestimate the unconscious sense of sovereignty that is the lot of spectators. Because that's why, as the status of hero was usurped by performers, the focus of the limelight began to shift—or, better, it was as if another limelight (infrared, off the spectrum) began to glow, began to shine in the other direction, in the direction in which the pop star so often points the mic these days, in our direction, a limelight for us. It shines invisibly upon those to whom all performances are addressed.

Over the years, the decades, the centuries even—the hidden blandishments of representation implanted a sense of entitlement, an envy, a desire for public significance commensurate with an unconscious sense of centrality. Fans, in their anonymity, got more and more restless. Celebrities held a monopoly on the most precious scarce resource in an increasingly mediated society. Attention. They were gorging on it. For spectators, the most basic of specifically human needs—the need for acknowledgment, for significance—was left unsatisfied. Unlike premodern monarchs, who were openly flattered when minstrels and jesters postured before them, postmodern fans, implicitly flattered more and more intensely, would eventually have to take action to make their covert centrality apparent—as would only seem fair. The surgical-makeover show *I Want a Famous Face* expresses the longing obviously, but all the reality shows are sustained by this reversal, and most fans would rather make their own face (plus enhancements?) famous. They are already performing their lives, as we have seen. Now they want to be *recognized* performers.

And we are returned to our inaugural theme of Method acting from another angle. If the performance of one's everyday life is the most comprehensive manifestation of the mediated self's centrality, it is also the subtlest, the most diluted. Something more obvious was needed. All that was lacking were the means.

Until recently.

Now the representational spaces have been technologically multiplied through cable, satellite TV the Web, all the usual suspects—and all that space and time has to be filled. That's the condition that allows the virtual revolution to take place. But spectators were primed for it, motivated to undertake what the technology only made possible.

Robert Murphy, who introduced me to anthropology at Columbia lo these many years ago, used to sum up the difference between modern societies and the small-scale hunter-gatherer communitites in which human nature took shape in this way: "everyone is famous in a tribe." He meant us to understand that, for human beings, the need to be recognized is almost as basic as food. The force behind the virtual revolution is primordial.

Now consider this. In the mid-1970s, introducing his late-night audience to Truman Capote—then keeping regular and much publicized company with the likes of Andy Warhol and Jackie Onassis—host Merv Griffin happened upon these words: "Our next guest is not only one of America's greatest authors, but a real celebrity in his own right." No irony, no 1990s self-awareness, just a statement of fact from a man completely immersed in show business in the early days of what would soon be known as "celebrity culture." In hindsight, Merv's clueless intro can be taken to mark a transition point, for the pure celebrity would be defined as someone who is "famous for being famous," a status transcending all question of achievement.

So why shouldn't anyone be entitled to that?

Now consider this little factoid from the mid-1990s, when Robert Shapiro was OJ's principal lawyer. The *New Yorker* ran a cartoon that showed a little girl introducing a friend to her playmates in the park. She was saying, "This is Robert Shapiro, except he's not the real Robert Shapiro."

Revolution was, by then, at hand.

And so it came to pass. Coached by performer heroes, seeking the recognition to which people naturally feel entitled, spectators pushed themselves forward as the technological venues opened up, and not only in what we call the reality show—that mother of all mixes, that most basic fusion of genres. Other reality shows, under other names, sprang up everywhere. What they all have in common is the celebration of people refusing to be just spectators, all the mini-celebrities, for example, who dominate chat rooms and game sites, hundreds of them, thousands of them—and the blogs, the intimate "life journals," illustrated with digitized photos. Think also of raves and flash-mobbing, mass marathons, karaoke bars, focus groups, talk-radio call-ins, e-mails to every news show, camcorders, home-made porn, sponsored sports teams for tots—and every start-up band in the world can burn a CD and produce cool cover art and posters. There are so many platforms now, so many performers.

Being famous isn't what it used to be.

Has it ever struck you, watching interviews with people in film clips from the 1940s and 1950s, say—or even just looking at them in photographs—how stiff and unnatural they seem? Even prominent people, but especially regular folk, the way they lean into the mic and glance awkwardly around as they say whatever they have to say in semiformal tones, almost as if reciting, and the way they raise their voices, as if they can't quite trust the technology to reach an absent audience, the way my grandmother used to when she took a long-distance call, feeling as if she had to shout to someone far away. But nowadays? Every man on the street, every girl on the subway platform, interviewed about the snowstorm or the transit strike—they are total pros, laughing in the right places, looking directly at the interviewer or into the camera, fluid, colloquial, comments and mannerisms pitched just right for the occasion, completely at ease.

And check out the wedding pictures and the little biographies in the *New York Times* announcements section these days.

Method actors all.

But, before we get back to more about you, let's polish off the old-style heroes once and for all.

Put your nostalgia on hold, if you have any, and ask yourself this: on the whole, aren't we better off without those real heroes of the past? I know some of you long for great causes, grand historic movements and events, but, really—think of the carnage. Looking back, don't the visions of those heroes appear to us now as intoxicating, masculinist fantasies that brought devastation to millions? Aren't we all hoping that the "war on terror" *doesn't* play out on a heroic scale? Aren't we better off limited to the kind of glory we find in the sports arena and the concert hall?

Alexander the Great? Napoleon? Douglas MacArthur? Really! Who did they think they *were*? I mean, there's a limit to how much self-esteem we want to encourage, right? Sometimes it's hard to believe that people were supposed to admire those egomaniacs. Okay, so you personally can balance the scales by referencing Gandhi and King, say—but then there are figures like Churchill and Castro, who get judged so differently by people on opposing sides of the historical ledger, and even Gandhi and King weren't universally admired, you know. You should check out what Winston had to say about Mahatma, for example. No, the issue isn't whether you admire a particular hero, the issue is whether the status itself, as a cultural given, was a good thing that we lost, or is it a good thing that we lost it?

This goes beyond the military and politics. Take the Big Thinkers. Plato? Augustine? Descartes? Kant? It suddenly hits you. The sheer brass of those guys, pontificating about the ultimate nature of reality and the proper purpose of *our* lives. I mean, who did they think they *were*?

Don't get me wrong, it's fine to put them in books and teach courses about them and stuff, so long as it doesn't get out of hand, so long as they don't impose on the rest of us, who are busy exploring our own options, choosing our own philosophies, our own lifestyles. That kind of imposition from above is not appropriate at a time when we have great leaders exercising great leadership everywhere, in every company and school and neighborhood and church, special people doing special things in their own special ways, local heroes one and all. And they are being recognized and celebrated for it too—as you well know, as well they should—though perhaps not as much as they should, but we're working on that.

Another aspect of the virtual revolution.

Of course, some people are more special than the average special person, people like Bill Moyers and Tina Brown and Colin Powell and Stephen J. Gould and Margaret Thatcher and Hillary Clinton. These people are so accomplished, so downright *prominent*, that you have to say they are especially special. But at the same time—and this is the nice part—they're regular people too. This is a kind of greatness everyone can identify with. The same goes for the villains. There's Ken Lay of Enron fame and Don Rumsfeld and Martha Stewart and Mike Tyson—and Margaret Thatcher and Hillary Clinton. I mean, they may be pretty loathsome, but you can imagine being in school with them.

The old-style heroes just weren't empowering, that's the point. They had an intimidating kind of greatness that could make you feel like not bothering to develop your own average greatness. We no longer approve of that demanding kind of greatness; what we want now is a supportive and inclusive kind of greatness.

So enough of da Vinci, Shakespeare, Newton, Jefferson, Beethoven, and all of them too. But it's not just the dead white male thing; that's old hat, in case you didn't know. Enough Frederick Douglass and Martha Graham too. They all come off like they have some historical dispensation that the rest of us don't have, that's the point. Again, this isn't about burning books or paintings or anything drastic like that. By all means, lavish attention on the heroes of the past, transform them into celebrities in their own right, because that's where we want them, up there in la-la land with Britney and Becks and Gandalf. Go ahead and drape those gigantic banners on the museum façades— the more gigantic the better—and celebrate their centennials, and all their other -ennials as well, the more the better, because the more of that we do, the more proportionality we get, that's the irony, and *that's* what this is all about. Proportionality. Keep treating the greats of yore like stars of the hour and they will all melt into each other eventually. A pudding of indistinguishable greatness.

The Blob is eating.

It's the same with inserting Ben Stein's face into the *Mona Lisa*, using snatches of the Ninth Symphony in margarine commercials, putting Einstein and Picasso on Apple/Mac billboards—stuff like that, over and over and over again, until everything gets absorbed and takes its place among the options, like everything else.

That's fair, right?

So now we see why people so often respond to the question "Do you have any heroes?" by naming someone local, someone in their personal lives, someone who struggled bravely with uncelebrated burdens.

You, again

We are also in a position to understand why traditional TV shows began to look contrived in recent decades. There were too many of them for one thing, so they couldn't stand out the way they used to. It got to be more interesting, and more plausible, to identify with regular people in extreme circumstances of some kind: competing for a mate, trapped on an island, winning a recording contract, being fired by Donald Trump, in a coffin full of maggots. Also contrived, of course—but not pretending not to be; once again, that's the key, the vaccination, there's no suspension-of-disbelief issue.

And there are so many little things to notice, when it's real people, revelations that reside in unintended expressions, affectations, mannerisms, little foibles. Real people responding to circumstances, no matter how unlikely, can't hide these giveaway traits the way good actors following a script can. It doesn't matter how hard they try, how much they may exaggerate their excitement or hostility for the camera's sake. It's so obvious when they do, like when the trailer-trash fat woman on *Jerry Springer* stalks over to her sister, who has just admitted sleeping with her husband (who is sitting between them), and starts to pummel her—it's so obviously being done for the camera, in conformity with the show's format, it's so obvious that, in some weird way, it is real in the very transparency of the performance. Compared to actors, that is, or their stunt doubles, doing digitally enhanced combat ballets.

Also the sister *really did fuck that guy*.

Who cares how much the woman on *Fear Factor* is exaggerating her trepidation—*she is eating a mouthful of live worms*.

And if you get to the point of appointment-viewing involvement with *Big Brother* or *Survivor*, then you can gossip about the people without feeling like the kind of moron who writes letters to characters on soap operas. You can pick the ones you like, the ones you hate, the ones you don't trust, and so on, just the way you do at work or at school—or, for that matter, the way you do watching some drawn-out real-life crime story, like the epic Michael Jackson molestation investigation. Things actually happen. You might change your mind about Sheri after she keeps her promise to Ron not to vote against Rachel.

In a nutshell: it could be you and yours up there, and what's going on is a lot more like your life than what the doctors and cops get into in the standard dramas.

But, who knows, reality TV could turn out to be a fad. The shift in focus, however, the shift to spectators will not. What is likely to last, for example, is the rage for the memoir—and for all the fiction that mimics the memoir, the whole *Bridget Jones's Diary* genre, for example, all those girly books, with the pink and blue jackets, kooky lettering, and female feet displayed in various postures of whimsical vulnerability. The jacket designs will change, no doubt, but the works they advertise will continue because they speak more deeply and directly to you than even a reality show can (unless you're on one).

So it's not just autobiographies of the famous anymore. We are inundated with stories of ordinary folk—shattered by drugs, stricken by disease, worried about the size of their thighs, stranded in the wild, captured by the mullahs, spending Tuesdays with Morrie, giving kidneys to their sisters, awakened from comas, being dumped by clueless boyfriends, on and on. What is it with these stories?

Identification. Self-recognition. It may be fact, it may be fiction, it may be comedy, or tragedy, but it's all aimed at eliciting responses that go "I'm *exactly* like that" or "Imagine how I would feel if . . ."

It is especially revealing to notice how people identify with confessional suffering even when they can't identify with the particular condition. There is a huge fan base out there for trauma memoirs (and on the talk shows again) and it goes way beyond the constituency that shares the specific malady. Why? Well, partly it's morbid curiosity, a ghoulish investment in gazing upon the misfortunes of others, of course that's part of it—that's the disdainful high-brow analysis and there is truth to it.

But there are other reasons. How often do you hear this refrain—when you witness these public confessionals—how often do you hear, "I felt so alone, I felt weird and ashamed, I thought no one would understand what I was going through." And so on. That's the mantra. And it's the key to understanding how people who haven't been, say, abused by their Siamese twin, can nevertheless identify with someone who has.

The fact is that a lot of people who have not had some socially or physically problematic condition thrust upon them by fate *feel as if they have*. Like fans of Harry Potter, they feel different. They feel alone and misunderstood and imposed upon. They feel unacknowledged, unappreciated. So they respond to the saga of redemption through recognition that is the underlying plot of all narratives of this kind.

That's the key.

They respond projectively with something that borders on envy. The specifics of the cases they identify with vicariously are symbolic condensations of the amorphous afflictions that burden them, and of the universal pain of anonymity.

All of which is not to say that there is a dearth of standard dramas or of autobiographies by the famous, of course, heaven forfend, there are still plenty of those too, and more besides, because, Lord knows, there's enough room in the Box and the MegaStore to accommodate us all, in every way—and this is mostly a good thing, once again, it's good that the famous have to compete with the rest of us for our own attention. Metallica may be the world's most successful heavy metal band, and they may have made a documentary movie showing them all in group therapy, but there's no guarantee they will get more attention than garden-variety drunks and their friends and relatives on the reality show *Intervention*—and that's fair, right?

And it is also seems fair that, when the most popular reality shows, like *American Idol* and *The Apprentice*, reach their climactic weeks, the news media cover them as real events, like they would an impending election—and not just because of corporate synergy. It's because, on this new plane of being, they *are* real events.

The Blob is obviously at work here. Some ironic doubling, some virtualizing effect of optionality must be lurking in the vicinity.

First of all, notice how stars of suffering typically derive therapeutic benefit from "telling their story," as the expression goes. It is a healing process, they all say that. And, not coincidentally, they often lay claim to a public service benefit as well—a provision of comfort and encouragement to fellow sufferers, whose story is also being told. And even practical consequences can follow when attention is drawn to something that can be presented as an "issue"—as with movements launched by relatives of victims to control handguns or crack down on drunk driving.

But public forms of therapy—memoir therapy, advocacy therapy, vicarious therapy—also serve to take the edge off the given, to leaven necessity with reflection, just as private therapy has always done. Personal intimacies validate public identities when the anonymous bare their souls in forums that cater to their longing to matter. Those intimacies get absorbed into performative categories. Repeated anecdotes, favorite punch lines, memories revisited so often they inevitably get honed into more poignant shapes. Of course, the process is relatively superficial on the talk-show and lecture circuit, compared to therapy itself, but the structure and function are the same. The 1960s therapist provided the model for the talk show hostess, just as she originally offered us an audience of one—at a price, the dramatic equivalent of the vanity press.

And the aim of all these therapeutic missions, the grail? A particular sensation, cherished by all the participants in this ritual of self-overcoming. It's that feeling that wells up, reaching for release, wells up and overflows when at last it finds expression in words and sobs, blessed self-expression and the liberation that follows the unburdening. Free at last from the weight of repression and self-loathing and self-doubt, admitted, at last, into the light of self-acceptance made public, welcomed, acknowledged, recognized—and, yes, celebrated.

Just for being you.

And lest you misread, overread, the irony, you hipster, you, I am quite sincere. I have been substantially helped by therapy myself, as have many people close to me, and I frequently advise a friend or a student to get professional help when things start going off the rails. No, no, you can't ironize yourself out of this, you can't get above it, you can't elude the play of this paradox. Therapy is mostly a good thing.

But the fact remains. Transforming a given condition, something that was imposed upon you, into something you possess through expression and description contributes to the virtualization of your life. What was ineluctable and necessary, determined by accidents of birth and circumstance, becomes something you have. It no longer has you. The act of self-acceptance through self-expression in the light of public recognition just *is* that transformation. That is why that moment is experienced as a liberation as well as an affirmation. The self that emerges from this process is, in effect, a chosen self.

Okay, it would be a stretch to say that it is an optional self, strictly speaking—at least in some cases. If you are stricken with a crippling disease, if you were abused as a child, if you are black or gay, such things can never be options the way, say, your political beliefs are options—though certain biotech possibilities are opening up, and a trend is discernible, even here. You can, in fact, decide to become a woman now, and more and more people are doing that. And vice versa, of course. Can race be far behind, as the age of the makeover dawns?

Imagine a reality show about that. And, trust me, there will be volunteers in all directions. And especially there will be volunteers who want to be "ethnically ambiguous"—that being the latest thing, according to a recent piece in the Style section of the *New York Times*. But all you have to do is look at the models to know that.

More mixes.

But leaving such possibilities aside for now, let's run with this premise: the conditions just mentioned are not optional.

But consider how it is to be a person on that spectrum of conditions in a culture of therapeutic mediation—think, for example, of how one moves, psycho-culturally as well as literally, from being crippled in an environment that does nothing to accommodate you to being differently abled in an environment with lots of ramps and special parking places. That just is a process through which living in a wheelchair becomes as close *as it can possibly be* to a lifestyle among others.

It can't literally be an option, in other words, but the central aspiration of this culture is to make it into one.

So, if you find solace and community and purpose in a group of survivors of, say, priestly pedophilia, if you recover some lost dignity in a movement to see justice done in your name and in the name of your fellow victims and, especially, if you contribute to the

127

security of youngsters not yet victimized—this whole experience of self-assertion and vindication in service of a common identity and common cause—none of that can turn what happened to you into an option, of course. But that dynamic of recovery *aspires* to transform what makes you different into something you can live with the way other people—say, members of a sect—live with what makes them different, even though they made a choice and you didn't. The inherent aim of the ethos of mediation is to turn everything into an option, even when it can't literally succeed.

That is why the Die with Dignity movement will certainly take hold and flourish as boomers come up against their inevitable ends.

And that is why the personal became the political.

CHAPTER 4

Identity Politics. Players and their issues. Why politics is so boring. Except when there is crisis or scandal. From Deep Throat to Monica. A people's princess. A president's penis. A president's heart.

Politics as Self-Expression

OVER THE PAST twenty years, I've done many workshops for students, faculty, and parents—mostly dealing with the effects of media on young people. "Political apathy" always comes up. Since 9/11—what with the reaction to Bush and Blair, the Iraq war, Howard Dean's campaign, MoveOn.org, and *Fahrenheit 9/11* duking it out with *The Passion of the Christ* (politics as box office?)—you don't hear this quite as much. But the basic conditions haven't changed. What has changed is the mood. Apathy receded before the reality of war, the blind certainty of a fundamentalist president, and the prospect of terror, but an affirmative (as opposed to reactive) commitment to politics is still unusual among young people (see coda). And there was one exchange I witnessed at a workshop that stands out in my memory because it taught me so much about why that is.

We were featuring a panel of students, fishbowl style, in front of an audience of maybe seventy-five adults. Each kid represented a political club in the high school. Environment Gender Issues, Asian, African-American—you know the list. The president of the Latino Students Organization had just finished describing an event they had recently sponsored, lamenting the paltry turnout for a prominent guest—someone who had worked with Cesar Chavez back in the glory days. There had been plenty of publicity, posters all over the place, announcements in assembly, flyers in the mailbag, but only fifteen people showed up, and nine of them were club members.

A woman rose in the audience. She was maybe fifty-five, solid, at ease with herself, graying hair in an up-woven braid, well dressed but casual—someone of substance in the academy or publishing or a nonprofit, you could tell. And you knew she'd been there way back when, been at People's Park or the siege of Chicago—she had recognized the snubbed guest's name, she felt entitled to speak with authority. And she did. Her voice shook with indignation as she said, "I can't believe that in a school like this there aren't opportunities for *all* of our students to bring their concerns to the community . . ."

On the panel, heads were shaking before she finished the first sentence. One girl leaned into her mic and interrupted, "No, no, that's not the problem. The problem is there are *too many* opportunities." The woman was taken aback, but only for a moment. She knew what she knew, and that was that. "How can there be *too many* opportunities?" she asked, but dismissively, rhetorically, before going on to suggest ways the administration could initiate this or outreach for that.

But I wasn't listening anymore. I was having a little epiphany. I was realizing that the welter of worthy causes that was the legacy of her generation seemed to this woman to be an invitation extended to successors—an invitation to choose. But to most of the kids she hoped to see engaged, inundated with exhortations to care about one thing or another since their *Sesame Street* days, that same array of causes amounted to a battery of demands they couldn't possibly meet.

Hence, so-called apathy among the many in the 1980s and 1990s, and—what's a good expression?—let's say "niche commitments" among the few, the few who made a choice. On what basis? Because they "identified with" the focus of one of the niches. By way of race, gender, or sexual orientation, obviously—but identification works more subtly as well. Kids who care about the environment are usually kids who love animals, who identify with them in that special animistic way certain children have of projecting their very souls into another living creature's moods and motions. "Identifying with" nature says something about them, in other words.

And what do people in each niche proceed to do by way of political action? The only thing they've ever seen done. They stage some kind of show, some presentation that will exhort others to attend to their cause—thus adding their mite to the battery of demands.

It was that evening that I first grasped the dialectic of "whatever."

For people coming of age in the 1980s and 1990s, politics came to actually *mean* presentations. Documentaries, movies, guest speakers, rallies, concerts. They saw the Army-McCarthy hearings ("Have you no shame?"), the Watergate hearings (Sam Irvin, the "country lawyuh"), civil rights sit-ins (the Formica counters, the generic napkin dispensers, the brave black faces), Vietnam war protests (draft cards burning), the war itself (GI sets thatch roof ablaze with lighter), Anita Hill's testimony, antiglobalization demos, anti-Iraq demos, on and on. They saw the whole series, you might say—because that's what it was like for them, that's what it *was* for them.

No wonder that, for those who do get politically engaged in these circumstances, for those who identify with one of the causes, political action means getting attention. Politics becomes the process of "giving voice to," "raising awareness of," "getting the message out." It is expressing oneself in terms of some shared identity—which is what makes it political.

The Dean campaign took the politics of self-expression to a new level of self-consciousness. Participants knew—they all said it, over and over again—that this wasn't about Dean; it was about the movement, the participants. It was about the "Deaniacs" themselves, those techie communards and the multiple niches they coordinated, online and off—so many flash mobs of Lesbians for Dean, Golfers for Dean, Acupuncturists for Dean—this was the ultimate manifestation of the event-story genre, the giant-improv-starring-everybody version. If you were part of that campaign, you were *being* the phenomenon as you were seeing it represented, in real time, unfolding before you. You could see the impact of your role on the national stage in essentially the same way you can see the impact of your button-pressing in a video game. You were the agent, you were the star. MoveOn understood this. That's why it held contests for political ads, judged by celebrity professionals, and then featured the winning ads. Dean himself understood it too. He was the political equivalent of a DJ at a rave that refuses to glorify bands. He acknowledged you at every turn, saying over and over again, ferociously, joyfully, pointing his fingers out at you, like a rock star offering the mic: "You have the power . . . You have the power . . ."

And so an ineluctably self-oriented quality emanated from the cohort of campaigners who invaded Iowa in their orange hats to round up voters—a clique unto themselves, brash as dot-commers in the spring of '98. And that, in turn, provoked the natives to express themselves in accordance with their own scripts.

I remember another occasion that brought the overall situation home to me from a different angle. It was a few years after that workshop, and I had affiliated myself that semester with the gay and lesbian students group. One day we had a guest, a young man in his late twenties who worked for a nationwide advocacy organization. His job was to go into various school settings and help students and faculty and parents get themselves organized "around" (as they say; why?) gay and lesbian issues. That's how he made a living. During a chat after his presentation, he happened to mention an "Advocacy Institute" he had attended—or maybe it was "Camp" or "Center," something like that—but it was enough to make me want to ask: advocacy of what?

And he said—anything.

I clamped down on my incredulity and asked a few questions, just to make sure. Yes, he confirmed, there are institutions out there that run programs to train advocates in techniques of advocacy, so they can advocate for—whatever. A would-be advocate for a classic identity group (like ACT UP) gets the same training as someone from a classic interest group (the American Association of Retired People or the National Association of Manufacturers) and someone from the increasing number of organizations that fuse identity and interest (National Association of Black Journalists, Emily's List). That's the sociological bird's-eye view. A whole industry can be devoted to the art and science of creating panels, retreats, orientations, CD-ROMs, Web sites, tours, workshops—because that's how many people there are out there who make a living presenting something, getting attention for something.

The grown-ups involved in all this presenting presumably understand that the aim of getting attention is ultimately practical—money, position, resources. Because that's what domestic policy comes down to these days, that's about all that's left of issues on the left since the "end of ideology": straight material payoffs, getting more for some identity and/or interest group—which doesn't make the political scene any more appealing to the young, by the way. Indeed, it makes all those presentations look more and more like what they are.

Ads.

Just what kids need. More ads.

So that's the driving force. As political activity becomes the production of representations, the dynamic of commerce is reproduced in politics. Because political representations must contend with clutter, they must be packaged in a certain way, they must grab the most attention possible in the least amount of time and get across some simple message.

Mainstream players in the game of politics have understood this ever since Johnson clobbered Goldwater with that little girl counting down to Armageddon on her daisy petals. But it took longer for them to realize that laws of representational competition were going to hold sway over more than campaign ads. It wasn't until the Clinton administration that players began to talk openly about governing as a form of campaigning—though Michael Deaver and Ronald Reagan pioneered the process, and the administration of Bush II has been pursuing it transparently. (The "mission to Mars" idea, trotted out with such fanfare, failed the laugh test because it so obviously turned policy itself into publicity. The fact that its exponents didn't realize how it would play shows how entrenched that thinking is.)

In any case, that was how the pros began to describe the effect of mediation on politics, that was their take on the fact that politics was *becoming* representation.

In concrete terms, this simply means that making presentations of some kind, and turning actual events into presentations of some kind, becomes what institutions are for. You can see it happening to some degree or another in whatever institution you are involved in, I'm sure, but it is especially true of political institutions. A random case in point, from a *New York Times* op-ed on December 8, 2003, by Philip Bobbitt. Struggling to account for why the consequences of our invasion of Iraq were not anticipated, he wrote, "It is an open secret that the National Security Council's strategic planning directorate is really devoted to communications tasks and the State Department's policy planning staff is actually a speech writing office." An empirical study would expose ramifications this little snapshot only suggests. The question would be: how much governmental time is spent preparing, giving, receiving, and responding to presentations today as compared with, say, thirty or fifty years ago? And the answer would be: lots.

Of course, the mainstream 24–7 political show they put on is mostly boring, unless it's during a crisis, unless it's like Bush doing his aircraft carrier thing, or footage of Madrid. Representations from the commitment niches can afford to be a lot more powerful. Kids today have been subjected to thousands and thousands of high-impact images of misery and injustice in every corner of the globe before they are old enough to drive. The producers of these images compete with each other to arouse as much horror and pity and outrage as possible, hoping that *this* encounter with a person dying of AIDS or *that* documentary about sweatshop labor or *these* photographs of recently skinned baby seals will mobilize commitment. But what the cumulative experience has actually mobilized, in the majority, is that characteristic ironic distance that aging activists mistook for apathy. But it wasn't apathy as much as it was psychological numbness, a general defense against representational intrusions of all kinds—especially painful ones. I mean, who wants to look at pictures of skinned baby seals?

Well, a few people, as we noted. People who identify with

natural innocence, who find in the human mistreatment of animals a moral allegory that gives meaning and direction to their lives.

And so on, across the niches.

But most kids didn't "identify with" any of this. As politics came to be about expressing identity, it couldn't compete with other identity-defining venues in popular culture—like the ones we just considered in chapter 3. How much more satisfying to belong to Hip-Hop Nation than to some dowdy civil rights organization? How much more fun to go to parties with all your clever friends and watch *Queer Eye for the Straight Guy* makeovers on TV than to join a conclave of relentlessly earnest Episcopalians stuffing envelopes on behalf of a gay bishop?

So political "apathy" took hold because political representations were boring—when they weren't painful.

So, since the 1960s—when it all began—mainstream political actors and story lines lost dramatic credibility as pop culture expressions of identity became more purely attitudinal, stylistic, life-stylistic. Jesse Jackson's rainbow blurred and dimmed from the 1980s to the 1990s, just as Michael Jackson morphed before our eyes into someone not white, not black, not straight, not gay, not young, not old, part flesh, part plastic—a riveting image of generalized otherness. Politicians were forced to become players in a never-ending show/game. They naturally moved to control it, to control their representational existence—and succeeded to the point of rigor mortis. Take, for example, the 1968 Democratic convention in Chicago, when a mob of Chicago cops beat demonstrators in the streets while a Jewish senator denounced their "Gestapo tactics" from the podium and a shot of Mayor Daley—last of the great Irish bosses—caught him spitting obscenities at the senator from his place in the Illinois delegation. Out of control. And live. Compare that with the canned productions the national parties have to put on now in order to maintain the brand.

And so on, across the board. Mainstream political representations as compelling as cable TV commercials for Vegematic accessories.

Except when there is crisis. And especially when there is scandal.

Of which more anon.

Players and Their Issues

But maybe it goes beyond boring. I'm something of a political junkie myself. I read a lot, watch a lot of news shows. And maybe it's just me, but I notice that I often want to switch away from, say, Colin Powell talking live and watch a panel of talking heads instead. Why is that? Because the panel is more entertaining? More spontaneous? Partly, but that's a symptom. There's also this subtle discomfort, this slight feeling of embarrassment I get when I watch the politicians themselves. It's because they are supposed to be real, but they're so scripted. Yet their real traits have a way of peeking through their performative masks. It's like catching a glimpse of someone you know only slightly sitting on the toilet, but less intense.

Talking head panelists are also performing, but they're supposed to be performing. Their personalities are the characters they play and vice versa. "Robert Novak" is Robert Novak. That's why it is so easy for them to do cameos in which they play themselves in movies.

But, for most politicians, it doesn't work that way. They are victims of the same irony we saw at work in the decline of heroes.

They face the threat of diminishment by comparison with virtual personalities, on the one hand, and, on the other, incessant pressure from journalists angling for a gotcha moment because that's the only interesting thing they can do. So politicians package themselves for protection—and end up looking phony as well as flawed. Not only do we get the strange hair and the unfortunate chin, but we also get obviously coached hand gestures not quite in sync with obviously canned lines masquerading as real reactions, and delivered much less realistically than actors deliver lines that are scripted by definition. That's why the most successful—the only truly successful—politicians since Kennedy have been good Method actors who deliver attractive and realistic performances over and over again.

Yes, political leaders have always been actors, but the model used to be theatrical. The stage invited grand gestures—watch clips of a Teddy Roosevelt speech, or just watch old Bob Byrd, elder statesman of the U.S. Senate, still performing on C-SPAN as I write, clinging to the tradition of oratory he cherishes, and you get a sense of that. They perform when the curtain rises, but when the curtain comes down, the lights go out and the show's over. But the close-up intimacies of constant TV coverage invite the muted nuances of naturalism, the subtleties of Method acting, the relentless necessity of being yourself, being real—*and* being on.

Sum it up this way: a lot of people don't think politics should be a show but they have learned that it is, so they tend to disdain the whole enterprise. Others, the ones who vote, accept the show and support whomever they identify with or support an opponent of whomever they identify against—above all, with the one they like or against the one they fear, for these elementary sentiments are central to the mainstream form of identity politics. But the first group, the disdainers, have decided that politicians are full of shit and simply ignore them. And they don't vote at all—in huge numbers. Even the intensification of the culture wars and the prospect of terror can't get them to the polls.

Again, this is not really apathy; it's more than apathy. It feels denigrating to a lot of people, to participate as if they were taken in, to act the part prescribed by the high school civics teacher, to submit, in the act of voting, to the stereotype of the ordinary person whom politicians (unlike musicians) address so unctuously and hypocritically from their spotlit perches. Not voting is refusing to play a particular role in the political scenario because that role is so insignificant, not without aggregate consequences but without public meaning in the anonymity of the deed. Alone in the booth you pull the lever, press the button—who cares? This is not what the flattered self has come to expect. Much better to be in a focus group; at least then you get some attention, even have some impact.

So, political alienation in general, on the one hand. On the other—where those who do engage in politics operate—media-savvy players representing various identity and/or interest groups through performance politics in a never-ending show/game for a fan base of identifiers.

Now players, almost by definition, understand that the horse race is what counts. Basic political and moral commitments are kid stuff. No serious player changes such commitments because of arguments, for God's sake. It follows that arguments are just performances designed to influence naïve opinion. Players are preoccupied with how to do that, with manipulating arguments and other celebrated items—people, lifestyle, grooming, events, legislation, anything that comes along—manipulating them for effect.

It got called "spin," because the expression so precisely captures the improvisational feel of this interminable enterprise.

But understanding that the horse race is what counts comes down to understanding that it's all about getting recognition and/or stuff—money, position, resources—for you and yours. Leading players in organizations that represent identity and/or interest niches therefore act as brokers between their constituencies and mainstream leaders who cobble together as many niches as they can under general rhetorical banners that can give an appearance of unity across a spectrum that stretches between poles of pure identity and pure interest. Being for or against gay marriage, for example, is almost entirely a matter of self-identification (or "values," as the pros say), while being for or against some provision in Bush's Medicare package is a matter of who gets what. Politicians whose careers depend on particular identity and/ or interest niches stake out positions at the poles (Al Sharpton, Gary Bauer). Those looking for the middle ground support civil unions for gays, split the difference on Medicare, and spin all their positions with rhetoric that expresses something about them as people (compassionate, resolute, reasonable, etc.).

Players working the middle ground assume that they are addressing not just identity and/or interest niches but also a broad mass of naïve consumer-citizens who fall into lumpier categories of the kind that market researchers use. Waitress Moms, Soccer Moms, NASCAR Dads, that kind of thing. Even here, the technology is allowing for more and more refinement and we are getting subniches like "Aging Blues" (as in "blue collar") in the Rust Belt and the "Young and the Restless" in hip urban environments. When politicians think of the "American people" it's groups like this that they have in mind.

And the point of all the spin and rhetoric is ultimately to influence their, presumably naïve, opinions.

No doubt it has worked that way in the past, and probably still does, to some extent—I mean, the pros must know what they're doing. Still, there are so few undecideds these days—why? It's not party loyalty in the old-fashioned ideological-issues sense, it's more like loyalty to one's own identity, to the self as a brand. In fact, it may be a popular version of the kind of loyalty professional players have. Big-time political types don't "decide"; they already know where they stand. They aren't undecided; why should we be? Sometimes, when I listen closely to the call-in voices on talk radio and C-SPAN, I sense something very similar going on more generally. A lot of those callers are *not* naïvely venting feelings and voicing opinions anymore. They are playing the game too. This may be the key to the popularity of these forums. The people are performing too—they are spinning, players in their own right, feeding talking points to the *really* naïve listeners who are not calling in, but will presumably carry the message to the water cooler upon the morrow? Is that how it's working? I bet a lot of people are even spinning the polls, by which I mean giving answers to create a desired effect. For example, I don't myself actually believe that Bush knew there were no weapons of mass destruction in Iraq before he invaded, but if I were polled on the question, I would be tempted to say otherwise.

I bet there's a good bit of that going on these days. Do the pollsters know it? They wouldn't tell us if they did.

But this would explain why politics, focused on issues, can only arouse the interest of interest groups, while politics focused on process—and especially on crisis or scandal—gets more general attention. The latter focus treats us all like insiders, a much more flattering position to be in.

But surely issues still matter, and for all of us, not just the identity/interest groups—perhaps more so at this moment than at any time since LBJ or even FDR. Bush's economic agenda, if fully implemented, will transform the polity, the New Deal will be all but repealed, something more like nineteenth-century capitalism will be restored—and God only knows what the doctrine of preemptive war will lead to in the long run. But it will definitely matter. To everybody. So how is it with issues in a mediated politics? How do postmodern issues differ from modern ones?

It's "the vision thing," as Bush the Elder put it so famously. But in order to understand what that means, progressives need to look in the mirror. Bush's original phrasing betrayed his own lack in terms that were easy to mock; quoting was enough. But quoters got away with implying, just by quoting, that, unlike Bush, they had authentic social vision—or at least understood what one was, the value of it. In fact, progressives have no such vision, none that is shared, none that links issues together reasonably, given some philosophy of human nature and analysis of history, none that implicates policies designed to advance that vision as a whole— nothing like classical liberalism, articulated and modified over centuries from Locke to Smith to Mill, or Marxism, spawning descendants in Bolshevism, anarcho-syndicalism, democratic socialism . . .

How quaint all that sounds today.

Call issues under those modern visions "grounded issues."

Today's issues are iconic. That means, above all, that they have no comprehensive basis, no foundation in principles rooted in serious thought about the human condition as opposed to blind dogma and one's sense of self. Take a position on an iconic issue— immigration, abortion, gay marriage, minimum wage, whatever—and what are you doing? Expressing your identity and promoting the interests of the group you identify with—and so on, down the list of issues, the items bundled in accordance with the needs and tastes of whoever does the choosing.

But why did grounded issues evaporate into self-expressive or self-interested options?

Because, in an age of relentless and ubiquitous representation, the scarcest resource is attention.

Some factoids.

One of the Lincoln-Douglas debates took seven hours. There was one break. The place was packed throughout. In 1960, uninterrupted speech by presidential candidates on the nightly news averaged forty seconds. That means we saw Kennedy or Nixon talking for an average of forty seconds before Walter or Chet interrupted with some "analysis." Do you realize how long that is, in TV land? Well, in 1992, the average time for uninterrupted candidate speech was nine and a half seconds. When Senator David Boren resigned he explained why by describing an endless round of "fourteen-hour days" in which there "was no time for reflection, no time to exchange ideas with fellow senators," as, for example, when "the president . . . asked four senators from each party . . . to work on a civil rights compromise" and "it took two weeks to find an hour when all eight could meet" and, even then, the "eight entered and left the meeting at different times" so that "no more than four were ever together for more than fifteen minutes."

Sound familiar? (See chapter 5.)

This quality of rushed busyness expresses in action the absence of vision in thought, the absence of principles that establish coherence and priority. You have to deal with anything that comes up when nothing but political pressure can tell you what matters. So issues multiply listwise, as a function of multiplying interests and identities. They become iconic rather than grounded. There is no authentic vision in popular political culture for the same reason that high-culture postmodernists have given up on universalizing intellectual enterprises.

There are just too many different things out there, and too many different things happening—and so fast. Things in general aren't comprehensible. No one can attend to it all, let alone comprehend it in a "vision."

That's just a fact.

Only an emergency or a threat to identity can establish priorities now. Only then can unifying purpose prevail. Like with Democrats uniting to defeat Bush. Like with evangelicals pouring to the polls to stop gay marriage. Or like the war on terror itself. When objectives take the place of ideals we no longer need an ideology to provide coherence—though, in the long run, the war on terror could give rise to new ideological frameworks. "Liberal imperialism" is a candidate ideology, you might say, and it may take hold—especially if attacks on the scale of 9/11 occur again. It has been articulated by a lot of people—Niall Ferguson, most prominent among them, and it has been most popularly represented by *New York Times* columnist Tom Friedman, whose casual style cannot mask a consistency of analysis and prescription, sustained by underlying principles, however arrogant, however naïve. If a genuinely liberal imperialism does take hold (in a Hillary Clinton administration, say), opponents will be helpless before it unless they find an alternative ideology of comparable sweep.

Depending on your point of view, then, the war on terror is either a godsend—or it is the occasion for a systematic misrepresentation of history on a truly Orwellian scale because it promises to become a global OJ story that could go on for decades, into the indefinite future, fueled by undeniably real acts of mass slaughter, by acts of terror and retaliation that will more or less permanently suspend the bubble of mediated culture in a void of possibility—a void which, in the nature of things, cannot be covered, cannot be represented at all (see coda).

The People's Princess

Crisis, then. Or scandal. Or, even better, both. Only when there's crisis and scandal can politics compete with sports and entertainment. Only then are politicians genuine postmodern performers, being in the moment, packaged *and* real.

That's why it's only then that we want to watch them. That's when politics becomes reality TV.

And how people loved to watch Princess Diana.

You couldn't call Di a politician, exactly, but neither was she an actor or a singer. She was an extraordinary synthesis of premodern and postmodern forms of social prominence, a fusion of royalty and celebrity. As a consequence—and especially in death—Diana brought into high relief the way successful politicians must address the identities of their constituents, how they must reflect back upon the flattered selves of spectators the attention they are giving to the celebrated. The circumstances of Di's death gave her fans a chance to perform in that reflected light, exposing features of our mediated political culture that are usually less apparent.

I mentioned Di's mourners in the introduction, to illustrate the way mediated people become Method actors. I only touched on the idea of virtual revolution, remarking on how her mourners took control of the script.

But now we can look more closely. The Death of Di was yet another "event-story," but a classic of the genre officially established with OJ. It emerged because of the new communication technologies—multiplication of outlets, speed and frequency of transmission, all that again. But here's why the cultural form took shape: the platforms only make these things possible.

Remember OJ in the white Bronco? That's the paradigm. The media make a story out of a reality *while it is happening*. Then they cover *that* so completely that story and reality fuse. Watergate was the first case in point, but people didn't really understand what was happening at the time. It was before cable, and because the coverage was pervasive on the networks—all three carried the hearings live—it made for an event-story even more dominating than OJ's was. During the spring and summer of 1973 there was, almost literally, nothing else on. But no one had enough reflective distance to see what this meant. No one noticed how the story was becoming the event. People just applied the old categories. The participants thought they were holding hearings, conniving, investigating; the press thought it was reporting on what the participants were doing; the spectators thought they were learning about what the participants were doing from the reporting.

That model crumbled over the next decades and some people (Michael Deaver and Jean Baudrillard, for example) had a precocious grasp of it all, but it was the OJ case that made everybody—participants, press, and spectators—aware that a new phenomenon had emerged to enfold them all. The threshold reflexivity criterion was met when the story itself became a story—and everyone talked about *that*.

After OJ, anything that unfolded over time and could be construed as having a plot was subsumed—cases like those of Marc Dutroux or Scott Peterson, most obviously, but also Monica Lewinsky and Bill, Blair versus the Beeb. Even the Bush wars and the election of 2004 were subject to this form, though the fit is necessarily looser in the case of events so dispersed and complex. But they tried, they tried as hard as ever they could. Media and politicians may differ over what a hybrid reality-story line should be, but they are both committed to the notion that there must be *some* story line. You can't just let things be.

The Death of Di was all that those event-stories were, and more. The obviously active role of the paparazzi press—who

literally caused her death—and the direct participation of spectators in subsequent events upped the ante on the genre, exposing its
internal structure. Everybody played publicly the part that, in
other event-stories, would have been surreptitiously or vicariously
enacted. Essential relationships between the virtual classes in the
mediated world were dramatically outed as celebrities and journalists jockeyed for position before newly empowered spectators.

FLOWER POWER sang out a headline in the *New York Times* over a
picture of that ocean of bouquets piled up against the gates of an
empty Buckingham Palace—and how typical of contemporary
headlines and titles that was, a cultural reference that makes you
feel hip if you get it, but still works if you don't. Yet another
flattering gesture, including you in the creative process—for you
"make" the connection, if it gets made. And how, while we are on
the subject, did the custom of laying flowers at the site of some
temporarily celebrated death get started anyway? I first noticed it
during the Central Park jogger story. But whatever the origin, this
custom clearly expresses spectator desire to play a part in the show.
The flood of flora for Di just brought this folk form to a new level
of significance, as the queen's eventual capitulation made clear.

But the queen wasn't the only one who had to grovel.

The always operative struggle between celebrities and media
for control of the plot in an event-story became explicit, part of
the event-story in itself—so much doubling, this was Blob
heaven. That happened because both classes were openly court-
ing the spectators, trying to make them allies. A piquant tableau
it was, all those famous journalists and actors taking turns
fawning over the public—directly soliciting the identificational
attachments they are always after, but less obviously. It was that
spectacle that first got me thinking explicitly about the flattery
inherent in representation.

Celebrities saw an opportunity to turn the public against the paparazzi press. They wanted Di's death to play as an extreme case of what they suffer at the hands of a gossip-mongering media all the time. Liz Smith reported that three major Hollywood stars had hired a team of private detectives and committed millions of dollars to a search for personal dirt on the editors of the major tabloids. Tom Cruise and George Clooney and many others spoke out in this vein, and photographers threatened to boycott them in retaliation. Like politicians refusing press conferences in favor of ads, celebrities were reaching out to spectators over the heads of the media, pleading for respect for their private lives, which were, they insisted (what a laugh!), so much like ordinary private lives.

Children were mentioned *a lot*.

So, for example, *Newsweek*'s My Turn section, which usually features columns by ordinary folk, was turned over to celebrities speaking out against media harassment. An interesting repositioning right there. The guest columns all asked the public to control its appetite for intimate stories. The gist was "we know we can't do anything about the money-grubbing press, so we ask you, as fellow human beings, to stop buying the *National Enquirer*."

Fat chance.

Paul Reiser offered a spin on Di that became an instant classic—"instant classic"? Sure, we have those now. "Everybody says she used the press and loved it," Reiser declared, "that's how people talk about rape victims!"

But, of course, Di *did* use the press.

When it suited her.

And that was the thrust of the journalists' response to the celebrity case. They saw it as a threat to their independence, a hypocritical attempt to turn the press into press agents. Again, the structure of the relationship between politicians and journalists is mirrored in the one between Sylvester Stallone and the reporters to whom he ostentatiously presented his back in front of Planet Hollywood. He had been eager enough to get publicity for the chain when he launched it—as reporters duly, and frequently, noted. They were inviting spectators to join them, to see through the machinations of celebrity, to be hip and cynical—which is what the media does implicitly all the time.

Now it was explicit.

The British tabloids were especially eager to ingratiate themselves with the public, of course, because they were the ones most likely to be hurt if the celebrity attack on gossip were to gain traction. They dutifully relayed stage directions from spectators to the reluctant royals with headlines like SHOW US YOU CARE!

Ah, yes, oh, sure—press and public, united as one, standing up for Di.

Talk about cynical.

In the upper reaches of the media food chain, respectable figures were intent on distinguishing themselves from the tabloids. How staunch they were in defense of the difference. Imagine! Who would dare to blur the line between the gutter press that brought you Monica, 24–7, and the venerable journalistic institutions that brought you—Monica, 24–7? At the very pinnacle, superstar journalists employed a revealing tactic. They began to confide in spectators about their very personal and private moments with Di. They hung out with her, you see! The message? Barbara Walters and Dominick Dunne weren't *really* in the media class at all; they were celebrities in their own right. Journalism was incidental to their status. They were more like Sting and Versace. They identified with the celebrity class as it consolidated around Di's death. They too understood that, in Di, celebrities had found their perfect representative.

Why? To see that, we must focus on the obvious, the life and person of Diana herself—her beauty, her days as a kindergarten teacher, her family, her bulimia, her sex life. Like so many celebrities, Di had no particular talent, no special gift. She was known by virtue of her exalted position. And how she was known! Known as the victim of a cold and distant husband, exploitative lovers, disloyal friends, neurotic urges, self-destructive habits— very ordinary misfortunes, all of them. But then, she was an ordinary girl (sort of) catapulted into a fabulous position, an ordinary, but lovely, girl who just happened to fill that position more naturally, more sympathetically, than anyone ever had. There was about her nothing of the scripted sheen of the politico, no rigor mortis factor—as was notoriously the case with the other royals. Di was suspensefully vulnerable, a natural Method actress, seeming always not quite comfortable being the center of atten- tion, which brought out her essential ordinariness. Her royal manners were so obviously assumed, but gracefully—she was like a lovely little girl learning how to greet grown-ups formally, ever so slightly tentative, emerging from buildings and entering rooms, the downcast eyes, the shy smile.

Spectators were mourning for themselves as they mourned for Di. She had "made a difference" in their lives (so many said that) because in her life they saw their own anonymous struggles elevated to the big screen. Maureen Dowd dubbed Di the "New Age Princess," and Tony Blair, himself a definitive embodi- ment of that age, also got it right—both in content and in the manner of his delivery—choking back the tears as he hailed the "People's Princess."

Di was the ultimate celebrity because, in her performance as fabulous victim, she managed to represent everyone who felt marginalized, unappreciated, misunderstood—for whatever reason—in all their millions. Multitudes could identify with her, in a manner essentially similar to the way fans felt about Judy Garland—but with an added intensity, an added dimension. It's the vicarious therapy phenomenon we looked at before, but so cogently enacted in this case, and on so grand a scale, embracing the entire international polis of mediation. When Reisner floated the rape analogy, he was playing on just one aspect of this icon of victimhood, an aspect adapted to reach women especially. But Di was loved by minorities, gays, the disabled—everyone who felt unjustly treated by society could identify with Di. Trevor Phillips, a black British TV executive, spoke for them all when he hailed her as "a heroine" who "embraced the modern multicultural, multiethnic Britain without reservation."

Phillips had in mind such improvised moments of heroism as Di hugging AIDS patients in their hospital beds. But there was also Di's association with Dodi al-Fayed and his father, Mohamed—those dark Muslims who, for all their wealth, were not accepted. Above all, were revelations of her personal misery and disastrous relationships. The marginalized millions, victims all, felt represented by her on this account and claimed her for their own. They seized the opportunity provided by her death and the queen's intransigence to take charge of the show, to rise out of anonymity and make a difference of their own.

For them, for those virtual revolutionaries performing their parts in the media-saturated streets of London over the course of that week, the personal and the political were utterly indistinguishable.

The President's Penis

Oh, those were the days, you know they were. He *represented* us, he really did—or rather they did, for they were a package from the start, and through all that followed, two sides of the same generational coin. The fate of the whole sixties cohort was enacted through and by them. Even if you loathed them—which I did; I was a Ralph Nader voter in 2000 (but if I'd lived in Florida, I would have voted for Al Gore, honest)—even if you loathed them, you *deserved* them.

I loathed the Clintons for sucking up to corporations and rolling over for globalization, for replacing hard-core economic justice with high-profile diversity as the defining characteristic of progressive politics.

But they *represented* me just the same. I'm a sixties guy with a retirement plan, after all. And I too have fudged things a bit over the years, you know how it goes.

I always meant well, though.

Will a future History Channel routinely refer to Bill Clinton as the defining political figure of our time? True, he only consolidated trends that had been developing since Kennedy's TV presidency, but he consolidated them on a whole new plane. With Bill, we crossed a threshold in the history of mediated politics.

Could the political get more personal?

Of how many presidents can this be said: for years, even to this day, his countrymen—and women and children—have been compelled to visualize his penis whenever he appears in public. They have been coerced into stealing glances at his crotch while he thanked assembled dignitaries, trying to recall if it was boxers or briefs while he discoursed on global trade, and found themselves wondering, yet again, what an enthusiastically delivered blow job in the sunlit silence of an Oval Office afternoon must have *sounded* like.

Ah, well, we had to visualize Robert Dole's penis too. I mean,

Viagra ads from a leader of the *Republican* party? What would Eisenhower say? And that codpiece on Bush's flight suit got a lot of attention too. Enough so you knew they made a conscious decision to go with it.

Maybe it's a trend.

But no one ever called attention to his privates, literally or figuratively, with the splendid abandon of Bill Clinton. His whole persona was performance intimacy. In the long run, that is what will make him the archetype of leadership for the media age.

To see more deeply into this abyss, begin by asking how someone so completely phony, so hard-core phony-to-the-bone that he makes the Babbitts of Sinclair Lewis's nightmares look like models of authenticity—how could he have succeeded and survived, and in spite of Monica? But, of course, it is *because* of Monica (and Gennifer Flowers and Paula Jones and not inhaling) that Bill, in his congenital phoniness, will qualify as an epoch-defining historical figure. It is *because* of choked-up, finger-flapping lies and questions about the meaning of "is" and pastoral therapy sessions with Jesse Jackson and walks to the 'copter with Chelsea between them and Buddy at his side. In the last analysis, it is Bill's incredibility, in every sense of the word, that will entitle him to that standing.

He took phony to a whole new level—a level where he could not be reached, could not be shamed, a level from which he could not be brought down.

He was the master player.

I mean, if what happened during that year had been forecast to you, the year before, would you have believed it? Incredible! But incredible also, in the other sense: of everything Bill Clinton said or says, isn't it pointless to ask if he's telling the truth, pointless to wonder if he really feels it when he gets sentimental about his loyal supporters, or does that drawling, chuckling, self-deprecating nodding thing, or that precautionary, hand spread to settle the audience, eyebrows raised to promise a rhetorical deal-closer, saying, "Because . . . lemme tell you, lemme tell you this . . . we *better* do X, or . . ."—is there any point in asking if it's real?

Would you ask that question of a Method actor, being in the moment?

It's not just Bill, of course; he's just the prototype. Take Tony Blair, the most exemplary of all Bill's progeny. Talk about legacy. Have you compared his shtick to the master's? You could swear he got hands-on lessons in expression and intonation management. But Blair just marks the trend. Leaders the world over are proceeding, more and more consciously, to turn themselves, their causes, departments, universities, companies, parties, nations, and regions into well-positioned brand names. "Traditional, but forward-looking" was what some PR advisory committee to the Blair government called their vision statement for the New Britain.

Says it all, doesn't it?

As with the greats of yore, Bill Clinton had his defining moment, the speech that made history. For Churchill it was "blood, sweat, and tears," for FDR it was "fear itself," for JFK it was "ask not what," for MLK it was "have a dream"—you know the top ten. For Bill, it was the Monica State of the Union. As with Lincoln at Gettysburg, it may take awhile for that speech to garner the significance it deserves, although, in Bill's case, it won't be because of what he said. It will be because of his performance. But that's generally true of political speeches and events now, isn't it? Political reporters don't even pretend to a discourse distinct from movie reviews. And speech writers understand they are writing for the part the politician is playing. That's why the Monica State of the Union performance will assume world historical importance someday. In that speech, Bill brought showbiz political culture to its apotheosis, forcing his vast appetite for dominion upon an enthralled planet like some Genghis Khan of virtuality. Remember how it was? With his impeachment trial getting under way, after cum stains on a blue dress had forced him into claiming he didn't think a blow job qualified as "sexual relations" in front of the *entire world*, for God's sake, Clinton had to face down Congress, the Supreme Court, his cabinet, foreign dignitaries, the media, and the *entire world*—again!

There they all were, in the well of the United States Congress. It *was* incredible. It was as if they were somnambulating, hypnotized, into a some newborn zone of being where hallowed custom and bizarre context were so surreally fused that the whole tableau seemed poised to shimmer off into the ether at any moment. Partly it was the peculiar nature of the suspense. A new form of stage fright was born that evening. It permeated those Hallowed Halls like swamp gas, and gripped millions, maybe billions, of viewers beyond. Leaders of the world's institutions, from prime ministers and CEOs to district managers and college deans, were riveted to the tube. They knew how central to their success was their ability to bullshit their way through awkward situations. This was the ultimate challenge! They felt an implicit solidarity with Bill, deeper than any substance. Would he fumble? Would he crack? If just one giggle broke the stillness, what then? Would people be able to go through with this charade? Most fundamentally of all: *was this really happening?*

But, as is the way of ontology, that most fundamental of questions went unarticulated, and so assumed what Heidegger would call its "grounding significance." How's that for an angle? The Monica State of the Union as a Heideggerian moment of decision. It works for me. After all, who knew, at that moment, what was at stake or what would come to pass? Only the one who must decide. And he did, by God, he did.

Plebeian as a Shakespearean watchman, the sergeant at arms managed his entrance and announcement. And Bill did the rest.

Under pressures that would have crushed a citizen of the old real world, which was passing away before our eyes, he strode into an arena without precedent, without definition, and slam-dunked it into a shape of his choosing. In that masterful performance, the personal and the political fused utterly, on a global scale, in real time. History shuddered imperceptibly and lurched into the future.

For we were all carried along, were we not? Bemused, admiring, repelled, ashamed, angry—no matter; we went with him down the aisle and onto the podium, through the handshakes and the first formalities, and gradually, as he picked up momentum, we realized it was going to be okay. And we were, at some half-conscious level, profoundly grateful. He kept it together, himself and the mediated world we all share, in that instituting hour. Without acknowledging gratitude, we were enabled to relax back into our accustomed roles—stand or not, clap or not, yawn or yell or switch channels—pretending not to notice that everything had changed even as it all went back to normal.

For if *that* could be normal, then normal could only be "normal" from now on.

One priceless shot caught Trent Lott—then Republican leader of the Senate—gazing up at Clinton as the speech came to a close. He looked stunned and depleted, but there was also a hint of awe in his expression. "Incredible," he was thinking. "How did he *do* that?" If Lott had been a chimpanzee, he would have been in abject submission cringe. Bill's enemies marched on, of course. Like zombies, they stumbled toward their inevitable humiliation at *his* impeachment. For it was during that evening, you recall, that the baseline of those job-approval ratings was set, and they did not waver from then on. That was how the people, out of unacknowledged gratitude, helped preserve what he had saved.

William Jefferson Clinton had indeed done his job.

Didn't you just love it when they used all three names? It gave the expression "make a mockery of " a whole new dimension. And that usage fit the impeachment trial so snugly, did it not? The utter absence of the intended sonority echoed the constant but hopeless insistence of attending journalists that this was a truly historic event. "Not since Andrew Johnson was brought before . . ." etc. Remember how they introduced the coverage on the evening news?

But none of the networks covered the actual proceedings. That's because everybody knew in their bones that it wasn't historic at all. It was "historic."

But apart from such defining moments, Bill served the Blob on a daily basis as well, with every rambling speech, with his great sprawling autobiography. He continuously created elaborate situations in which people could make adjustments in their politics to accommodate the performance requirements that Bill brought with him.

Remember when Bob Dylan sang at Clinton's first inaugural in front of the Washington Monument as fighter-bombers flew overhead in battle formation?

That was a good one.

But don't confuse Blobby moments with good old-fashioned hypocrisy and rationalization. The self-deception involved here is of an entirely different order. As we shall see in chapter 7, among Blobsters, self-deception is indistinguishable from self-overcoming, in the Nietzschean sense. This is a new form of personal growth and self-actualization. So, to take a small example, when Bill said he felt your pain, he meant it, *and it was true*. He felt it each and every time, and he probably still does. He is that protean.

We are beyond old-fashioned concepts like "sincerity" here. There is no limit to Bill's empathy, to his absorptive capacities—he is himself a walking psychoblob. That's why people have always been so impressed with his one-on-one skills, the way he listens, the way he understands, the way he makes you feel important. Even very smart people, who got face time with the Blobster in Chief, and knew they were getting the treatment, did not, on that account, resist. Not at all. They wanted the treatment. It made them feel like insiders to be so treated, and to realize it at the same time.

The Blobby benefits of this doubling were multiple, of course, as all things Blobby are. On the one hand, there was a gesture that passed for autonomy: describing the encounter later, in confidence to friends and relatives, re-creating every little stroke and tone, you got to come off so knowing. On the other hand, in that knowing retelling, you were collaborating again with the original treatment—like Swann, remembering Odette telling him something he needs now to believe. Finally, there was so much to be learned from the way Bill did it. It was a little leadership tutorial. To be blobbed by Bill was to collaborate in your own seduction.

But that's just the beginning. More was involved than traditional amorality and blind ambition. Recall the notorious loyalty Bill generated? Nixon had John Deans to tattle on him, and Elliot Richardsons to resign from his cabinet—but not Bill. Old-fashioned leaders and followers couldn't understand how Bill could betray and abandon so many people and principles and still retain such loyalty; they harped on that a lot, remember?

Now we can see why. His subordinates couldn't turn against

him, outraged at betrayal, because they weren't really betrayed. They weren't really fooled; they were sort of fooled and sort of not—he told them this, he told them that, there were a lot of ways to read him, always. But neither could they desert the sinking ship. They rightly felt ownership of it, just as it was. Blobsters all, they had, like Bill himself, signed up to serve the old progressive causes in a new political context they understood so well and had done so much to shape. They knew that, in the performative politics of a mediated world, the appearance of loyalty matters more than loyalty, that players worthy of the name can never quit. War room. Take the heat. Tough it out. Rajin' Cajun. Grrrr.

Suave Mike McCurry, press secretary to Bill during the unfolding scandal, perfectly embodied this form of allegiance. Adapting his official role to the needs of the moment, he acted it out publicly. He knew but he didn't know, you know? Remember how clear he made it? In words, in tone, in his superb demeanor, he conveyed the essential message. He wasn't loyal, he was "loyal." As a result, he couldn't be charged with any real responsibility, yet, at the same time, he got credit for handling the pressure that would have gone with the responsibility if he had really had it. How cool was that? Talk about attitude.

The press held Mike in high esteem for this remarkable performance, of course. In coming as close to candor as reflexivity allowed, Mike became their role model. He showed them how to be in the thick of it, but above it all at the same time—the very state to which power journalists aspire.

Blobsters all.

But Bill's most profound achievement was to provide Blobby moments for people with no direct connection to him or his administration, people who had been vaguely on the left for years, out of fashionable habit—but the circumstances of their lives were changing, they were getting older and wealthier and more conscious of their place in society. This process was necessarily more subtle, but it entailed that same collaborative dynamic. What he did for them was this: he betrayed them in ways that allowed them to complain but still acquiesce, and thus avoid a moral reckoning.

Bill picked out just those issues on which such people wouldn't want to waffle publicly, and he did it for them. Ever since he put teacher testing into his education initiatives and pulled the switch on that retarded murderer during his second term as governor of Arkansas, Bill had been facilitating this delicate process. People who themselves would not support the death penalty or criticize Sister Souljah or institute the Republican workfare program or abandon gays in the military or promote global capitalism were enabled, by Bill's actions, to avoid acknowledging that they didn't like bullying rappers and whining panhandlers or had never quite understood how sexual orientation was a political category or didn't want to openly confront the fact that, nowadays, they were really counting on the stock market or affirmative-action-inspired sinecures in positions of substantial power and prestige where it was difficult to keep the focus on conditions in the ghetto, what with all the conferences and book tours. In a nutshell, a lot of people got to tsk-tsk at Bill for his New Democrat compromising, even as he was doing things they didn't object to *that* much. Like some weird variant on the theme of the savior, he took a generation's sins of expediency on himself.

So intimate a service. And so inclusive. There were so many ways to identify with the Clintons. Maybe it's true, maybe liberals really *are* more complex than conservatives.

You could identify with Hillary as a victim of a philandering husband and, at the same time, admire her for sticking by him in the face of Kenneth Starr and the vast right-wing conspiracy, and, when she went on to run for senator, you could give her props for striking out on her own. Talk about having it both ways! Or, if you were a certain kind of guy (you know who you are) you could think, hey, Monica snapped her thong, go for it, you fortunate rogue, and you could take pleasure at the embarrassment of feminist talking heads, reduced to making light of "private conduct" with a subordinate in the workplace after years of condeming the very idea of it. You could loathe Bill for his smarmy charm, and be charmed by it as well. You could recoil from Hillary's ambition, her cold-blooded control, but confess to a certain admiration for it too, especially in the long run.

No wonder, when it was all over, after Gore got robbed in Florida and Hillary secured her beachhead in New York and the Bushites brought their (by comparison) cartoonish style of personal performance to our political existence—no wonder so many people came to realize how richly and intensely they had identified with the Clintons after all. They may have been morally compromised—but Lord, they hung in there. They made the show go on.

And that's something we all need to be able to do—more and more as the years go by, right?

The President's Heart

It's usually progressives we think of when we think of identity politics, but that's a big mistake. The National Rifle Association and the Right to Life movement are all about identity and self-expression. Reagan and Thatcher were all about identity too, even more so than Clinton or Gore or John Kerry, who have to spread themselves more thinly across more diverse identity niches. Reagan, especially, made American self-love the central theme of his presidential performance; think of the orgy that was his funeral, aided and abetted by the mainstream media, leaping at the chance to show its lack of liberal bias in this easy way.

Identity politicians on the right used the culture wars to convince folks in the heartland that *they* had been marginalized, even victimized, by a politically correct elite promoting the warm-fuzzy and/or decadent legacies of the 1960s. Especially the way they played their roles, the way they performed *as* one of those folks, rising up to set things straight, to clean up the mess the hippies left behind, restore free enterprise, crack down on muggers and bureaucrats, and, above all, give ordinary people reason to feel good about themselves again. That was Reagan's genius.

And Dubya inherited Reagan's mantle in more ways than one. Not just in policy and constituency—but as an actor too. In more complex ways than Reagan, to be sure, because Bush is not at all professional, as Reagan was. On the other hand, and paradoxically, the habit of acting goes much deeper in Dubya's character. That seems unlikely at first blush, of course, since Reagan actually was an actor. How could that be?

Reagan started out in radio, and not by accident. He was a very old guy. There was no TV back when he got launched.

That's all you really need to know. The Hollywood that shaped Ronald Reagan dates from a time when mediation in general had not reached saturational levels, a time when stars were openly artificial, haloed in studio stills, a time when acting was a relatively superficial exercise—effective posing, certain looks, certain mannerisms and intonations—and a star was a definite and compelling "personality." It was the time of Clark Gable, Jimmy Stewart, Humphrey Bogart, Lauren Bacall, Joan Crawford, and Bette Davis. Among such striking figures, Reagan was too dim to be a real star, and thus he was prepared to play the modest part of spokesman, first for corporations and later for a conservative movement.

Put it this way: Reagan belongs to an age when the paradigm of self-presentation was set by Dale Carnegie's *How to Win Friends and Influence People*, not by Lee Strasberg's Actors Studio.

But Bush is a child of a later time, the 1960s, when the age of mediation took hold. He could not escape its fundamental dynamic, no matter how adamantly he refused its more obvious expressions, the political and cultural "revolutions"—which he did refuse, he certainly did. But, alas, he did so consciously, there was no other way—which is to say self-consciously, reflexively. He had to *decide* to become a regular guy instead of adopting fashionable styles and opinions. It was a lifestyle option. So Bush is a Method actor too.

But not a good one; in fact, he's quite bad at it. His reflexivity skills are lacking because he is suspicious of all reflection; he thinks it will dilute his realness. Ironically, though, this lack works to his benefit among people who identify with him. They made the same decision he did—proud to be that "Okie from Muskogee" Merle Haggard celebrated, a figure with whom all the regular folks who rejected the 1960s could identify. But that posture is as mediated as any other.

When George W. Bush plays his role as protector of the 'Merican people, you can see he is performing. If you watch as he runs through those lists of evangelical/Manichean truisms, you will see he is performing the simplicity he thinks of as his principal virtue. He actually recites (rush of words, pause and stare; rush of words, pause and stare) little bromides like "We are a good people," "Our enemies hate us for who we are," and "Our cause is just," and his eyes light up after each nugget is delivered, as if he is proud to get his lesson right. It is as if he were hoping to ingratiate himself with parents he disappointed.

Which is the basic plot of his life's story.

Bush, as method actor, is still a boy. He never reached the stage where the self he chose to be as an adolescent became habitual enough to pass for real. It is as if he is still convincing himself that attitudes and mannerisms he once decided were ideal are really his own. You can feel him listening to himself, watching himself, rehearsing, practicing, just as he did all those years ago when he first assumed the postures of Texas manliness—the arms held out from his body, fist side forward, swinging as he strides, and all the rest. That was how he decided to distinguish himself from patrician Easterners back home, people among whom he failed so utterly to be otherwise distinguished, coasting through those intimidating schools, clowning for the hackers at the club. And it was his adoption of those postures that allowed real Texans to exploit him and his connections through the simple flattery of including him in their doings during his oil years in Houston, just as they later allowed the tough and canny men around him—older, deep-down confident men like Cheney and Rumsfeld—to guide their prince's policy through the simple flattery of deferring to him personally.

But he would cut them loose if he had too, don't doubt that. He *is* the prince. Just as he will abandon Iraq to chaos if it becomes expedient, regardless of all the talk about "finishing the job." He'll just say we did finish the job ("removed the evil dictator"), and it was the Iraqis who failed to "step up to the plate." Or he'll bomb Sunni cities to smithereens if that feels more authentic to him. Or both. It'll depend how he feels in the moment.

All his life, Bush has been protected by his birthright from the consequences of pretensions he might not have been able to live up to, standing alone. Invulnerable because of his position, he became tough and confrontational, but without risk. So he could never more than half believe that it was him.

That accounts for the spoiled-bully quality in Bush. He is driven to assert himself constantly, looking for the resistance that would test his mettle if it were ever there. The compulsive teasing, admonishing, nicknaming—the symbolic subordination of people around him, people with no choice but to collaborate with his humor at their own expense—these forms of dominance can never be entirely convincing. Hence the aura of puppetry around him, arising from the repeated deployment of mannerisms that have never quite settled in.

All of this means that Bush habitually breaks the cardinal rule of Method acting. He commits the sin of "indicating."

As opposed to just reacting and being in the moment. "Indicating" means that instead of *letting* your face and voice and body do whatever they do when you react to whatever is going on around you or try to fulfill whatever intention you have within you—instead of that "letting," you impose some expression on yourself that signals what you want to get across. Think silent movie actors striking poses, for an extreme example.

But they can't be accused of indicating because they weren't Method actors to begin with. For them, acting *was* posing. But Bush is trying to be himself, to act himself. He is indicating because all the little ways he has that don't quite ring true are attempts to perform who he is, or thinks he is. But this awkwardness helps him with his followers because, like him, they think of it as an emblem of authenticity. They never did like Slick Willie.

In any case, Bush took up the tropes of world-historical leadership after 9/11 in the same way he assumed his Texas-style manhood. He practiced them as diligently as he followed his workout schedule, one day at a time, never deviating, with Laura presiding, you may be sure—for it was she who first set him on the straight and narrow. And he was sustained in this discipline by his cast of courtiers, all of whom understood their fundamental role. After all, if you were in the Bush White House during the months leading up to the Fall of Saddam, you were, above all, thrilled with your proximity to power in a truly historic moment. Everyone in your life knew you were there, and when you went home for the holiday, the hush around the table when you told your stories was almost reverent. So you had a big investment in the credibility of it all. You understood that in order to make the whole show convincing, even to yourself, you had to believe in the boss's act. You had, for example, to be inspired by his bizarre serenity in the run-up to the war, even though, on some level, you knew that he was congenitally hyper, the very opposite of serene. He may have been indifferent to the consequences for foreigners of his decisions, but that wasn't serenity, and you knew that, but you stuck to the script because your own particular luster derived from it.

The investment of the courtiers in the script only deepens as a function of media coverage, of course. Watching it, for them, gets to be like watching the dailies with the director in his trailer after a shoot. They watch, and they compare what they see to coverage of comparable moments—the Cuban missile crisis, say—and, inevitably, they find themselves playing to the coverage they hope to get when history tells the tale. This may be the most self-conscious crew of historical actors that ever lived, but, unlike Clintonian hipsters, many of whom would have enjoyed speculating about their own reflexivity, the Bushites have been willfully clueless. No irony allowed. The man's man's rule in this White House has been—as Bush the Elder used to put it—none of that psycho-analyzing stuff around here. Too 1960s, too bicoastal, too blue state.

Okay, that's an option.

Above all—beyond the cast of courtiers, beyond the daily schedule, beyond even Laura's loving, chiding eyes—Bush has been sustained in his performance by the kind of sentimentality that motivates the revenge movie.

You've noticed how, in those action-vengeance flicks, there has to be a moment near the beginning where some very bad guys, led by this incredibly bad guy, slaughter the partner or the wife or even the kiddies, so that Van Damme or Stallone can emerge from the moment fully justified, seared by a transcendent loss, by a grievance so ultimate no judgment could encompass it, emerge to commit mayhem for the whole rest of the movie, that being what you came to see in the first place? You pay for the thrill of relentless carnage by enduring a few moments of sickening bathos, a brazen sentimentality more repugnant than any violence— Steven Seagal in the yard tossing a baseball with his soon to be rubbed out son, doom hanging over the scene, you know what's coming during the lingering close-ups of that innocent face under Seagal's tender supervisional gaze, the awesome martial arts prowess tucked away, it's there, but it's folded under—the ideal American man at home.

After 9/11, Bush was animated by this emotional syndrome, and so were those who followed him. That current of feeling shaped his subsequent performance. Hence the baffling references to his "heart," the maudlin bottom-line intensity with which he insists that he has one, that he feels with it or in it, that it cannot be questioned, that he is who he is because of it. Bush's heart was elevated on 9/11 from a personal to a historic plane. He understood his role after that day in terms of divine election, don't doubt that, and take it literally, no metaphor obtains. He experienced himself being chosen by God to lead a war on terror—a war against evil, a war to save the American way of life—in exactly the same way he once experienced his personal salvation: in his heart, where floods of feeling admit no doubt. So conceptualized, this sentimentality has appeared to Bush as his own essential goodness, a goodness that merges with the greater goodness of the American people, binding them together; for millions of them also identify their best selves with this same kind of sentimentality.

It fell to Bush to act it all out for them.

From this vantage point, then, uplifted by a transcendent feeling of collective virtue, Bush contemplated the enemy. Osama and Saddam, two manifestations of a single malignancy, aliens as loathsome as any that might burrow their way into Sigourney Weaver's bowels. Moral clarity? Not a problem. He considered— with some attention to gory detail, the kind of attention reality cop shows lavish on descriptions of crimes—he considered the barbar- ities of Baathists, the villainy of guerrilla tactics, the whining ingratitude of hysterical Shiite mobs. Then he thought about how much time and money his military spent on target selection to minimize, to the degree possible—for war is cruel and accidents happen—civilian casualties *on the other side*, and when he thought about that, well, what further manifestation of national goodness, of his personal goodness, could anyone possibly ask for? Imagine that, he would think, choking up at the very idea of the care his military took selecting targets, imagine such magnanimity and compare it to Saddam, and, really, if you weren't on America's side after making that comparison, then you stood beyond the pale of common sense, wallowing in some baleful territory of the spirit where envy and guilt, cultivated since the 1960s by America haters—many of them Americans themselves, which is just plain perverted when you consider how lucky they are to be Amer- icans—in some decadent territory, then, where envy and guilt and a lot of academic verbiage combined to blind you to the simple truth. Because, for Bush, this was an obviously valid comparison, in just these terms. He has no notion of historical context at all. None. The world is as flat as a set to a man who always equated learning with affectation—which Bush has all his life, that has been axiomatic for him, and that made him all the more vulnerable to the few books he did read, the ones that confirmed and embellished his prejudices. So the comparison between his goodness, which was the goodness of his people, and Saddam's evil was all he needed. It was that simple, and Bush has always prided himself on simplicity. Simplicity has been what allows him to follow his heart.

But so minimally developed were Bush's habits of reflection that he could get misty-eyed contemplating the decencies of American restraint in war even as he calculated that, up to a point at least, minimizing Iraqi civilian casualties was a tactical and even strategic necessity—what with all those al Jazeera cameras around. But knowing that he was making such calculations, and even knowing that the priorities might change with circumstances—such hard-nosed considerations in no way diluted the tide of good feeling that sustained him.

One is good, but one is not weak. As every action hero knows, to defeat evildoers you have to have what it takes to do what is necessary.

And so, as we slide over to the other side of this emotional seesaw, we meet the other Bush, the complementary Bush, the one who refers with evident relish to death and destruction, to the terrible fate of enemies, the Bush who sneers and gloats and drops laconic Eastwoodisms into his addresses, the Bush who cannot resist tough-guy moments like, after a slight pause, during which we were to imagine that he was considering more graphic language, he finally decides on "let's just say those folks are no longer a problem for the United States of America," another pause, a "get it?" glance around the room, the bloodlust visible, but contained, as is only proper in mixed company, but the signals are there for the guys, the real guys, to read—in the mocking little downturned grin, in that classic rhetorical gesture of the American West, the slightly overemphasized understatement.

The gloating and the bloodlust were justified you see—by the sentimentality—just like in the revenge movie. More than justified. Necessary. A practical requirement, and Americans are alive to those, God knows, you can't kick ass if you don't want to kick ass, whole-hog want it, and so, by this alchemy, what sentiment originally justified we were at last enabled to indulge.

The grievance, instantly iconic, also gave Americans permission to ignore the history of our involvement in the Arab and Islamic worlds. "Nothing could justify what they did on 9/11" functioned as a blanket pardon for continued indifference and ignorance. Systematically conditioned by media to avoid anything they couldn't understand in a minute, these multitudes have learned to think of their indifference and ignorance as sturdy common-sense. They have internalized the flattery heaped upon them by generations of political shysters, serving various agendas, all of which have this in common: they rely upon the nation's civic laziness. The vaunted "wisdom of the American people"—even more vaunted than Iraq's Republican Guard—is the more to be cherished for being theirs by definition, effortlessly acquired, no tedious study, no demanding ethical reflection required, yet another convenience in a convenient world. It is sufficient, for example, to declare "you have to take a stand at some point!" in tones that thrill with conviction because such platitudes seem adequate to the tiny sphere of one's own life experience. Projecting such maxims onto the complexities of world affairs follows automatically because representations of that world have been reduced to terms that invite just those projections. Performing such reductions is the whole business of journalism and the whole business of politicians is to align their personalities and policies with them.

In the case of Bush, no particular exertions were required when he moved into the political spotlight—beyond the no-doubt considerable effort it took to reign in his bratty temper. The indifference and ignorance were long entrenched, already cast as virtues in his own mind. And people in his constituency have been drawn to him for just that reason, as they were once drawn to Reagan. They recognized one of their own. It made up for all evidence of privilege. Jokes about Dubya's mangled vocabulary, revelations of his inability to identify important foreign leaders and significant historical events the educated classes in the blue states might have been gleefully appalled, but folks in the heartland, folks who took pride in describing themselves as "ordinary Americans," they were neither gleeful nor appalled. On the contrary. They resented the pedants and snobs who jeered at Bush's natural awkwardness and innocent errors in an ill-disguised attempt to draw attention to their own suave ways, their own erudition. Never doubt it. Bush's hold on his constituency has depended not only on the rhythms of sentiment they share, but also on their common antipathy to all things intellectual and refined. Bush's people know the difference between being smart—as in quick, cunning, focused—and being educated, overeducated, pseudo, verbose, affecting an interest in the useless, the unintelligible, the foreign. Unlike so many who mocked him for stupidity, they always knew that Bush was smart; it showed in the way he looked people in the eye, always gauging them, a gifted salesman scoping out the client.

Because Bush's people aren't stupid either. What they are is willfully ignorant and unreflective, just like the president with whom they identify. They don't read anything either, so events like 9/11 occur in a historical vacuum for them too—and TV coverage relentlessly maintains it. Above all they don't think about what they really mean by highly charged phrases that cement their political identifications, that make their hearts beat as one with their leader's. When they talk of love of country and pride in being American, what happens is that very rich and deep and, above all, specific feelings for family and friends and neighborhoods, for places they vacationed as children and hung out as teenagers, places where they courted their wives and husbands, places where they lost them too, all the places they belong to—the particular smell of a school hallway, the mood of an empty intersection at the center of town, when you stop at the traffic light, just before dawn—a host of genuine attachments like that get projected onto the giant geopolitical categories presented to them in the media. The striking symbols and stirring anthems, images of people-like-us suffering, images of people-like-them enraged, on and on, until you can no longer distinguish between what you identify with directly and caricatures of that larger reality that concerns the Leaders of Big Entities to whom the media attends.

Except when they are doing their human interest "plight of ordinary people" segments, of course, but those only serve to reinforce the Blobby fusion of local attachments and fabricated entities.

So when Bush triumphed, his people triumphed. When Bush confounded his legions of highbrow critics—the tenured radicals, the effete Frenchmen, African diplomats with thousand-dollar suits and Oxbridge accents—all those masters of gray nuance, weaving their paralyzing webs out of distant causes and obscure consequences, when Bush the Bold confounded them all with simple words and simpler deeds, well, his people naturally rejoiced, for they were themselves vindicated, they were right all along, right to be ignorant, right to be parochial—right, by God, just to be American.

Bush the war leader performed that vindication after 9/11. It was the most personal of political services—though none can tell, as of this writing, if he can sustain it. So many of his façades have been shredded, and the age of terror posits a reality that media cannot cover (see coda).

CHAPTER 5

All about time. Crunch time. Time to get a life. **Busy, busy,** *being numb.
You don't need a BlackBerry, you need a chief of staff. Quality time.
Down time. Even the food is fast. Real time. She runs marathons too. The
end of the day.*

Crunch Time

CAPITALISTS MADE OUT like bandits in recent decades—
literally first of all, but in subtler and more consequential ways as
well, mostly having to do with time. Ours. Ours becoming theirs,
and we have been falling all over ourselves to give it to them, for
our own reasons, of course, but that's what makes the whole scam
so pretty. I mean, take the most obvious example, the phone line,
the waiting, listening to dozens of pretty abstruse descriptions of
options that don't apply to you—but you have to listen to them
pretty closely so as not to miss the one that does.

That's everyone's favorite example of corporate time robbery,
especially if you are of a certain age. But guess what? They've done
research, and it turns out that more and more people prefer
dealing with automated phone services for the same reason they
prefer ATMs to bank tellers. They want to avoid the little psychic
shock that necessarily accompanies any engagement, however
fleeting, with another human being. If you deal only with digital
interlocutors, it may take more time, but you can do it in your
underwear, figuratively speaking as well. And more and more
people like doing things that way. It's a virtual extension of the

175

casual pandemic that has shunted formal manners to the sidelines since the 1960s. You youngsters out there might find this hard to believe, but middle-class people used to dress up for social encounters of all kinds. They dressed up to go out—to a restaurant, to a play, to a museum, to travel by train or plane—a certain formality was expected of private people when they appeared in public places. The rise of the casual was an aspect of the rise of naturalism in our social performances generally, a development that echoed the shift to Method acting in specifically theatrical contexts, as we have noted. And, of course, all of this was ultimately an expression of the flattered self's new claims upon the world. I mean, if Mr. Rogers loves me just the way I am, why shouldn't you?

Virtually extended, such claims become authorial. Not only are you free to be just the way you are, and free to change as well, but everything around you also reflects that. Interacting with digital entities contributes to the construction of that portable bubble so many of us are getting accustomed to living in. Remote-control sovereignty over every gizmo in your environment, your living space, your online nooks and parlors, of course, but even when you are physically on the move. The iPod. Chatting on your hands-free, caller ID–equipped cell phone as you walk across the park, everything that isn't summoned by you, for you, flows by like streaming video on some random screen in a foyer—that's what the external world gets reduced to when we are snuggled down in MeWorld.

Or take a much larger, more traditionally sociological example of time robbery. Women in the workplace. I'm all for it, of course, some of my best friends are women in the workplace, but I just want to focus on the two-career (or -job) family phenomenon for a moment, because that's where the great time rip-off gets its initial choke hold on our lives.

Not so long ago, when families dependent on salaries or wages stood before the bar of social justice and called Big Capital to account, they could say something like this (picture Jimmy Stewart in suspiciously clean miner's overalls, rising from the pew to confront crusty old Charles Bickford at the town meeting):

"By golly, Mister Meanman, I've worked in the mill all these years like my father before me and now I can't put food on the table for my wife [Joan Fontaine with a peasant scarf over her shimmering hair] and family, and, what with my oldest [Natalie Wood at fourteen, limping] needing another operation and . . ."

And so on. The general idea was: one family, one breadwinner. And basic justice said that the economic system owed that family a decent living on those terms.

But it doesn't work that way anymore. Now Mr. Meanman gets to throw a skeptical glance at Joan Fontaine and say, "Well, what's *she* doing?"

It's not that obvious, of course, but that's the net effect. Women entered the workplace under the banner of progress, for the sake of independence, equity, and fulfillment, and now the unwritten understanding is: one family, two breadwinners—or, if it's jobs rather than careers at issue, sometimes several jobs among the breadwinners, just to stay afloat.

You don't have to be Keynes to figure this one out. X number of citizens for the system to support, and twice as many of them working for the same standard of living (lower, recently, but whatever). So where does all that extra productivity go? You don't have to be Marx to figure this one out. Profits.

But it gets better. The men and women who dominate the opinion-shaping classes are working too, just like everyone else—but they're working especially hard, they're working like caffeine-fueled gerbils, twelve-hour days, chained to their cell phones and e-mails every waking minute, frantically stuffing more than twice as much of that productivity into plutocratic pockets for less than half as much in return. And not only that: they're supposed to like it!

And not only that: they do like it!

That's the neatest trick of all. This is another case of the Justin's Helmet Principle. People may be stressed to the gills but, by and large, they're all for it. Recently there have been some signs of retreat, of people letting up—simplicity movements, more women opting out of careers, couples sharing the same job, Gen X parents giving more time to their kids—but, on the whole, the beat goes on.

That's why bosses onstage at the Orlando Hyatt employee-bonding retreats sound like directors giving notes to the cast after the final dress rehearsal. "Let's have fun with it!" they say, and clap their hands as the team breaks from the huddle (metaphor switch alert), hoping that they've become the beloved coaches they learned to want to be at *their* retreat, the one in June when the exces got three days on leadership by the author of a best-selling management excellence book. The point being that you (if you are of a certain class) aren't supposed to just work for a living anymore. Work is supposed to be fun and fulfilling. Work nurtures you, helps you grow; work appreciates you and, in exchange, you do a whole lot more of it.

So what is it with all these career hounds? We will see shortly, but for now just focus on how splendidly the macho cult of multitasking, bring-it-on busyness serves the powers that be. From interns to associates, the expectation of dedication is higher than anything the man in the gray flannel suit ever dreamed of. Those nine-to-fivers in the old economy were napping their way up the ladder by comparison. Of course, those old-time employees signed up with Acme for a lifetime, while today's go-getter on her new job is polishing her résumé before she finds out where the restroom is, but that's part of it too—part of a specific form of ambition nurtured by the culture of mediation, the one captured by career advice titles like *Me, the Brand*.

No wonder you lost sympathy for labor unions, or never had it. Now, what you really think when you see transit employees or doormen or maintenance workers or the hard-hats on those endlessly proliferating highway construction sites that make getting out of town for a weekend so inconvenient—what you really think is that they've got a pretty cushy deal. I mean, they do seem to be just *standing around* a lot of the time, don't they? Waving flags, leaning on things, gathered in small groups over some hole in the road—consulting, maybe—while one guy steers the one rig that's actually doing something, the rest of them watch and wait. I mean they *look* like they've been working very hard, they've got dirty rugged clothes and battered gear and sweaty bandannas, and they lean against things in that almost-exhausted cool way, big arms draping, hands dangling. But sometimes it seems like they are extras on a set because, so often, so many of them just aren't doing anything at all when you pass by. Plus, you know they don't have to take any of it home with them. Punch in, punch out, coffee break, lunch break, sick days, personal days, overtime—all in the contract.

Unlike you, that is, *they don't have to care*. They don't even have to pretend to care.

On the other hand, those illegal immigrants in the produce stores, on the delivery bikes—they really do work. They work sort of like you do, the same relentless rhythm. I mean, obviously it isn't as *interesting* as what you do, but that pace is there, that sense that there isn't much else in life but this.

I remember the first time I understood that one could *manage* one's life as an enterprise, as opposed to just living it as it happened to be, scheduled, if at all, by institutions you happened to be in. It was at Columbia College, where I was pretty much wasting my nineteenth year, at least as far as scholarly endeavor was concerned. I never went to class. On the other hand, I was in the greatest city on earth, meeting very interesting people.

One character appealed to me especially, a classmate of mine, a huge, shambling, oh–so–New York–Jewish kid named Ethan Geto. Ethan was given to announcing, in his great booming voice—so richly accented that he seemed to be flirting with self-parody—that he intended to be mayor of New York someday, and he just wanted whoever happened to be listening to know that he was counting on their support when the time came. He would proclaim all this with great good humor, obviously alive to the comic improprieties, but also letting you know that he was serious, that he was laying the groundwork for legends those who knew him when would one day tell.

I was entranced by this guy. So, one evening, I dropped by his dorm room and found him poring over books and papers, seated on a standard-issue dorm chair at a standard-issue dorm desk, seated but looming, because everything else was so small. He seemed to have no place for his elbows and knees; his enormous feet barely fit between the bunk and the bureau. But he welcomed me as grandly as an emperor in his throne room, and, after an exchange of pleasantries (I was inclined to tease, addressing him as "your Honor," and so on), he inquired as to the purpose of my visit.

Now, from within my little frame of reference at that time, you didn't need to have purposes for visiting friends and acquaintances. You just dropped by. So I was taken aback by his question, but he was so transparently glad to see me, and the way he asked the question was so obviously customary to him, that I recovered myself discreetly and said something like "Oh, nothing special, just thought we might hit the West End, grab a couple of beers?"

Hearing this, he reached for an appointment book.

I couldn't believe my eyes. I had never before seen an appointment book in the hands of anyone even close to my age—let alone seen one used to apportion time for friendship. I was stunned. I was a bit insulted too, but I also felt that I was looking at something with a larger significance.

And I was. Nowadays, in our more competitive schools at least, twelve-year-olds have appointment books and family lives are scheduled as if they were presidential campaigns going into the last week before an election.

So that's what you are getting into when you decide to become an adult—whenever that may be.

Getting a Life

So you finally grew up, got married—or coupled up seriously in some way. Most of all, you got busy. You got a career. Or you haven't done any of it yet, but you will. Maybe.

How does this happen?

Of course, it could be that you were like Ethan Geto—worthy goals set, time managed, networking habits entrenched, essentially an adult at eighteen, or even fifteen. Or maybe you started up a band in high school and went right on with it afterward, and you haven't looked back, or even sideways, since. Or maybe you let institutional cues nudge you along and went off to medical or business school right after graduation, then took the most obviously desirable job after that almost as if you had no choice, maybe not wanting to have *this* choice; who needs the vertigo? But maybe you resisted the consolation of following cues as if you had

181

no choice, maybe you jumped feetfirst into the vertigo of options, stuck studs in your tongue, tattooed your buns, and took up DJing or blogging in some loft in Williamsburg. Maybe you took off for a couple of years, traveling in South Asia, say, or living in Prague. Maybe you thought you would be a writer or an actor, and you fiddled around with that and waited on tables a lot. Maybe you decided to go to graduate school to give yourself more time to decide what to do. Maybe you experienced complete FTL (failure to launch) and you're living at home, sleeping in the same room you had when you were in eighth grade, surrounded by stuff you owned as a thirteen-year-old. Maybe you pretend you don't mind it—and maybe you sometimes don't.

Lots of possibilities is the point.

So which of the myriad paths to adulthood that we can only gesture at did you, or will you, finally, take? *If* you did or will, that is. Because the extended adolescence we noticed on the child side has been extended—indefinitely, in some cases—in the other direction as well. Some sociologist coined a term for the phenomenon "Adultolescence." Cute. Catchy.

But let's say you're one of the ones who decides to shift out of adolescence, however extended. What does it amount to, that shift, what marks it?

Well, first of all, what precedes it, what drives you to so drastic a move?

It's the drift factor. For a lot of people it begins in college; that's why the counseling services have multiplied, to give the drifters something to hold on to. Because, after a certain point, you start to feel like a little hunk of junk washing around in the eddies of some endless stream—on the one hand a prisoner of habit, on the other a plaything of whimsy. There's no reason to do anything in particular, and there's no reason not to. And, if you're still adrift after graduation, it just gets more so. You get bored with the porous circle of friends and roommates, the same old slang, the same old jokes. What used to make you feel like a member of a select society starts to border on pathetic. Like you are all clinging to each other, trying to pretend time isn't going by. But you are definitely getting visibly older, some of you notice that your hair is thinning and certain lines are settling in your face in a particularly stubborn way. And there's no denying the number of years you have to say you are, when you are asked. At the same time, you may still be spending way too much time on video games, or maybe you are still going out to the clubs, not having that much fun anymore, if you ever did, usually ending up with someone kind of weird, or no one at all— hard to say which is worse at this point; at least when you're alone you don't have to keep up an act, except the ones you perform for yourself, of course, you can never get away from those. Your love life is a mess in some way, anyway, that's for sure. You get hurt or you inflict pain, or both, over and over again, or you're stuck with some bunion you sort of love, but he or she is getting annoying in a very specific and entrenched way, and it is obviously not going to change no matter how many times you talk it through; but you can't face breaking up without some big dramatic reason, and there isn't one—or even couldn't be one anymore, or so it seems. Or you've got nobody at all, or nobody in particular, or a few people occasionally, most of them embarrassing in one way or another—and the whole STD thing begins to feel like Russian roulette, and now, when you go home for Thanksgiving to take stock of the damages it feels as if some great bell in the sky is tolling the end of another year that will never come again.

Yes, that's the mood that marks the decision to make the big shift to adulthood. The years just keep on keeping on and you are realizing that there isn't going to be an automatic resolution to this—no puberty onset, no graduation day, no nothing to determine a transition, no rite of passage that comes at you from wellsprings of nature or tradition and thrusts you into the next phase of life with a defining force that cannot be resisted and might, for that very reason, be all the more welcome. Just time going evenly by. And there's a fear factor too, like a buzz in the background, more insistent lately, louder. It's not a stream you're adrift on, it's an ocean, and if something safe to hold on to were to happen by, well, you just might be ready to cling really hard. Because, if you're going to arrest this drift, you'll have to do something, anything; that's what you realize, that you will have to perform a major self-defining act, no matter how arbitrary it feels.

But that will mean closing off options, and you have learned to identify yourself with those options, and you may still be reluctant to give them up (especially some of you guys). That's why this process can take so long, that's why drift is so hard to arrest. It's a hell of thing to take on, the responsibility of just up and *deciding* something like this, deciding to be this as opposed to that.

But then you realize, at some level, that you aren't *ultimately* giving them up after all. It's a relative thing. It's more that you are choosing something that will be hard to unchoose—not that you categorically can't change your mind about it somewhere down the line. You can't switch careers the way you can change your hair color, that is—but you *can* switch careers. In fact, more and more people are doing that these days, aren't they? And you can't get divorced as easily as you can change personal trainers—but you *can* do it. Everybody understands that these days, don't they? It's the unwritten prenup. You can even get divorced after making the one commitment left to us that still has the feel of the irrevocable about it, the one change you can still choose to make in life that has something of the weight of nature behind it.

Having kids.

And having kids *and* having a career means taking the busyness of adulthood to a whole new level.

Busy, busy, being numb

Remember that T-shirt from the 1980s? HIGH ON STRESS, it said. It was funny because it was sort of true and sort of a way to bluff it out and sort of a protest—it had that Blobby "any number of meanings" quality we now prefer to depth. That's because that "any number of meanings" quality keeps you in motion, but depth asks you to stop. Depth is to your life what dead air is to a talk show. After you've made the big self-defining decisions that transform you into an adult, you don't want depth—you want routine, and the busier the better.

Because you've still got options, large and small. Alternatives still surround you, endlessly presented and represented, and at some level you understand that. Depending on the particular ups and downs of your adult life—your career, your family—you may or may not want to look them over now and then, even act on them in some covert and compromised way. But to the extent that you remain committed to adult roles, you need to be convinced that "this is me," that this self you chose to be really is you—and to that extent you don't want your options highlighted. It's dysfunctional. You want them muted, dimmed down. You want to live as if they didn't exist, to forget them. You don't want the stillness of depth; you want the bustle of perpetual motion.

Ever notice how, when your hand is numb, everything feels thin? Even a solid block of wood lacks volume and texture. You don't feel the wood; your limb just encounters the interrupting object. Numb is to the soul as thin is to the field of representational surfaces. A guiding metaphor for adult experience in a mediated world.

The best way to achieve the insulational state of numbness is to be swamped with routine activities. The old-fashioned super-ficiality of routine blends seamlessly with the new superficiality, the surface quality of ubiquitous representation—and this hybrid accelerates constantly, as you take on more and more. Adult busyness is constituted, as we all know, by innumerable things we "have to do." People we have to be nice to, meetings we have to go to, events we have to attend, and, above all, deadlines we have to meet. And, of course, by little interventions of chance, glitches in the flow that you have to deal with as you move from one thing you have to do to the next thing you have to do. The result is a simulation of reality convincing enough to pass for the original, for most of us, most of the time. It is only when the ultimately real descends upon us in the form of tragic accident, illness, death, or a miraculous recovery, the birth of a child—only then does that simulation stand revealed for what it is.

And then we remark upon how things have been put in perspective, how we now know what really matters, and we see that we don't really have to do the things we have to do at all.

But we can't live on that plane for long. We don't want to. Only artists and metaphysicians (and adolescents) can endure that kind of contingency on a regular basis. Most of us want to be, as the old saying goes, "creatures of habit"—even though we know that those habits are constructs, we can mostly forget it if the pace is sufficiently demanding and our roles are sufficiently rewarding.

And "roles" now means more than sociology intended, don't forget, more than "mother," "neighbor," "boss," and so on. The term also refers to character and personality, to Method acting—even though, when you perform yourself out of habit as a busy adult, you can forget that it's a performance in a way you couldn't when you were an adolescent.

But you can be reminded. Let's say, for example, that you like animals. You really do like animals, this isn't about being a phony, this is about being so reflexive, so mediated, that you can't help but live through various performances. The fact that you like animals also means that you see yourself as a "person who likes animals," or, even better, as a "person who *has a way* with animals." That means that when you visit someone's house for the first time, say, and the family cat comes slithering into the room with its tail twitching and its back arching, you will fall into a well-worn groove of words and deeds that show that you are a person with a special connection to animals and that, in turn, will say so much about how down-to-earth and authentic you are.

And so on. Do your own inventory.

Are you a "no-nonsense kinda guy" who is "good in a crisis" and "doesn't suffer fools gladly" but "doesn't hold a grudge" either? Or maybe you are "sort of wacky" and people "never know what you'll say next," but you are "always there" for your friends, and you "really listen" and "give good advice" too? Whatever the particulars, to the extent that you are mediated, your personality becomes an extensive and adaptable tool kit of postures of this kind. As you immerse yourself in routines of adulthood, they ramify in all directions, in various combinations, depending on settings and likely consequences—which you assess automatically at all sorts of levels, from the moment-to-moment flicker of expression on the faces of people you are with, to the long-term likelihood of professional advancement. You become an elaborate apparatus of evolving shtick that you deploy improvisationally as circumstances warrant. Because it is all so habitual, and because you are so busy, you can almost forget the underlying reflexivity.

But it is obvious to other people. I mean, you see it in others, don't you? Why should you be different?

And it's especially obvious to your kids.

That's why, after they reach a certain age, they find you so embarrassing. They are sensitive to every little nuance of your tone and deportment, and can trace them automatically to various aspects of your elaborate self-image, especially when you are in public situations. Long after you have learned to bury performative self-consciousness under layers of habituality, they can almost literally see through you.

Now, there's a spectrum, of course. People vary with respect to how reflexive and performative they are. We all know certain individuals, blessed with impenetrable innocence, who live out their lives in the most sophisticated and relentlessly mediated circumstances as if the utterly ersatz were simply real, people who adapt automatically to every cliché in circulation, people for whom scare quotes have no function. And it would be a stretch to say, even for those who can recognize themselves immediately in this overall description, that these habitual characters we play are fully optional. If you've been "measured and judicious" for thirty years, you can't just up and decide to be "impulsive and intuitive" from now on. It would take a really good reason, and a transformative process, to get you to stop being the person you've been being for so long. And this applies to people with "low self-esteem" as well—the yield in secondary gain for *that* performance is notoriously addictive.

But, given a reason, we can change a lot, and sometimes we do. Unlike our parents or grandparents, most of us are capable of revising deeply ingrained habits and reforming long-held images of ourselves. We are subject to crisis and willed self-transformation to a degree that they simply were not. Again, most of us can't make such changes on a whim, not after we've grown so accustomed to our performances. Drastic changes in character typically occur in tandem with drastic changes in context—through divorce, in new families, new careers, and also, of course, through therapy or a twelve-step program—but (there's a sliding scale) in multitudes of smaller ways as well: diet and exercise, Viagra prescriptions, an inspiring book or leader, meditation, and on and on.

Summing up: Performative habitualities in a mediated adulthood that dims down the horizon of options through immersion in a numbing routine allow many of us to feel relatively real.

Especially if we have a lot on our plate. And that is the ultimate reason we make sure that we do. That's why we take on more—more appointments, more projects, more health and grooming aids, more acquaintances, more appliances, more pastimes. Besides, it's all good, or might turn out to be good, so why shouldn't I have it? Why shouldn't I have it all?

Overscheduled busyness might seem, at first glance, to be the opposite of numbness. But it is the active aspect of living in a flood of surfaces, keeping pace with everything that's coming at you. Consider the guiding metaphor again. The (absence of) sensation that is physical numbness is constituted by a multitude of thrills and tingles reaching a level of frequency and multiplicity beyond which you feel nothing. The numbness of busyness works on the same principle, but it is less obvious because it relies upon its agents to abide by an agreement they must keep hidden, even from themselves.

The agreement is this: we will so conduct ourselves that everything becomes an emergency.

Under the terms of that agreement, stress becomes the way reality feels. People addicted to social and professional busyness—

for example, people who don't just use their cell phones in public places but display in every nuance of their cell phone deportment a sense of throbbing connectedness to Something Important—these people would suffocate like fish on a dock if they had to stop, if they were ever cut off from the flow of events they have conspired with their fellows to create. To plugged-in players, the feeling of being busy is the feeling of being alive.

The irony is that, *after* we have worked really hard and fast on something urgent for a long time, we do escape numbness for a while—stepping out of the building, noticing the breeze, the cracks in the sidewalk, the stillness of things in the shop window. During those accidental and transitional moments, we actually get the feeling of the real we were so frantically pursuing when we were busy.

But we soon get restless. We can't take the input reduction. Our psychic metabolism craves more. A constitution sustained by representations can never get enough. It needs to have too much.

Down Time

So it's no wonder that we rush, even in our down time. We need as much as we can get, and there is a lot of it out there, multiple avenues to recreation, all pressing for our custom. Think of all the movies and books and magazines and exhibits and games and CDs and videos and TV channels and restaurants and bars and sports sites and parks and malls, all the fun products everywhere. Think of all the offerings at those gourmet take-home food places that have sprung up recently. Exurban supermarkets in the middle of Nebraska have sections like this now, but it's the really fancy urban emporiums that embody the significance of fast food most cogently, precisely because they are not McDonald's. They charge so much they can afford to let half the food in those bloated displays go bad, just for the sake of the succulent vista of possibilities that greets us as we enter, and we are willing to pay that much just so we won't have to waste a minute of our precious down time getting ready to eat and cleaning up after—such laborious, outmoded tasks, the peeling and chopping, the handling of breakable china and glass, the water that takes so long to boil, the soap that takes so long to rinse away. Drives you nuts, the handling, the waiting. You want to just click and be done with it.

That's what microwaves are for. To let you get right to the screen.

Of course, for all I know, you're into gourmet cooking and wine tasting and you've taken courses on how to prepare various exotic cuisines from scratch and attended little seminars at your local high-end liquor store to sample their newly acquired Australian vintages.

But, either way, we learn to surf our recreational options too. On some level, we're rushing even when we're relaxing. That's why we spend so much of our time scheduling the rest of our time. Even if we're poleaxed for hours on end in front of the TV, our minds must keep pace with the hyperpacing of the ads and shows, and the remote lies ever ready to hand. We seek busyness even then.

That's why television (and movies) provides us with all those stress dramas. It's so we can keep virtually busy, even when we aren't working. The bleeding, writhing body on a stretcher arriving at the ER, every personjack on the team yelling numbers from monitors, screaming for meds and equipment, especially for those electro heart-shocker pads—that's the paradigm scene. All the other scenes in stress dramas derive from it: the hostage-negotiator scenes, the staffers pulling all-nighters in the West

Wing, the detectives sweeping out of the precinct, donning jackets, adjusting holsters, snapping wisecracks. Sheer speed and lives on the line. That's the recipe for feeling real.

Actually, though, stress dramas are about the working lives of the media people who make them. This is a fundamental insight, another example of the unnoticed ways that media saturates experience. Stress dramas purport to be about the White House or hospitals or law firms, but what they are really about is what it is like to make shows for a living, about high-stakes teamwork in the land of celebrity where, by definition, everything matters more than it does anywhere else, a land that welcomes diversity and foibles as long as the job gets done, a land where everything personal, unconditional, intimate—everything unbounded by the task—takes place on the side. That's why, in these shows through which the celebrated teach the rest of us how to be like them, moments of heartfelt encounter that make it all worthwhile are stolen in the corridors of power, while the verdict is awaited. Now and then, we get that real-folks-rushing-to-get-out-of-the-house-in-the-morning scene, but that just underscores the priority of the flow of events that protects the busy from the danger of being left alone in the stillness with what supposedly makes it all worthwhile. Lest direction be lost, motion must be maintained.

So life in a flood of surfaces that demand attention means a life of perpetual motion, and TV provides the model in other modes as well. Take the transitions from story to story in newscasts, that finishing-with-a-topic moment. "Whether these supplies, still piling up on the docks after three weeks of intense effort by these frustrated humanitarian workers, will actually reach the victims [pause] remains to be seen." A hint of a sigh, a slight shake of the head, eyes down-turning; the note of seasoned resignation. Profound respect is thus conveyed for the abandoned topic even as a note of anticipation rises to welcome the (also interesting but less burdensome) next topic—and a cut to a new camera angle back at the anchor desk makes clear that a stern and external necessity, rather than any human agency, governs the shift from two minutes on mass starvation to three minutes on Janet Jackson's tit.

Judy Woodruff is especially good at this, her particular little head nod, or shake, as the case may be, and the way her lips tighten up a tad indicate to us that "If it were up to me as a human being, I would *never* leave this coverage of thousands of dying innocents, but, as a newscaster, of course, I have to." And her speaking voice says something like. "All right, Jim, we have to go to a break now, but we will be following this story as it develops—and thanks again." The extra thanks lets us know that Jim can smell it. "Thank you, Judy," says Jim, echoing her gesture, and we are given to understand that he too, as a human being, would never allow us to move on from so ghastly and demanding a reality, but, of course, it isn't up to him as a human being either. It isn't up to anybody, actually. There's only one reality, one thing there is no choice about. Moving on.

It would be irrelevant to object by demanding, "Well, how *should* it be done?" There isn't any other way to do it. That's not an objection, that's the point. This isn't a consultant's memo. This is a serious diagnosis of a serious condition. Would we rather not know about it because it's incurable?

These conventions of the media, conventions of gesture and rhythm, consolidate the most fundamental agreement of our public culture in ways we rarely notice. This goes much deeper than subject matter, or the political bias we so regularly detect, all the usual fodder. It determines the way we frame everything. For, if you don't accept *this* agreement, you are either a child or a nut or some passed-over tribesman—charming or dangerous, as the case may be—but not a participant, not a player. Like all that is most profound in human custom, this agreement is almost physical, an attunement, more music than semantics, a form, indeed, of attitude. It takes priority over everything to which we consciously attend as it instills and expresses, moment by moment, the *way* we live in this world of surfaces.

So, for example, you don't have to wait for the anchorperson to change the topic. You can change it yourself, and you don't have to nod or sigh or clench your lips as you make the transition. But you do. Monitor yourself the next time you zap away from some disturbing something on *The News Hour with Jim Lehrer* to catch the action on a *Law and Order* rerun. You mime those same little gestures to yourself as you punch the buttons. These are the constituting habit structures of our culture.

And we've touched already on what awaits you when you join the gang on *Law and Order*. The stress drama re-creating, more elaborately, the basic gesture of the news show, the gesture you just performed when you slid away from those refugee visuals. Everything's in motion, elliptical, glancing, fungible. You see the sides of faces, the slope of a shoulder, the beginnings of expressions but not the ends, the ends of expressions but not the beginnings. No matter what happens, no matter the horror, no matter the injustice, no matter how passionate McCoy may feel about this or that, no matter how angry Bratt gets at Briscoe (actors or characters?), no matter how obnoxious the defense attorney or impatient the judge (especially in chambers), they all keep moving. And the camera keeps moving too, gliding, peeking, glimpsing (and this is *Masterpiece Theatre* compared with split-screen stress dramas like *24*). Frightened witnesses, incoming lawyers, outgoing suspects, they're all moving too—as is the traffic, the doors, hands, phones, everything in motion, every which way. Meaningful personal encounters are bound to be interrupted, and the performers, like would-be fighters in a bar relying on friends to keep them apart, anticipate the interruption, rely on it. Ferociously or tenderly, they emote in transitional interlude, awaiting the inevitable rescue by events, and, gratefully regretting the passing of the moment of communion, they watch the DA step into the elevator and deliver the homily as the door slides shut across his grizzled visage, a homily that is never merely upbeat or despairing, never final or conclusive in any way. Because the one thing people in a TV series know is that tomorrow is another show, and they will be ready to roll. They are pros, and pros know how to deal. It's not that they're indifferent or cynical. They care. Sometimes they win, sometimes they lose— but, either way, they move on. That's the lesson, the ultimate homily of all shows. The way we live now.

Real Time (The Bottleneck)

Yet another revelation in a slang expression that bubbled up and caught on. "Real time" as opposed to what exactly? Well, as opposed to representations that aren't simultaneous with whatever they represent. Instantaneous stock market info—but not just snapshots, the flow across the mediational screen *as* events occur. Hence, "real time." That's the paradigm case.

Anything less than that must count, by implication, as "unreal time." Any representation that lags behind or previews and/or otherwise selects from the actual stream of events is in unreal time.

It follows that we live in unreal time a lot of the time. Of course, we are always in real time at one level. While you are absorbed in a movie, you are also ticking along biologically, moment by moment, in the same way that you would be if you were peeling potatoes (do people still do that?) or walking the dog. So unreal time should be understood as an add-on, a dimension attached to real time that takes us out of it and inserts us into alternative flows.

Of which there are so many. You could be absorbed in a book instead of a movie—Abigail Adams's biography, say. Or listening to messages on your answering machine or reading your e-mail or watching TV, of course, especially that—though, come to think of it, TV is often live, which has to be reckoned as real time I suppose? That means that, with TV, you are sort of flickering in and out of real time depending on what's on, in addition to always being in your own real time, in the sense that you are lying on your couch. But that formulation leads to the realization that, when you are absorbed in any representation, you are nevertheless aware, at least peripherally, of the medium—of the book or the remote in your hand, the keyboard under your fingers, the screen as a screen. So we are living a fusion of real and unreal time, an ongoing undulation of overlays and intersections.

You know what it's most like? It's most like the way good old-fashioned thinking and imagining work in relation to sensing and perceiving! How obvious that is. But what it says is pretty consequential. It says that back before representational technologies developed, before literacy itself, people were also living in a fusion of real and unreal time because they were often daydreaming while they were doing this or that. Just having a mind is to be in unreal time as well as in real time.

But what *that* says is that representational technologies have colonized our minds. That may be the simplest, deepest way to characterize the whole history of representation. To the extent that our thoughts no longer wander along on their own, stocked only with materials drawn from direct experience, to the extent that they follow flows of representations instead—to just that extent we don't think our own thoughts. Literally.

There should be no need to reiterate the extent of that extent. And yet, by virtue of a by now familiar dialectic of mediation, the colonization of minds by representation resulted in more self-conscious and autonomous selves.

I'm not sure how this works, actually, I can't discern the internal phenomenology of it. But that it has worked this way is evident.

When the term first arose, "real time" implied speed, intensified velocity. The medium doing the representing was transforming reality into representation immediately. The expression was first used in connection with digital processing of information (as opposed to typographic or manual). It was a term of praise that focused on how fast a computer could record and file transactions as compared with paper-shuffling clerks. It wasn't until the fact that computers could keep up with events was taken for granted that we noticed that security cameras in public places were real-time media too. And nothing seems slower than those! How strange. Why is that?

No editing.

No manipulation of what is presented.

In the same way, an innovation like video conferencing could surprise us with a real-time capacity that the telephone had all along. But we only *noticed* that a lot of analog media were in real time after computers achieved sufficient processing speed to do it too. It was the malleability of digital transformations that made the difference. The fact that we could now manipulate what had once just been conveyed on a screen or over a wire, that's what got the juices going. That's why "interactive" became the mother of all buzz words. The idea of real time emerged when we became players on screens we had once viewed passively. The fusional loop of subject-object that is a video game expresses most cogently the thrill of real-time existence in unreal realms. You tweak the joystick and press the buttons and virtual swords flash and machine guns blaze in some tunnel on an asteroid in a distant galaxy—not as a result of, but as a function of, at the same time as, your fingers on the console. You exist as agent and instrument simultaneously in two places, in the meat world of fingers and consoles and the virtual world of cyborg warriors. Representational being incarnate. The primordial aim of the human imagination realized—literally "made real."

So "real time" is a compliment we pay to representations that reflect our agency either directly or in the way they conform to our designs subsequently—as with a computer program that browses the Web for things we might be interested in, a virtual Mini-Me who never sleeps. Incidentally, remember when people thought that the Web was going to build bridges between communities and inspire cross-cultural understanding, etc.? Hah! The multiplication of niches has been so intense that the word fragmentation doesn't begin to describe it. What with these search worms and filters and custom advertising hooking you up with stuff you're already interested in—why, you can spend your whole life online and never leave your own head.

Anyway, it was when real time emerged as a category that we began explicitly to cope with unreal time. We had to, because that's where time pressure comes from. Just do the math. Your real time is now clogged with how many representational devices? And they are all chiming and beeping and blinking and popping up at you constantly, all of them demanding that you respond, that you push this button or that button, that you listen to this or scan that, that you point and click this way or that, copy and paste, CC and forward, delete and download and print out and xerox—on and on. So you equip yourself with speed dial and Tivo, call-waiting and chain mail, split screen, spam filter, buddy list, and avatars—on and on. Which equipment proceeds to feed back positively into the representational existence of others, similarly equipped—and on and on again.

And I haven't even mentioned the time it takes to learn how to operate these devices, depending on how deeply you plunge into their layers of functionality, into manifolds of esoteric possibility so numerous and intricate that only designers and operating instructions writers ever plumb the full potential of the gizmo.

And I haven't even mentioned coping with upgrades. Sometimes I think that all the techies were initiated into a secret society where they took a blood oath that, no matter what institution they ended up in, they would explain to their techno-dependent bosses why they needed to upgrade a system that had just been upgraded six months ago, and that's because, if they don't, they will fall behind everybody else because everybody else is upgrading. So everybody upgrades. It doesn't matter that the system they had before worked perfectly well, did everything that needed to be done, and that everybody had finally learned how to use it.

But they probably don't need to take an oath. They probably understand that their jobs depend on lagging user-learning curves and that arbitrary alterations in software interfaces ensure that the lag will be perpetual.

And I haven't even mentioned coping with your kids time. Talk about busy, ask any working parent—this is where the whole vehicle of the life you decided to get spins just this side of out of control, and you can't do much more than hang on as it plummets along. This is when the word "vacation" gets to mean "taking care of the kids somewhere else." Nannies? Day care? Camp? Sure, of course, but that barely takes the edge off. This is when you come to understand that getting a life for yourself amounts to giving it up to others. This is when you learn what they meant when they said that the days go on forever but the years go flying by.

The decades, even.

No wonder they invented quality time, that most plaintive of pop concepts, expressing, as it does, the forlorn hope that the tide of busyness might be stemmed long enough for you to just *be* with your children.

You wish.

Either busyness will intrude and sweep aside your little structure like so much balsa wood, or you will have to turn the damn thing into yet another project. The Family Sit-down Dinner on Tuesdays and Thursdays Project, for example. Did you read about how the citizens of Ridgewood, New Jersey, passed a town ordinance making one evening a week an official "Family Night," prohibiting local residents and institutions from scheduling events on that evening? They made a law.

They must have been *really* busy.

The essential point is this: cell phones and answering machines and digital telemarketing messages and Xerox machines and Web sites and BlackBerries—these are all representational technologies too. They all siphon your attention into unreal time. They represent what is not present and confront you with something else you have to deal with, if only to discard it. Consider just the answering machine. It used to be that you called and, if no one was home, there was no answer. The phone just rang until you gave up. Time would go by. Maybe you would try again. Maybe you would get no answer again. By now, sometimes, it was too late for whatever the call was about in the first place or some other way of dealing with whatever it was came up in the meantime or the whole thing wasn't that important in the first place and you could just forget about it. Or, if it really was important, you would keep trying until you got through, but even in that case, a lot of time would go by before the person you were calling had to deal with whatever it was. Looking back, having no answering machine provided a built-in buffer, an automatic prioritizer, an automatic time expander.

Now, of course, it would just be rude.

And similarly for all these technologies. And as the input multiplies it ramifies across the various platforms, breaching the boundaries of the locations and time periods that used to divide our lives into separate sectors. So those buffers collapse as well. Work follows us home, school follows us home, family follows us to work, friends follow us on vacation— —in a nutshell, if you are sitting on the Acela Express to Boston, you may be hundreds of miles away from the New York City places in which you live and work, in transit for, in principle, untraceable hours, but if you've got your cell phone along for the ride you might as well have never left.

Of course, this is mostly a good thing.

Isn't it? I'm so confused, I can't tell anymore.

And don't forget. Though everything in this fusing environment is conspiring to cram more and more into the instants of our consciousness, our basic psychological apparatus hasn't changed since the Stone Age. True, the boosterism got so bad in the late 1990s that some dot-com visionaries were hyping studies purporting to show that human processing capacities were expanding to accommodate the flood. They hailed marginal increases in multitasking abilities as if an indefinite potential were being revealed, as if the mind itself was as expandable as a microchip, as if they really expected that someday people would be able to *pay attention to everything at the same time.*

Wouldn't *that* be cool?

Huh?

What does that even mean?

There's only so much a human being can pay attention to in a given moment, obviously. That's what "paying attention" means, for God's sake. And there are only so many moments in a day—in a lifetime. So there's an unbreachable bottleneck right there at the tail end of the funnel, where the representational flood comes up against the human sensory system and the screen of human consciousness. And that's where all the interesting psychological effects related to speed and volume occur. If you don't want to sink, you learn to surf; you have to. You learn how to go fast, but smooth, through a huge amount of stuff—at work, at home, in the store, in the street. Multitasking means learning how to double back and reshuffle at the least hint of resistance, it means missing most of what goes on around you but learning not to regret it because nothing is that much more valuable than anything else, it means learning how to coast through meetings on zero information, it means learning how to ripple through your face-to-face dealings in the meat world as adeptly as a star techie navigates a new piece of software.

For the "lightness"—let's try that expression—of digital transactions sets a standard, stylistically speaking, attitudinally speaking. You are compensated for the loss of buffers and boundaries built into the old real world of separated times and places, by an overall muffling of experience in general. The muted, gliding, plasmic poofs and puffs and pings of desktop alias and window behavior, the rippling minimalism of point-and-click transactions, the murmur of shuffling e-mails—it's all so *easy*, so you do more, more checking to see, more forwarding, more CCing, more browsing; it's all so easy, so insulated, compared with actual human encounters and the clumsy stubbornness of implements and furnishings in the physical realm, things you have to handle, things with weight, things that have other sides, things that insist on being what they are.

Maybe this lightness, and the moreness, like so much we have been considering, will prove to be a net gain in the long run. "What's so great about reality?" a techie friend of mine used to say when confronted with earlier, more conventionally Luddite versions of this book's argument. He meant it too. And maybe he was right. I'm not kidding about the Justin's Helmet Principle, I hope that's been clear.

Still.

At the End of the Day

My grandfather, as I remember him, became my model for a little enterprise I undertook recently. Released by good fortune into an expanse of unstructured time, I decided to get back in touch with the real on an everyday basis, to refuse the insulations of representation and busyness. I decided to unplug and slow down.

It turned out to be amazingly difficult, in spite of the inspiration of my memories of his way with things—I mean actual things, physical objects. That was what I undertook to imitate, as if serving a long-delayed apprenticeship. He had been a surgeon in his day, and widely admired for his skills, but in the years when I was trailing around after him he had long since retired. I knew him as a fisherman of infallible technique, a hoarder of all things useful, an inspired tinkerer, a classic *bricoleur*. In personality, he embodied the old New England archetype: taciturn, skeptical, a plainspoken master of the deadpan put-down. Complete with accent. An irresistible figure for a glib little boy with no roots.

But it was his hands that I remember most of all, the care they extended to everything he touched, one by one, no haste, no waste, to each its due. That much was obvious. But subtler internal qualities made for beauty in even his simplest actions. Before using things, he took time to assess them. Just for a second, when he was buttering bread; more intently, when the task was less routine. His eyes supervised, but it was his hands upon which he most relied— constantly gauging and accommodating, hefting, balancing, fingering for edge, flexibility, fit. He never held anything too tightly, but nothing ever slipped his grasp. And he loved to prepare—to unwrap, to lubricate, to sharpen. To lay everything out. When at last he executed a task, the outcome followed from the preparation like a dénouement. And he attended just as respectfully to cleaning up, to returning and replacing.

No wonder that the things he owned, seen in repose, apart from him, showed the history of this treatment in gradations of their wear, in just those places that reflected implemental purpose. No wonder that they always seemed to be waiting for him to come back.

So I have been trying to emulate him. Whenever I think of it, I slow down and focus and try to do it his way, whatever I'm doing. But I usually lapse after just a few minutes, especially when I'm in transition, leaving the house in the morning, say, or getting back after a long day exploring the outer boroughs with my backpack full (a book or two, a yellow legal pad, a bottle of Poland Spring, a towel, sunscreen, bug spray); and the external zip pouch stuffed to the limit (address book, wallet, army knife, Ray-Bans, Halls cough drops, comb, nail clippers, portable stapler, three or four pens, aspirin and Tums, gum, paper clips, loose change, eyedrops, a few matchbooks)—and, somewhere in there, my keys.

The keys being the point, because I've stopped off at the deli for a few things on my way home, so I'm carrying a plastic shopping bag too, and, somehow, there's this rule.

The rule says that I should not have to stop walking in order to get to my keys. I should not have to put down the (sure-to-flop-over-due-to-skewed-48oz-soda-bottle) shopping bag. I should not have to remove the backpack and place it upright in front of me on a stable flat surface and look through the zip pouch in an orderly manner until I find the keys. No. What I am required to do is continue walking and release only my left shoulder from the backpack strap, hang the pendulating shopping bag from my left wrist (where it can snag on my watch), maul the backpack around under my right armpit (where it will be tilted so I can't see into it), and steady the whole scrunched-up bundle with my right hand while I unzip the pouch with my encumbered left, so I can plunge in and grope blindly (under a certain pressure, the pouch will spontaneously unzip all the way down on both sides) for the keys I must find before I get to the door.

Well, you can see where this is going. Inspector Clouseau redux.

An extreme case, granted. But all my encounters with inanimate objects incline in that direction. Drawers, appliances, packaging, car dashboards, newspapers on crowded subways. In my heart, I know that emulating my grandfather will not lead to radical change in habits so ingrained, but the effort has been yielding insight.

Most fundamentally, my problem is simply this: I don't *want* to pay attention to these damn things. I am impatient with them. They have some nerve, the way they take up space, asserting their positions and solidities, obstructing me at every turn with their intrusive points and angles. And my reaction is to tumble and shove, which usually results in more obstruction. When I handle things, I am inclined to gesture in the direction of the result I want.

My touch should be enough. It indicates my purpose. The rest, the details, the actual execution, should not be my concern. It should be up to the things. After all, their whole reason for being is to function, right? You'd think they'd catch on after a while. Why should I have to go through the whole process myself, step by step, every time? I'm a busy man. I've got a lot on my mind.

That's the core attitude. Where does it come from? Maybe it's a character flaw. But I suspect it is the cumulative influence of all the devices in my life—from dishwashers to microwaves to computer programs—that do so many things people like my grandfather used to do for themselves, when there was no other way.

It's also mass-produced disposability, as a feature of so many of the physical things we are still obliged to handle. Razors, lighters, cups, cameras, pens, plastic utensils, the list goes on and on.

You can't respect such things. They aren't even things, really; they have no singularity. I want to say that such objects come as close to being desktop icons as physical utility allows. After all, when you throw them away there's nothing to miss. But that was exactly why my grandfather kept things. He respected them. He respected their singularity. Above all, he respected their potential. Even broken things had potential—one never knew how this thing or that might serve in some way in some future circumstance, for even broken things still had whatever edges and points and holes and leverages they stubbornly had. My grandfather respected things for the very characteristics that make me impatient with them.

So that's how I tried to get in touch with the real as I began to understand that the end of the day would come after all.

But there are other ways. Lots of options. Again.

For example, some people, some still very busy—young enough to have open futures, and others who feel the narrowing ahead—

they decide to invest themselves in demanding and time-consuming hobbies, especially in some sport, golf or tennis or marathon running, whatever it may be. Why do they do this?

Some of them are into health and vanity and serotonin levels, of course, but that's just a fringe benefit for the ones who make a real sports commitment. They want a whole different level of involvement. Maybe they get lured into it by a friend, maybe they played in college but let it slide for some reason, but, however they come to it, they find themselves drawn into a new world, a world that is— what a blessing—on the side of the one they rush through so routinely now. And this world on the side has certain compelling characteristics by comparison with the one they mainly live in— which often gets more confusing and incomprehensible as they settle into it. Ominous undertones make themselves felt, lurking recesses, things left unsaid and overlooked, intimations of dread that even the most established routine can't quite paper over.

In sport there is redemptive simplicity. You always know what's at stake, and you always know where you stand. This is a world with clear boundaries. They are marked. There are defined ends and obvious means. A stick of some kind, a ball of some kind, a goal of some kind, so elemental. And all the more so when the place where you play is laid out nicely, a place that's not too crowded, that's well kept up; there's a certain feel to the space, even the sounds of the game have a purity in that space, the whacks or bongs or clinks of good equipment, skillfully handled. In these circumstances, even the most impatient consumer of disposability can give to physical things the respect they deserve.

It would be hard to overstate how important all this can become to some people, no matter how busy they are otherwise. There is a magic to arriving, early in the morning, the shadows still long across the field, the dew still on the grass. A place to come home to—and an arena as well. Here real limits can be reached and tested. Up against extremes of exertion, discipline, and concentration, the possibility of transcendence is open for any serious player as much as for a celebrated champion. Here you can triumph against the odds, or go down to honorable defeat, and here, no matter how devastating your loss, there is always another day, a new beginning, another chance to achieve your personal best. A place to perform.

No wonder sports metaphors abound.

But others of us long for something more than even a sport can provide, especially as we get older, as our children turn away from us, as our careers settle into final form, as we realize that we will no longer be getting better at the games we play. Then, especially, we—some of us, anyway—look to nature for redemption.

CHAPTER 6

On saying "awesome." **The fate of nature**. *Mixed feelings about the disabled person who "climbed" Mt. Everest. The fate of the exotic. On taking pictures of the Other. Our unseemly access to everything. Outer space, anyone? The transcendent significance of the Weather (Channel). A blasphemous aspiration.*

Awesome

MY NOMINEE FOR the saddest *New York Times* op-ed piece ever written is called "Capturing the Light" by Alan Lightman, an MIT professor who is both a talented novelist and a working scientist, a latter-day C. P. Snow. He wrote to express his ambivalence about a recent achievement of his colleagues. It seems that, in their laboratory, they had somehow "succeeded in slowing light down to a crawl, and finally a dead stop."

That's what they did. They stopped light. Did you even know? How could you have missed that?

Now light had always been an absolute for the professor—like the "swift thought of God," he said. Seeing God's thought conquered was not a comfortable experience, of course, but as a scientist, he had to celebrate the achievement. At the same time, as a person, he felt a kind of grief— one less transcendent phenomenon in the cosmos.

But here's the really sad part. In the required solution-to-the-problem paragraph at the end of his piece, Professor Lightman concluded that "the great challenge to us as a species of thinkers and doers is to maintain our awe of nature while at the same time subduing and shaping it."

Hello?

It's up to us to *maintain* our awe of nature?

That can only mean that nature is no longer up to the job.

What are we supposed to do? Would a CD-ROM from Steven Spielberg help? Units on awe in the science curriculum? *More* I-max movies?

Once again the vernacular rises to the occasion, distilling a cultural condition into a dialectical package, an idiom that catches on because it accommodates the mediated mind so deftly. "Awesome," the young folks say these days, as in "these are awesome french fries." On the one hand, there's the obvious devaluation of the very idea of awe, which originally shared connotations with its companion concept "awful," even as it registered admiration on a par with reverence, but more intense, more immediate—above all, overwhelming.

Which is just what a conquered nature can't do. Overwhelm.

On the other hand, oddly, the slang use of "awesome" is also an effort to retain something of the original meaning in a quasi-ironic sanctification of the everyday. It is as though the miracle of being retreated to the nooks and crannies of ordinary life to escape the onslaught of virtualization, hid itself in the mundane, where disclosures of the miraculous are still possible. After a lifetime's experience with digitized wonders depicted so fabulously that the human imagination begins to feel like a vestigial organ, there is redemption to be found in a plate of fine french fries.

The Fate of Nature

But, like the early Romantics reacting to industrial fabrications, some of us still turn to nature for relief from the insular feel of the surfaces we navigate so relentlessly all day long. We turn to nature because we want to be with and in something that wasn't put there for us, something indifferent to us, something massive and gritty, something vast, something we can't penetrate, can't get to the end of, something incomprehensible—something as big and powerful as God used to be. We long for the beyond. We want to be in awe.

But we can't get there from here, as the old joke goes, because the professor's unintended point was right on target. Nature doesn't really make it anymore.

Why? Well, first of all, there isn't much of it left. That's just a fact. It doesn't follow from any fancy theorizing about mediation. The earth and its oceans were finite after all, and now it's over. There are still a few unlabeled species around, a few acres of untouched jungle or tundra, a Pacific trench or two off the Philippines, but, basically, psycho-culturally, recalling the epochal sweep of events on a planet that was once unbounded—it's over.

And don't start up about outer space, please.

The end of nature is, of course, a spiritual catastrophe. The appeal of mediation rests in large part on its capacity to distract us from the monumental grief and guilt we would feel in the presence of this loss, if we were not distracted. It is no accident that, as we succeed in conquering the world, the trope of conquest falls from fashion. We don't want to talk about it that way anymore. Our complicity, though obvious, must be disguised—and the most effective of all disguises is custodial.

The conquest of nature drives us to domesticate whatever is left in an effort to preserve it. This is a crowning irony, perhaps the most comprehensive of the Blob's osmotic processes, for, with this one, reflexivity comes to haunt the whole planet, the very universe.

For starters, think of it this way: people who are *least* concerned with protecting nature, people who want unrestricted drilling and logging and hunting and snowmobiling—they are the ones who come closest to experiencing nature as real. For them, in their ignorance, it still registers as an inexhaustible given. But people who know better, people dedicated to protecting and conserving, people who "love nature"—they are the ones who experience it as limited, contingent, fragile, and, above all, *contained*. Contained by ecological understanding, by maps, by laws. And "contained" implies packaged—which always means optional. Optional, both in the sense that it is threatened and in the sense that one chooses to save it, to be in it, to appreciate it. The core experience of such a person, hiking the back country of Alaska, say, is best rendered in this way: *the wilderness around her represents itself.*

Take another example. You go to Yellowstone, hoping to see the wolves. Thanks to the restored *Canis lupus* population in the park, you can do that these days. But you probably know this already, even if you haven't been. Unlike the capture of light, this was a big story for a while, lovingly covered from all angles—the teams of experts who managed the process, alternative strategies for reintroduction, the dynamics of pack formation, confrontations with local ranchers—it was all in *Newsweek*, on CNN, in the *Times*, all over. Anyway, let's say you go, and let's say you get lucky, you time your ride through the park just right, you notice a cluster of cars and a battery of cameras and scopes arrayed at the edge of a particular turnout along the road, and you pull over and join the assembled wolf-watchers—and, by God, you see wolves.

Except you won't see wolves, you'll see "wolves." You'll be murmuring to yourself, at some level, "Wow, look, a real wolf, not in a cage, not on TV. I can't believe it."

That's right, you can't. Natural things have become their own icons.

Is that why you will get restless so quickly if the "wolf" doesn't do anything? The kids will start squirming in, like, five minutes; you'll probably need to pretend you're not getting bored for a while longer. But if that little smudge of canine out there in the distance continues to just loll around in the tall grass, and you don't have a powerful tripod-supported telelens gizmo to play with, you will get bored. You will begin to appreciate how much technology and editing goes into making those nature shows on the Discovery Channel.

When all is said and done, the family vacation to Yellowstone can be summed up this way: you may have some great pictures to illustrate the list of exciting creatures you saw—some of them from right up close, almost like at a petting zoo. But the truth is that if some no-account chipmunk just happens to come around your campsite every morning for crumbs from your picnic table, he will have meant more to you than any "wolf."

Precious accidents.

Accident—and necessity. Back to that again. Together, they constitute the real, and nature once reigned supreme as the source of both. Where they hold sway, we do not. They are what comes from beyond. Preserved, contained, domesticated—nature can't deliver like she used to but some folks go to great lengths trying to recover her original power and meaning. People in remote corners of the globe make a pretty good living providing their customers with the most strenuous and risk-loaded encounters with nature that the entrepreneurial imagination can contrive.

And there's plenty to choose from. Tornado chasing, shark hunting, volcano descents, survivalist backpacking. The common thread? There's a goal—and it's hard to reach. That's because you get closer to nature when you do something in it —even if it's just fishing—than you do if you go to gawk. And hardship, intense discomfort, enhances the intimacy because it puts you in such close relation with the necessary and the accidental. Hardship endows the most routine activity with authentic edge. Struggling to make a fire in a wilderness downpour when you are exhausted and hungry is like skinning the palm of your hand on the sidewalk when you fell very suddenly—as a small child, running down the driveway to greet daddy, laughing and yelling when, whack, boom, no warning—down. Hard. The welling burn, the shock, the grit in the gouged skin, the elemental injustice of pain. Edges of hardship in encounters with nature work like that, except in superslow motion. They make nature more real, and, after a while, you feel more real yourself.

That is, if you're into that kind of thing. A lot of people aren't. It's an option.

Encounters with the necessary and the accidental in remote and uncultivated places that are utterly indifferent to your existence— that's the underlying formula. An implicit scale, a sort of reality quotient, lets you gauge relative intensity. A ten-day white-water rafting expedition down some roaring canyon cascade, with a professional guide in each giant dingy and crash helmets and life jackets for all? Pretty awesome, but you can take the kids along on that one. You alone on a mountainside, ascending the sheerest, highest escarpment in the hemisphere—rock climbing the sucker, pinion by pinion, four days and three nights, with no more gear or provisions than you can fit in a backpack? Clearly on a whole different level. What about you all alone in a twenty-five-foot sailboat crossing the Atlantic? Think about what that would be like for a minute.

Encounters with nature on that level are the gold standard. In such circumstances, in the most majestically indifferent settings on earth, accident and necessity unite under the sign of mortal danger to yield the purest possible encounter with the real.

Now that's awesome.

Awesome in the original sense or the slang sense?

Here's the problem. Encounters with nature of that ultimate, superintense type seem to morph into something like . . .

Extreme sports.

And that means it's not so clear what the object of awe is.

I remember one of the first women to climb Mt. Everest making this point apparent in some interview I saw years ago, on TV. She had an answer ready when asked why she decided to climb the mountain. "Because I'm here," she said, cleverly inverting George Mallory's original reply to the same question. He had said, "Because it's there."

I got the gender politics—but found myself wondering: Where does that leave the mountain?

It leaves the mountain where it now belongs. At our beck and call, significancewise. It turns Mt. Everest into "Mt. Everest."

This is not curmudgeonly nostalgia. The point is not "so many people have climbed Mt. Everest that it isn't a big deal anymore." It is a big deal. Climbers die. Frequently. No, the point is that Mt. Everest isn't Mt. Everest anymore because it has become its own icon. Materially it is the same, of course (though apparently there is a litter problem now)—but that's exactly why mediational reflexivity can't be confronted or opposed in these paradigm cases. Mediation crosses an ontological threshold when a thing can become its own simulation. At that point, mediation transcends physical platforms of representation. It's everywhere and nowhere. It's like a shadow—we've made that comparison before—or like a ghost, a haunting.

It's a way things are.

A man with no legs, with very special equipment, got to the top of Mt. Everest recently. Anyone with a disabled friend, or with sufficient moral imagination, will celebrate his achievement, of course. The Justin's Helmet Principle applies. Only a mean-spirited reactionary would begrudge that brave fellow his moment of glory.

Still. Something has been lost. If we are tempted to deny it, it's only because there's nothing we can do about it.

Here's the overall situation. When people reach for the real through such strenuous encounters, natural settings get transformed into performance sites. Extreme sports is itself a form of reaching for the real, of course. And "raw," used as slang encomium, suggests how far you have to reach to get there. We have only to eavesdrop on the legendary Z-boys, reminiscing about the glory days of skateboarding, to understand the particular rush of a gritty encounter with necessity and chance in an improvised arena where the unprecedented is still possible. The proliferation of fusion sports of all kinds follows their example, their original fusion of skating and surfing—surfing on waves of cement.

Yet *more* mixes, more Blobbing—the mixing of what's already been done in the increasingly unlikely hope of finding something that hasn't (see chapter 7).

Because they are reaching for the real, the elite of extreme sports face the same dilemma as alternative rock bands getting mainstream attention. Going commercial means becoming unreal in a panoply of subtle ways involving modalities of representation—production values and performance standards, if you will, and the classic "compromise your art for cash" dilemma only symbolizes what gets lost in the bargain.

So let the phrase "domesticated wilderness" sum up the fate of nature in our time—the basal dialectic of mediation dons this specific garb in this department of experience. But modes of domestication we deploy unintentionally, when we go to nature to recover the real, pale by comparison with what we do when we purposely seek out natural things in order to present them to ourselves. As, for example, in the deluge of books and movies and TV shows about nature that we've seen in recent decades. Those that focus on natural disaster—*Twister*, *The Perfect Storm*, *The Day After Tomorrow*—constitute the archetype of virtualized awe. But the same basic process is at work in more scholarly and scientific works and also, of course, in our zoos and museums. If you are of a certain age, you will have noticed how those places adapted to the demands of presentation and representation. No matter how august the institution, it was upgrade or perish—and effects ramified in countless ways, governed by the overriding irony. Two examples.

Take a recent ad campaign for the Bronx Zoo. Photos and pithy copy scattered all over the subways, filling every available space in a particular car, you know how they do that now—so there's no place you can look that won't be dipping into your head on behalf of whatever it may be. The photographs reminded me of Annie Leibowitz's celebrity portraits, those super-close-ups showing stubble on the chin, broken veins on the nose, purple pouches under the eyes. So real, more than real, real plus—hyperreal. Only, instead of celebrities, these pictures showed animals. Celebrity animals, you might say, because they chose the ones with the most cumbersome and colorful beaks and noses, crests and tails, the most cavernous jaws, threatening claws, outlandish tusks—and all in close-ups so extreme, from vantage points so unusual, that they verged on distortion.

Ads for the New York Aquarium out in Coney Island were similarly inspired—only they seemed to be mostly on the sides of buses rather than in the subways (I bet there's a marketing reason). Similarly inspired, but of course with a new angle, because that's what good ad people do, find new angles.

Instead of hyperreal, expose-every-pore-and-wattle, round-lens close-ups, the aquarium went with horror comics meets faux carnival (Coney Island, see?). Faded painting of bearded lady on the side of a trailer meets *Tales from the Crypt*, circa 1957. So they would show, say, a huge man-of-war jellyfish, the tentacles drawn to look a bit more focused and grasping than jellyfish tentacles actually look, and then, in staggering, jagged-shock typography, the caption would read:

"It Lives! But it has no Brain!"

Stuff like that.

Very clever, both campaigns were, but there was a concession being made, and it's a sad one when you state it explicitly. They were trying to convince you that creatures of nature are as wondrous as they actually are.

The creatures themselves weren't enough.

You can't just say, "Come and see the elephants!" and expect a reaction, even though elephants are as unlikely in form, as huge and gentle and intelligent as they ever were.

The Fate of the Exotic

A once hostile tribe now leads tours in the Peruvian Amazon, past monkeys and parrots

Whales and New Age therapies draw laid-back types to Byron Bay

Sheep herding is part of the fun on a working ranch north of Sydney

—Titles of articles in the Travel section
of the *New York Times* (10/26/03 and 11/16/03)

We are moved to mark our passage through this life. That goes with the human condition, an anchoring response to the ephemerality of consciousness. The primordial impulse that moves us to place stones on graves and erect monuments at the sites of historic events also moves us to arrange our belongings around us as we take a seat on the train, to make it our own for the length of the journey.

And the same impulse moves us—to take pictures!

Pictures at weddings and birthdays. Pictures of family and friends. Pictures of colleagues and classmates, all in a row. And pictures of the places we travel in and through, pictures of foreign lands and natural scenes, of exotic architecture and costume, native peoples, wild creatures. And, of course, of ourselves against those backgrounds.

Capturing the moment. Was that an advertising slogan? For Kodak maybe? Well, it should have been because *it* captures the essence of shutterbug culture, an irresistible global phenomenon wherever it is not proscribed by dogma, the severities of which serve to highlight the existential allure of images, graven or otherwise.

Saturated as we are, we forget the simple magic, the miraculous effect of—*producing a likeness.*

Oh, that's a devilish power. Plato understood the danger. As did Old Testament prophets and Protestant Puritans. And the Taliban. A devilish power—to re-create creation, to create a second creation. It so manifestly bespeaks a blasphemous aspiration when you look at it that way, does it not?

And that's what this book is ultimately about. The consummation of that aspiration, as our second creation supersedes the first— so there's more on the agenda here than a bit of tourist bashing.

It is in the hands of tourists, though, that the camera most poignantly displays its capacity to activate the hopeless longing of consciousness to become permanent. A tour, a tour of wonders, a tour that must go on and cannot last. Could there be a better metaphor for life?

No doubt it was always thus. When Thomas Cook hosted his first touring parties in the 1860s—great barges of European luxury gliding up and down the Nile, laying over here to view the Sphinx and the pyramids and there to view the fabled Karnak Temple— no doubt among the passengers there were ardent diarists and artists, devoted amateurs who gave themselves over to the capture of special moments. And soon enough some photographers as well, lugging their unwieldy equipment. Perhaps you have seen some late-Victorian sketches and paintings and photos of "Europeans in the Orient"? If so, you were made immediately aware of a simple difference between then and now.

Just as it took hours to complete a drawing, it took months to complete a tour.

But our tours take days—and we cover ever so much more terrain. Fortunately, we have more than enough representational technology to make up for the difference. If we hurry.

Have you ever watched a slot machine addict? She's the victim of what psychologists call "intermittent reinforcement," the most powerful kind. The idea is that a pigeon will peck a button most frantically if the goodies are delivered randomly, as opposed to every twentieth peck or something. It's the suspense factor. You can feel it if you just think about it. You're rushing to get to the next pull of the lever before you can fully process this one.

It gets like that with cameras on vacations, but not because of intermittent reinforcement. It's because you don't want to miss anything. Just seeing something counts as missing it.

That's the basic tension. Of course, the typical tourist doesn't click away incessantly—but the tension is there. It shows in the way people finger their equipment as they move around the attraction sites. In the back of the mind the question is nagging away: Should I take this? Should I get that? Is this something I don't want to miss?

The result is that you don't really see anything. You either skim over it because it isn't worth taking a picture of, or you take a picture of it. When you take a picture of it you feel as if you have it forever so you don't have to really look at it. You are free to move on, looking for the next thing you can't afford to miss.

And so on.

Of course, most people get some kind of a control over this dynamic, restrain it in some way. They put the camera in a relatively inaccessible bag or even leave it back at the hotel when taking an impromptu stroll. But that requires discipline. You never know. You might miss something.

Then there's the whole process of showing pictures to family and friends when you get back. They serve to remind you of stories, that's one thing. It's also sort of a way of proving you were there, to yourself as well as to them, because when you are back home the memories of your trip have a very dreamy quality, much more so than ordinary memories. That's because they don't include all the familiar stuff that you normally perceive around you in the present, stuff that anchors ordinary memories. Pictures are substitutes for that stuff, you might say.

But there's a deeper reassurance at work as well. It's in the tone you use to say "This is where we stayed in Venice . . . That's our window there . . . We couldn't see the Grand Canal from the room, but the terrace where we ate breakfast had the *best* view . . . See, here's John with our waiter—he was the sweetest guy. Most of the people were so sweet, so warm, I know it's a cliché, but it's true . . ."

There's a specific impersonality in that tone, a narrator's distance from the subject that echoes the distance between the pictures and the pictured. It provides you with a certain perspective on yourself. But there's also a special warmth. Seeing yourself and people you know so intimately in pictures—any picture, but especially those taken in unusual settings—has the effect of letting you know that you are as real (and as insignificant) as any other random person in the world, hence real in the realest of all ways. Yet you are not any one of them, you are only the one you are—hence real in that way too. The mystery of your being is lodged in a picture that fixes you, like everything else, in the there and then, while your particular fate is always to be here and now. The contrast between the frozen image of your body, seen from without, and the unstoppable ongoing of your mind, seen always and only from within—that's what's being expressed in the tone of bemused and affectionate detachment you bring to the telling of the illustrated story of your visit to a foreign land.

So this isn't about tourist bashing at all, but even if it were, there's a flip side to that well-worn groove. It's easy to bang tourists—they make such juicy targets—but the latent implications of foregrounded mockery are very tricky, very problematic. As long as you leave it unarticulated, you can reap the props that go with being "for" the authentic and pristine, you can feel respect for native traditions without having to look too closely at what they actually are, you can feel like a defender of unspoiled wilderness without having to look too closely at the economic needs of the inhabitants. You don't have to deal with the fact that resident Inuits *want* big oil companies to drill on the Alaskan shelf. They want to hunt whales too. In effect, you don't have to deal with the fact that the largest single source of income for people in the postcolonial world is tourism—and what's the alternative? I mean, realistically. Just bashing tourism means not having to deal with the excruciating evaluational paradox of global mediation.

Yes, it's that time again, time to apply the Justin's Helmet Principle in yet more vaguely embarrassing ways.

Tom Friedman—impenetrably flippant as ever—once wrote a column called "Honey, I Shrunk the World" (*New York Times,* 9/12/99). He reported that the "Australian government set up an ethnic TV station called Imparja, to give a cultural voice" to the aboriginal peoples in the outback. In highest demand on the Imparja channel? *Seinfeld.* Other American sitcoms too, but especially *Seinfeld.* Think about that. I mean, I could understand, you know, *CSI* or MTV—but *Seinfeld?*

Do you recoil from this tidbit of info? Does it feel like evidence of human nature's corruptibility, the addictive potential of television, the inherent wickedness of American pop culture—or all of the above? But, if you do recoil, hold on a minute. Who are you to say that Australian aborigines should prefer traditional activities to kicking back with Jerry and the gang? Haven't they got a right to be hip? No one's forcing them. It's a choice, right?

Here's a deeper case. Front-page story (*New York Times,* 8/29/99) with a picture showing some South American Indians in authentic native garb gathered in a semicircle in what looks like a very rural schoolhouse. Hands raised. Lots of grins. The caption pegs it as "a workshop in Vicus, Peru" where "Indians learn to handle psychological problems brought on by the long Shining Path rebellion." We read in the article that they're mostly women because the men are all dead or gone to the city. We're told how the "peasants who resisted the rebellion gained a new sense of confidence" from the workshops, which are part of the infrastructural and social process initiatives being undertaken by a coalition of international humanitarian workers, anthropologists, government social service providers, and leaders of the local mothers clubs. This is obviously a good thing, right? Better than Shining Path anyway. Better than Che Guevara? Better than traditional lifeways and thousand-year-old rituals?

Well, no matter. They're doing the workshops. They *like* the workshops.

Okay, that's a couple of representative cases. The point is that it's getting harder and harder to find anything that might qualify as exotic, because everywhere it has been encountered it has also been subjected to mechanisms of mediation too numerous to itemize—but the core dynamic is evident in the little examples just cited.

(And, by the way, the fact that some of you may be looking askance at my use of the term "exotic," at least the way I've been using it up until this sentence—without the scare quotes—that's a consequence of the same dynamic. On the other hand, if you don't see the need for this parenthetical remark, you soon will.)

Anyway, the point is this: the essential dynamic by which the exotic gets mediated into the not so exotic doesn't just work from the outside in, but from the inside out as well. That is, it isn't just that Western scholars and artists and tourists and cameras and the Escapes section of the *New York Times* have turned all things native into objects of consumption—thereby "exoticizing" them at the very same Blobby moment that de-exoticization gets under way. It's that the exoticized "natives" become active and reflexive participants in the whole process, and in myriad ways—ranging from calculating self-commodification to making their own arrangements to tour us, to systematic (and, one suspects, ultimately futile) efforts to cherry-pick technologies from modernity's cornucopia while otherwise preserving, sometimes by violent and/or totalitarian means, supposedly traditional ways.

Ultimately futile, perhaps—but undeniably dangerous in the meantime, especially when mass media representations get implanted in contexts that are essentially tribal, where habits of ironic distance have yet to take root.

There's a long history to all of this, of course, and deep thinkers have been weighing in on the subject ever since Montaigne wrote about the "cannibal" brought to France by the explorer Villegagnon for the entertainment and enlightenment of the monarch and his entourage. More recently, Edward Said's *Orientalism* (1979) established the now dominant view, at least in academic circles and among those who fall under that influence. It is the proximate cause of the fact that, hopefully, you say "Asian" instead of "Oriental" these days, when you need a word for it.

That dominant view of the idea of "the exotic" hinges on the notion of "the Other." You've probably run across this expression even if you never dip into the humanities offerings at our major universities. There is, of course, a great deal to say about it—thousands of people have to say *something* about it as a condition of their employment—but we've just seen the underlying structure, the perpetual back and forth that is entailed.

The leading idea is that, instead of treating the Other as an alien something—threatening in some cases, alluring in others, but in all cases an *object*, whether of conquest, exploitation, proselytizing, study, or tourism —instead of that, you recognize in the other an autonomy and agency equal to your own and place yourself in a reciprocal relationship of dialogue with the Other, etc. This is the most visible, the positive, aspect of the otherness trope. The cardinal rule is to acknowledge the Other as *other*; that is, as categorically *different* from you. But that's a good thing; difference is good. We've already touched on how difference is to be embraced and celebrated, not just tolerated or romanticized—let alone conquered or gazed at.

But there's another aspect to this dynamic that necessarily gets obscured, not to say repressed, by the celebrating and embracing, the tricky issue that the two excerpts from the *Times* bring out so starkly. Modernity's encounters with traditional Others, no matter how dialogical, seem bound to change them more than they change us. Sure, you can find reverse influences in the global polyglot of mediation—American Buddhists, tai chi and acupuncture, reggae, and on and on. But in the aggregate, over the course of time, the primary direction of influence is clear—and determined, of course, by overwhelming imbalances in various power relationships.

Often, of course, this "influence" took the form of naked conquest and exploitation, genocide, slavery. More recently, less overtly, the imposition of lopsided trade arrangements, environmental degradation, inequitable subsidies. Other influences are not so easily condemned—women's rights, for example, though we like it better if the initiatives can be construed as coming from within. Other influences just make us cringe—Rambo's worldwide popularity, *Seinfeld* in the outback, Starbucks, the Plague of the Yellow Arches, etc.

But, either way, the truth is that—when it doesn't simply result in devastation—the encounter with the Other tends to make the Other less, well, *other*.

(The rise of the "X, well, X" figure in breezy journalese deserves an analysis all its own. But I already did "whatever," "like," and "awesome," so I'll leave this one to you.)

Anyway, making the Other less other is not something most people steeped in the discourse of otherness have typically wanted to encourage. That shifted in some quarters after 9/11, but, by and large, people still want to believe that you can aspire to a multicultural culture that celebrates difference and, at the same time, provides everyone with medicine, literacy, good roads, sewage treatment, universities, representative government, religious liberty, free speech—and on and on. But, if all that were realized, then there wouldn't be much left of multiculturalism beyond a really big selection of interestingly spiced foods, intriguingly designed clothes and accessories, distinctively rhythmic music, and lots and lots of holidays.

Differences that don't make *that* much of a difference, in other words.

That's the ironic fate of the exotic, in outline. And I guess it's mostly a good thing—or would be, if we could get past the devastation and exploitation part.

Still.

Our Unseemly Access to Everything

I remember when a certain judgment, long taking shape on the horizon of my mind, just beyond the reach of words, first got articulated. It was in the mid-1990s. I was at one of what seemed like seething millions of conferences on the educational applications of the new technology—of which there were, in turn, more seething millions. But the keynote presenter at this particular gathering had everybody beat. He had a videotape of an educational application of the new technology that left the assembly agog at the possibilities—that was the sine qua non in these presentations, by the way, the prospect of limitless possibilities out there in the haze of the future.

Anyway, what his videotape showed was something he and his colleagues at, I think it was the MIT Media Lab, had cooked up in consortium (what else?) with more colleagues at, I think it was the Woods Hole Oceanographic Institute—but whoever they were, they were funded big time, and no doubt expecting to be funded bigger time, if only they could establish the educational value of their enterprises.

That's where the bucks were. Education.

What they had was a multimillion-dollar drone submarine gizmo laden with cameras and seismographs and robotic appendages designed to do research on the ocean floor. The videotape showed their device at the bottom of some particularly interesting stretch of the Atlantic. I forget exactly why it was interesting. Shipwreck, maybe? Fissures in the earth's crust? Anyway, it was rigged so that you could put it through its paces by remote control from aboard a fabulously equipped research vessel or from an even more fabulously equipped laboratory—only, in this case, it wasn't being controlled from there. It was being controlled from a classroom full of twelve-year-olds who were taking turns at the joysticks, steering the thing toward this or that object of presumed oceanographic interest at the bottom of the damn Atlantic Ocean, for God's sake. All in service of their collaborative "science project." You know, learning through hands-on exploration.

Some hands.

I felt myself grimacing during the presentation, feeling almost offended for some reason I couldn't quite put my finger on. Then, during the Q&A, some other big shot from some other major institute got up and—addressing the presenter by a diminutive form of his first name in order to signal their relatively equal positions in the academic firmament—he proceeded to sketch out a *further* possible educational application of a similar technology that *his* consortium was working on. It involved the possibility (!!!) that you could have an astronomy class sending out instructions to the multigazillion-dollar Hubble Space Telescope or something like that, instructions that would point all its intergalactic data-gathering power at some particular sector of the cosmos in order to test some hypothesis they had come up with for *their* collaborative science project.

At this point I physically recoiled. I got up and walked out, feeling downright indignant. I wasn't thinking about the silliness of it all, the utter impracticality of the idea if you thought about taking it beyond the holy moment of the demo. I was morally aroused. I was thinking No! No!—stop, *twelve-year-olds just shouldn't be able to do that.*

It's just wrong.

What had hit me was how horrifyingly out of proportion it was. I hadn't yet developed the "flattery of representation" idea explicitly, but this put me on the track. Enough already with this *access!* People shouldn't have such access, it's unseemly, this access to anything and everything, access from anywhere, access on demand, access so smooth and fluid, so effortless—and, so inevitably, bound to be taken for granted eventually.

It should be hard to access the extraordinary. Unless you *want* to make it ordinary?

Weather

Some people barely notice the weather unless it complements or disrupts their plans and doings. Others are sensitive to every nuance. Some people walk from place to place and almost never look up at the sky unless it be to assess their chances of getting wet. Others cannot emerge from a building without registering the shapes and motions of the clouds above the canyon streets. Some people turn only to other people for solace and good cheer. Others can feel forgiven for a lifetime of sin by the touch of a vagrant breeze at the end of a compromised day.

For the weather-sensitive among us, it is as if the world has an emotional life, as if the world has moods we cannot help but share simply by virtue of being in it—as if the ebbings and surgings of the weather were vast sensations caused by cosmic hormones in the body of the world, and one's own body a member of the whole.

The weather may be the only thing left that can so regularly remind us of our place in what my mother used to call the "great scheme of things." Reserves of nature, vast and dramatic still in certain corners of the globe, can, of course, provide the same reminder—in that iconic form just described. But everyday weather manages with more success to elude—though it cannot escape—the ministrations of mediation. It offers its appreciators a subtler metaphysic on any average day.

And "metaphysic" turns out to be the right word. I have lately come to understand weather as more than metaphor because, like a lot of people reaching a certain age, I find myself more open to religious experience than I would have imagined possible even a decade ago. Intimations of mortality, cumulations of tragedy among friends and family, have something to do with it, of course, but not in the obvious there-are-no-atheists-in-foxholes way. It has more to do with the tone of the moment still to be lived against that background, a contingency to the time remaining, the line of what's left of a life, like a musical phrase anticipating conclusion.

I was told as a young man that the Greeks believed the gods got so involved with people and their doings out of envy. Because only mortals could know beauty. I didn't quite get it at the time, but it makes perfect sense to me now.

Anyway, because my particular religious turn was so informed by philosophy, I felt estranged from friends who were also turning to religion—but to established congregations or practices. I felt the need of a church, but found I could not join, though I tried a few times. (This was before 9/11.) Attendance meant the most at the beginning, when it was anonymous, when arcana of ritual and coincidents of light and music were all I had to attend to. As people became individually known, as greetings and coffees and projects made their demands, the specifically religious quality slipped away, and so did I.

But lately I have realized that I belong to a church after all, and have since I was a boy: a spontaneous congregation, summoned by occasion rather than by schedule, cherishing anonymity and insignificance. Call it the church of storms.

This church's members come from all walks of life, from the highest to the lowest, as the old expression goes. They never plan, they never organize. Most of the time, they go about their disparate business, each one keeping private company with whatever the weather happens to be. But when a storm hits, they gather. It might be Ocean Drive in Newport or the boardwalk at Far Rockaway or the shore of a lake in the middle of Maine. The congregants gather to bear witness, to be exalted in the presence of the almighty. They come singly, in pairs, in small groups. Some are laughing, some in love, some in despair, some rooted in a comfortable routine. They form a gathering only incidentally, hence most profoundly, the purest of gatherings. But taking communion nevertheless, cradled in the power, in a force that singles out each grain, each leaf, each strand of hair—but lifts, at the same time, the heaving sea and the swaying forest to the uttermost horizon.

What I have learned, by way of worship in this church, is that there is no need of metaphor. The storm is not a symbol of something else, of some being about whom questions of belief might arise. A consciousness that understands thunder to be the voice of a god is not making a mistake because it lacks a theory of ionized air masses. For such a consciousness, a storm is a god, and thunder is its voice, and that's all there is to it. The mistake is to ask for something else, for something more, for something other than what is given. Members of the church of storms don't need anything else. They are willing to bear the unbearable lightness of being.

But even so. The fact that I can write this, that I do write this, and that you read it and compare my description with this or that in your experience—that's mediation, and the merest indicator of how, even with weather, we now contain what once contained us all.

I remember the exact moment I realized this, in relation to storms specifically. I had pulled into a scenic turnout along some New England shoreline drive—I forget where, exactly—and left the car to walk around a bit, taking in the view. I spotted a modest plaque built into a modest stone at the crest of the overlook, and ambled idly over to it. Nothing elaborate, the stone well worn, maybe knee-high, straightforward brass for the plaque, no decoration, an almost military simplicity. Browning tufts of grass grown up all round, thrusting every which way—no one was tending this little monument, that was clear, and nothing else was set up in the vicinity to call attention to itself, just the grassy fringe between the asphalt and the steepening slope from the overlook ridge down to the rocky shore and then, of course, the ocean stretching out to meet the sky.

The plaque said something like "To the memory of those who lost their lives in the Great Storm of 1908," or 1928, or whatever it was. An "8" figured into it, I recall. And suddenly it hit me.

No name.

No "Hurricane Hugo," no "Andrew," no "Isabel." And it began to dawn on me, waves of understanding, the implications. In the days when storms were nameless, they were beyond human supervision in so many other ways as well. The insouciance, the familiarity, the impudence suggested by the naming of storms is a sign of the difference in the way they came to be viewed once we were able to represent them—viewed, quite literally, from above, from within, from all sides, from before and from after as well.

Imagine what it must have been like before representations allowed us to view storms in those ways. No tracking the tropical depression from its point of departure in the Azores, no daily progress reports on its westward progress as it gathers intensity and organizes itself into that giant spiral—you can see the whole of it in the satellite photos—as if some monstrous drain were opening up in the middle of the Atlantic. And, of course, no calibrated monitoring of the likely consequences. No level two or level four, no storm alert for Daytona but only a storm warning for Cape Hatteras, no interviews with locals as they stock up on bottled water and board up their bungalows. In a word—that word again—no *coverage*.

What must storms have been like back then?

Like the rest of the weather, but more so. Barely predictable, in broad accordance with the season and the near-term guesswork of people with nurtured senses whose living depended upon the signs they had learned to read—"red sky at dawning, sailor take warning," that kind of thing—supported, I suppose, by indications from the barometer, the needle's shift when the glass was tapped. But beyond predictability, there was the unknowable size, the incomprehensible extent of it; that's the main thing. No one in a storm back then could also be outside of it, in any way. The Great Storm of 1908 came down on everything from out of nowhere and, in its own time, passed on, leaving people and their properties scattered every which way—like so many bugs in a field mowed down by a giant McCormick threshing machine.

That was awesome. No quotes.

But nowadays? Hey, if weather is your thing, you have such access! Maybe, for example, you participated in the dot-com poll that the Weather Channel featured on the eve of the millennium? The audience was asked to vote for the top five storms of the century. Cool idea. Very interactive. A panel of storm experts was assembled to evaluate the results of the poll in light of their own choices—with call-in lines open for the fans, of course.

Okay, so that's a gross example. The Weather Channel is subtle too. It has hypnotic qualities. Strangely soothing. A perfect companion, in a way. I often keep it on in the background when I'm puttering around my place, even when I'm writing, sometimes. I remember when it first came online, I thought, yikes, they can't possibly fill up twenty-four hours with weather reports! Hah! Little did I know what the agents of mediation can come up with in their never-ending quest for ways to *fill that screen.*

But why is it so comforting? Partly it's the patter of the weatherpeople. They are somehow smaller, less intrusive, more modest, than newscasters. Nowhere near as self-important. The standard shot of them is middle distance as opposed to close-up, which only emphasizes their relative unimportance—relative to the weather? Or is it relative to the urgency and complexity of regular news? I'm not sure, but the effect is that they aren't demanding anything of us, whereas newscasters are implicitly nagging us to understand some place or event, to respond, to have an opinion, to care.

The weatherpeople have been coached to use lots of gestures. All the talking heads do that now, have you noticed? They take tutorials on hand moving. It's the human equivalent of zooming graphics and whooshing sound effects. Motion, motion, constant motion—the experts say motion is what keeps us from clicking the remote, you see, that's why they've all learned to talk with their hands. Anyway, the weatherpeople also use hand gestures—but they're *so* gentle, check it out. They caress the air with little imitations of slowly moving fronts and descending temperatures. Their wrists are lax and their fingers tentative and hovering. It comes off as an expression of deference, of respect for their subject.

But there's an insidious other side to this, isn't there—as with all things mediational? What happens to us when we are continuously exposed to satellite images of weather patterns moving across the face of a continent? What is the latent message in a format that shows the world's weather in tableau, presided over by a person, however modest in bearing, who ushers high-altitude jet streams down to Florida from the Arctic Circle with a wave of her hand?

Here's a hint. The infinitely soothing Heather Tesch, my very favorite weatherperson, habitually uses a formulation that captures the implicit effect. She says things like "and we have cloudy skies and gusty winds for you folks in the Chicago area today . . . and for anyone traveling in the Dallas area, we've got heavy rains, so budget for delays."

You don't notice it right away, but after a while you realize. So comprehensive and continuous and detailed has its representation of the weather become that, in its ethos and idiom, the Weather Channel isn't just bringing you a weather report—it's bringing you *the weather*.

Now that's "awesome."

With quotes.

It's all about an implicit shift in the focus of attention—from the object to the subject. From the world to us.

The Cosmic Pathway to the Hall of the Universe

But heck, that's nothing. If you are out for "awesome" experiences, why settle for a piddling planet when you can check out the whole universe. You can do that in twenty minutes for a cost of thirty dollars if you get your "Passport to the Universe" (that's what they call the ticket) for this show at the new planetarium in the Museum of Natural History in New York City. It's really cool, and I'm not just saying that; it really is, I enjoyed it a lot. The big velour seats in concentric circles under the sky dome tilt way back so you can take in all the projected effects—and I hope you aren't thinking a display of stars rotating staidly from solstice to solstice, with connect-the-dots outlines of the major constellations for a climax and some astronomer dork in horn-rims droning on about how a pea on Staten Island is to a basketball in Yonkers as Earth is to the Sun, etc., etc.

If that's what you are thinking, you haven't been getting out enough lately. The planetarium isn't what it used to be—in fact, the whole museum has been made over, giant video screens and interactive exhibits (so you can perform too) all over. Those once marvelous still-life taxidermy dioramas look like Madame Tussaud's waxworks by comparison. *Upgrade* is indeed the word. Especially the planetarium.

Instead of an astronomer dork, we get Tom Hanks—his voice I mean. He's in full family-values mode, congenial but responsible, serious about the science but not too detailed, nothing boring, and he's reverent about the universe too—especially about its size. Size matters here. And he's ready with a folksy metaphor and a joke or two to keep things moving along—a very specific type of joke, actually, a type that's become so intrinsic to the tour-narration formula that people aren't even aware of it anymore. Call it the "break the spell audience acknowledgment" joke. Yet another instance of the flattering bring-the-viewer-behind-the-scenes gesture we have noticed so often.

But what a spell to break in this case—and what a revealing motive.

But we'll get back to Tom in a minute. Before joining him in the Great Sphere (also called the Space Theater), we get to take a stroll down something called "The Cosmic Pathway" to a place called "The Hall of the Universe." The pathway is a huge spiral ramp, maybe three hundred feet long, under a huge glass arboretum-type structure. You start in a round dark room at the top of the ramp. It has a concave screen, a little amphitheater pit in the middle, and you lean over and watch the big bang happen while Maya Angelou describes it all in sonorous tones. Then you walk at your leisure down the ramp, starting at thirteen billion years ago when the big bang happened. The rest of the ramp is scaled to represent the passage of time. When you get to the bottom, you get to now.

Scale is the key, that's how the underlying message gets across—and there is a message, you betcha. Along the outer edge of the ramp, attached to the spiral banister, is a sequence of exhibits—plasma screens and photographs, diagrams and descriptive info-plaques. They show stuff like the earliest consolidation of galaxies after the big bang, the formation of our solar system, the formation of the oceans, the appearance of oxygen, the first single-cell life-forms, the first plants, sponges, bugs, reptiles, mammals, hominids—you get the idea.

So, for example, you shave 4.5 billion years off the original 13 to get to 8.5 billion years ago when our solar system formed. You're about one third of the way down the ramp. Ten billion years pass before bacteria produce oxygen in the ocean and another billion until it appears on land. You don't reach the first multicellular life-forms until 12 billion years after the big bang, when you are almost at the bottom of the ramp. The first trilobites, so dear to the hearts of paleontologists, are a mere half billion years ago. Dinosaurs appear 240 million years ago—you could spit to the end of the ramp at this point. The first hominids, 4.5 million years ago—and you are just inches from now at this point. The first *Homo sapiens* are 100,000 years ago, and you are, like, a centimeter from now.

Now gets represented this way: they've got a very fine strand of hair glued down under a very big magnifying glass. It represents the time between the first appearance of human art and now.

One side of the hair is the most ancient extant cave paintings, or whatever, and the other side of the hair is now.

As compared to the whole Cosmic Pathway you just strolled down.

It's very effective. And all about the size—in this case, length—of time. The manifest intent of the Cosmic Pathway is to "put things in perspective," as one of the Cosmic Pathway Explainers (a volunteer, wearing a button that called him that) said when I asked him for his take on it all. That's a nice way of saying the point is to make you feel very, very small.

As small as you in fact are.

Then I asked the explainer, if people ever got uncomfortable when shown so graphically how small they are, and he said yes, but that he could usually make them feel better when he told them to think about *who was responsible for knowing all this.*

In a way, he explained, since we evolved from the universe, and are now representing it, you could say that we *are* the universe reflecting back on itself.

Well, that *is* a boost, isn't it?

Turns out Tom Hanks will make exactly the same point, with

exactly the same spin, when he takes us on our journey through the cosmos.

There's a darkened foyer where you wait to enter the Great Sphere. They have that shapeless, surging New Age music piped in and a dozen plasma screens of streaming video artfully arranged all round—suspended from the ceiling so that anyone anywhere in the foyer can see one, and all of them are displaying factoid nuggets, like on the Cosmic Pathway, only now in the form of a little quiz. Questions appear, then fade out over some beguiling visual, then fade in with the answer. Very engaging. Never an empty moment. *Never.*

Then Tom comes on the loudspeaker and invites us all to enter the Great Sphere. We shuffle across a little suspension bridge to get there, sort of like the ones the astronauts used to get to the *Apollo* nose cones—remember them?

The basic plot is established. We are going on a trip.

Your "Passport to the Universe" calls you a "Citizen of the Cosmos." That is the foundational metaphor and it neatly points the way to the self-satisfying resolution of the dramatic tension that underlies the whole exhibit. The sea is so wide and my boat is so small, as the poet said in an age long gone, before we could hop across the pond.

Our boat may still be small, but whoa—the things it can do!

Your passport goes on to say that you are "empowered by knowledge and imagination to travel anywhere in the Universe," and Tom—and the mere existence of this installation—will be reinforcing that message of empowerment in all sorts of subtle ways, even as we are exposed to facts about our place in the great scheme of things that might otherwise make the most complacent egotist feel irredeemably diminished.

Here's how they do it. Even before we leave the foyer, Tom says: "There comes a time in our lives when it first dawns on us that we are not the center of the universe . . . that we are part of something larger than ourselves. As it happens to each of us, so it is happening to our civilization . . . right now."

First we are challenged, you see, challenged to grow up. It is never overt—much too controversial—but "growing up" means jettisoning traditional religious beliefs about the nature of things in favor of science. But, given what science has to tell us, a lot of people might be understandably inclined to cling to stories that reassure them about their importance in God's plan and all that. So Tom goes on to tell us about the "golden age of astronomy" we now live in. He describes some of the fabulous technologies we have created by means of which "we are mapping the grand structures of the universe, tracing its ancient past, finding our place in its great story."

We are up to the challenge, that's the point. Explicitly, we are up to dealing with the truth about the universe because we are part of it, we belong to "something larger than ourselves" and share in the greatness of it all. More implicitly, we are up to the challenge because we are on top of the whole damn thing, unfathomably vast though it may be—we are mapping the sucker. The cosmos is under our eye. We can represent everything.

That means that while the manifest content of this tour is showing you how small you are compared to the universe, the latent content, the message of the fact that this tour is possible at all, is that you have a God's-eye view of the universe, yourself included.

That tension is what accounts for the undeniable pathos of certain moments in the tour—which is structured as a quest to provide us Citizens of the Cosmos with our "Cosmic Address." We start with a view of the night sky as our prescientific ancestors saw and understood it (a two-dimensional bowl of lights, us at the center) and we end up at the limits of the known universe entertaining the in-principle possibility of parallel universes. But it's the steps in between that drive the message home.

We journey first (rocket sound effects, the chairs vibrate) past Mars and out to Saturn, passing each planet along the way—the 3-D digital representations are breathtaking throughout—and we glance back at Earth from various distances, until we get to Saturn, from where we have to pick out a "pale blue dot" in the night sky, represented exactly as it would appear on Saturn (all simulations are scientifically exact, unless otherwise noted). That is, you pick it out the way you pick out Saturn from Earth. With difficulty. It's just one in the great swarm of dots.

We have had "our computer on interplanetary drive" so far, but now we switch to "interstellar drive" (Tom's nods to sci-fi lingo always get a chuckle) and travel millions of miles out to the Orion Nebula. In about four seconds. Thanks to the Hubble telescope, we get to see it from within, a vast starry, gassy cloud, amazing colors and shapes in motion, completely enveloping. Tom tells us that this is a "stellar nursery."

So we hang out for a while to watch stars being born.

While we are watching stars being born, Tom tells us to take a deep breath, "No, I'm serious," he says. "Really, everybody, do it." So some of us (what are the stats on this kind of thing?) do it and then Tom says, "Every atom of oxygen you just inhaled was made deep inside a star. The carbon in our muscles, the calcium in our bones . . . all the heavy elements were cooked in the hearts of stars. As Carl Sagan said, we *are* star stuff."

So you see, when Tom tells us that, as Citizens of the Cosmos, we are part of something larger, it's not just a poetic expression. It is a material fact—and that piece of information suddenly makes our representational participation with the cosmos seem physical as well.

A moment of participatory uplift.

And so it goes on. The most affecting moment, I found, began with a view from outside the whole Milky Way galaxy ("hundreds of billions of suns"). Then a tiny blue-sphere mappy thing pings out to encompass a minuscule portion of the galaxy and we are told that all the stars we can see from Earth fall within that little sphere. Right after that, we switch to "intergalactic drive" and make our way, in seconds, to a position from which we can view the Virgo Supercluster of several thousand galaxies, of which the Milky Way is one—and then *it* pings out and now *it's* a dot.

Then we glance around at thousands of other Superclusters of thousands of other galaxies—and, well, "feeling small" doesn't begin to express it. But, at that very moment, Tom is there to bring out the latent message, the one built into the fact that we made the devices that made this tour possible. He says, in a whole new tone of voice he says, "We may just be little guys, living on a speck of dust. But we don't think small. We managed to figure this one out. And we're still figuring."

His tone, until now, has oscillated between dreamy, stretching, reaching, almost incantatory—as when he recites the colossal numbers, times, and distances—and folksy break-the-spell joking about interstellar drives. But this is a whole other level of breaking the spell. The tone here is a weird blend of consoling and defiant. His words are meant to comfort you, but also to compensate you.

Empowerment.

Then we find a black hole and take a thundering great ride home, the lights come up—and you're outta there.

Twenty minutes exactly.

Okay, you get the general idea. Unseemly access. You've been *everywhere*, you've seen *everything*. We've touched on examples, but we could go on and on. Not only have you seen through the Hubble to the ends of the universe and clambered around on the ocean's floor and entered the eye of a hurricane and descended into the mouth of a live volcano, but you've also watched the dinosaurs become extinct, and the first hominids take up the first tools, you've been on Mars, on the moon, at Hiroshima, and at Buchenwald, and you've penetrated to the interiors of atoms and toured the circuitry of chromosomes. You've got 3-D sonogram photos of your first grandchild as a fetus in your daughter-in-law's womb, and your son is going to videotape the birth. And you've watched how many total strangers in what kinds of circumstances? Thousands of them, in their most extreme and intimate moments. People dying, people being born, being tortured, being saved, being operated on; you've been up their colons, in their wombs, you've navigated their blood vessels, you've entered their skulls to monitor their brain activity, you've watched them in their kitchens and bathrooms and bedrooms, you've watched them fucking and sucking, engaging in every sexual act imaginable, you've watched them as they hear of the death of loved ones, you've watched them marry and divorce and cheat and lie and forgive and forget—is there anything you haven't seen, anywhere you haven't been?

The whole of history, the whole of nature, striking poses—just for you.

Is this right? Are you *entitled* to this access? Who do you think you are?

Origins of a Blasphemous Aspiration

Remember John Locke, from high school history if nothing else? He's the one who said that the mind is a blank slate, a tabula rasa, also known for inspiring modern constitutional governments with his account of natural rights in *The Second Treatise of Civil Government* (1690). Only Descartes could compete with Locke for the title "founder of modernity."

But we aren't going to be interested in what Locke is generally known for right now. We want to check out his fantasy life. No, not sexual fantasies—technological fantasies. Though there is a whiff of the licentious about them, come to think of it. He was definitely flirting with temptation.

Locke was conflicted, you see. His life's work was a struggle to resolve an unresolvable tension. He was, first of all, a partisan and practitioner of the "New Reason," of seventeenth-century science—Galileo and Newton and all that. But he was also a devout Protestant, a biblical literalist, not a deist like most of those Enlightenment types. These incompatible commitments animated his philosophy and gave him a profound, if only half-conscious, understanding of the deepest aspiration of modernity, the blasphemous aspiration to which we have only been alluding so far— to install ourselves at the center of a Second Creation that will reflect our own desires and designs.

Here is Locke indulging in a moment of speculation—something he typically resisted, but not always successfully. He's wondering about the "substance" (meaning essential nature) of man, and he says:

Had we such a knowledge of that constitution of man . . . as it is possible angels have, and it is certain his Maker has, we should have a quite other idea of his essence . . . and our idea of any individual man would be as far different . . . as is his who knows all the springs and wheels and other contrivances within the famous clock at Strasburg, from that which a gazing country man has of it, who barely [meaning, only] sees the motion of the hands and hears the clock strike.

When Locke tested, in fantasies like this, the limits to knowledge he always ended by accepting, he was at his most prophetic.

In this particular fantasy, he went on to imagine a man with "microscopical eyes," a man who could discover "the texture and motion of the minute parts of corporeal things" and so perceive "their internal constitutions." In other words, a man who could look at another man and see his essential nature, his substance, the very corpuscles he was made of—just as a technician can see the workings of the famous clock at Strasburg.

But as soon as Locke conceived this being, this seventeenth-century cyborg, he pulled back. With palpable relief, he remarked on how unsuited his fantasy man would be to "our present condition." He went on at some length about how his "acute sight would not serve to conduct him to the market and exchange," how he "could not see things he was to avoid at a convenient distance" and "could not endure bright sunshine, or so much as open daylight," and how "he and the rest of men could not discourse" about anything. Such a man might penetrate to the essences of nature's biological clocks, in other words, but he would not be able to tell the time!

Locke realized that he had imagined a freak, an ancestor of Frankenstein a helpless, blundering, isolated creature, miserably maladapted to this world.

So it turned out (as it always did, for Locke) that God had equipped His human creature in just the right way, limitations and all. We couldn't know essences, but we could go about our business—and you don't need Max Weber to tell you that those early modern Protestants were all about business.

But the fantasy was not so easily dismissed. Piety had returned the restless speculator to his place, but another "extravagant conjecture" pressed willy-nilly forward in this form: "One of the great advantages that some Spirits have over us may . . . lie in this, that they can so shape or frame to themselves organs of sensation or perception, as to suit them to their present design [meaning, purpose]." Locke was now imagining beings with *adjustable* microscopical and macroscopical eyes, beings who would be able to see molecular essences *and* tell the time. That image forced itself on him, inspired as he was by the apparently unlimited possibilities of that early modern technology (yes, it was ever thus). Spectacles were a reality. So were telescopes and microscopes, and they were adjustable. What else might come to pass?

"For how much would that man exceed all others in knowledge," mused Locke, "who could so fit his eyes to all sorts of objects, as to see *when he pleased* the figure and motion of the minute particles in the blood." (Italics mine.)

Locke just couldn't stop himself from thinking this way, no matter how hard he tried.

And lots of other people weren't even trying to stop.

Telescopes and microscopes. Do you remember the first time you played with a pair of powerful binoculars as a child? Instantaneous out-of-body perceptual mobility, and in either direction—because looking through them backward was even more fun, as I recall, but amazing either way. Still, your childhood experience is only a dim echo of what those very basic representational technologies did to the people who first devised them. It was stunning. To see mountains on the moon and debunk, at a stroke, the doctrine of millennia concerning the geometrical perfection of celestial spheres. To put a drop of your own blood on a slide and discover that this apparent liquid was in fact composed of particles—not in some theory, but to actually see them.

And don't forget how these early representational devices came to be invented. By analogy with mammalian eyeballs—just as scientific and technological innovation generally was based on analogies with the closely studied workings of nature, the devices of the divine Maker. No early modern who looked through telescopes or microscopes could fail to see them as fundamentally comparable to God's constructions.

Stunning achievements—and even more stunning prospects. And a power rush like nothing human beings had ever known.

That's what accounts for the licentious note, and the guilt-tinged back and forth, in Locke's fantasies. He was on the brink of conceiving of himself as God's successor and he didn't want to go there.

But the rest of us did.

CHAPTER 7

Bogus predictions and lame solutions you think you need in order to attain closure for your social criticism reading experience. Plus a monster vision of what it all means. The fate of originality. Jedermensch ein Übermensch. The Nietzschean Overman turns out to be a really nice person. He is you. You are so special that you should ask yourself this: how would it feel to make love to your own clone?

The madman jumped into their midst and pierced them with his eyes. "Whither is God?" he cried; "I will tell you. We have killed him—you and I . . . But how did we do this? How could we drink up the sea? Who gave us the sponge to wipe away the entire horizon? What were we doing when we unchained the earth from the sun? Whither are we moving? . . . Are we not straying through an infinite nothing? Do you not feel the breath of empty space? Do we hear nothing as yet of the noise of the grave diggers who are burying God? Do we smell nothing as yet of the divine decomposition? Gods, too, decompose. God is dead . . . And we have killed him.

How shall we comfort ourselves . . .? What festivals of atonement, what sacred games shall we have to invent? Is not the greatness of the deed too great for us? Must we ourselves not become gods simply to appear worthy of it?"

—Nietzsche

Bogosity Inc.

AN EARLY MEMORY. Fourth of July parade, small New England town, around 1950. Sunny day, everything sparkling. At the head of the parade, this old guy—*very* old—in a wheelchair. He is being pushed along at the head of a phalanx of other guys, various ages, variously uniformed, and my mother leans over me, points discreetly at the one in the wheelchair, and confides in a whisper that he had been a drummer boy in the Civil War.

He had drummed his drum at Appomattox, and there he was in front of me. In a world with airplanes and atom bombs.

That was my first encounter with history. It was the first time I realized that the distant past was once as real as now, in every detail. The Cosmic Pathway to the Hall of the Universe makes you realize that too—only this was more intense because it happened by chance, took me by surprise.

Much later in life I realized that when he was a little boy, that old man had known some old men who had played a part in the American Revolution. Even more recently, I realized that just two more such connections get us back to the days when Galileo and Descartes and Locke—with some help from the Protestant Reformation and the printing press—launched the whole shebang we call modernity.

The point? This whole technology thing, representational or otherwise, is only just getting started. It seems like a long time because of the way modernity works, because so much has happened, so much has changed, the world literally made over, the sea, the sky, the moon, the atom, the gene—all conquered, with so many consequences, some of which we have considered. Technology and all its consequences are stacked up behind us in layers so high and dense that it feels as if a long time has passed since it all began.

But it hasn't. If you tried to represent the period since Gutten-berg on the Cosmic Pathway you would have to slice that hair lengthwise thousands of times, and then use a very powerful microscope to see one slice. This whole technology thing has just started.

But it is accelerating at a tremendous rate.

That's a good reason to mistrust anybody who claims to understand what's going on.

You know how it feels when you are driving too fast on a snowy road and suddenly—poof—your car loses traction and starts to glide around, ever so gently, fishtailing this way and that, ever so slowly. You tap the brakes, turn into the skid, all the stuff you're supposed to do—but basically you just pray. It can seem to go on forever, until finally the car straightens out and traction returns and you drive on; but very cautiously now, because your knees have turned to jelly and your shaking hands are telling you a truth that's lodged in the Darwinian marrow of your bones.

It could have been otherwise. And next time it might be. Next time, the skid might extend itself a tad and the car proceed serenely off that steep embankment and, in an instant, you would become a mangled corpse, of no more significance to the universe than a squashed toad.

The universe doesn't care what happens to you. Or me. Or any of us. Or all of us.

Here's what you can safely say about the history of modernity. We've been through some periods of increasing complexity, you can definitely say that. But that doesn't necessarily make for "stages" of anything. Or maybe it does. There is no way of knowing because, if there is an unfolding pattern of any kind, it hasn't been unfolding long enough for us to detect—even if we could, which now seems especially unlikely, given the stupefying intricacies and velocities we've gotten into. Things have been getting bigger and faster and more complicated so quickly, for so short a time—and most of what is now happening is happening for reasons no one can fathom.

That's about all you can say. So far, we've survived. No nuclear holocaust or ozone meltdown or unstoppable mutant virus. So far.

The point being that our motion through the last few centuries has been more like that of the skidding car than the steady march of progress we sometimes kid ourselves into believing in. That was what Tom Hanks didn't want to tell us during our tour of the universe; he didn't want to tell us about its indifference to us— that's what he was covering up with that misty, reaching, questing tone, a tone suggesting that if we are big enough to reach the ends of the universe with our devices and theories, then we must be big enough to matter. But it ain't so. The next time the whole damn planet could just drift off the embankment.

That's why I don't trust all the jut-jawed leaders out there who presume to set directions for us with their world-spanning enterprises. It's also why I don't trust the futurist gurus, the psycho-cultural-eco-media mavens with their "visions," and all the business and cultural leaders who adopt their style and rhetoric. I have a sneaking suspicion that some of them don't even believe themselves after a while. In an era when every midsize enterprise in the Western world seems to have its very own visionary, grand predictions and sweeping solutions become a genre requirement. If you want to play this game at all, you have to act as if you enjoyed a special dispensation, a private pipeline to evolution's plan. But, of course, if you act that way all day, every day, year in and year out, you inevitably become a person who actually exists in some nether region between real conviction, blind faith, hopeful guessing, and pure bullshit.

Case in point? The Bush neocon visionaries.

But enough politics. Let's have fun instead.

Here's one of my favorite examples, much less tragic, way more piquant. I'll never forget—it was during the Christmas season of 1999, during those heady dot-com days, and Jeff Bezos was sharing his vision with the masses in a TV interview on ABC's *This Week*. As I recall it, one of his interlocutors, greatly daring, said something in defense of brick and mortar, maybe suggesting that shopping in stores was fun, something like that. The visionary of all things Amazon was not offended. He seemed to understand and even sympathize, and he said reassuringly, quite earnestly, no trace of irony—Bezos saith unto the multitudes:

"The physical world is a wonderful medium, and it's not going to go away."

What must it be like, to feel entitled to say something like that? And not even notice?

These guys toned it down a bit after the new economy went south and the war on terror began, of course. But they're regrouping. They'll be back.

After a while, listening to futurist visionaries gets to be like listening to evangelical literalists on the Christian Network. If you haven't treated yourself to a visit with these Christian Network folks, you really should, I mean it. Especially now. It's very educational. They sit around—the sets are quite luxurious, almost a parody of gracious living in a gated community—and they share. Boy, do they share. And what they share are stories about their personal relationship with Jesus Christ, specific stories of His intervention in their lives. They never get tired of this. Neither does their audience. These are people who can't get enough of Jesus, that's the basic fact. It's as if they are all addicted to a particular rhetorical gesture, the inevitable redemptive climax to their multifarious tales of woe. It's as if they gather to provide themselves with fixes for this collective addiction. And, if you listen for a while to their leaders, the ones who create the figures of redemption, you realize that the secular visionaries of the InfoAge and the fundamentalist visionaries of GodLand took the same psychological step. *They learned to trust.*

Whatever occurs to them in a certain way, whatever wells up in them with a certain feeling—that they trust. They feel authorized by the mere fact that these thoughts and feelings *come to them.* They feel literally inspired.

Most regular folks "get" ideas too. Feelings "arise" in everybody. When you look closely at the phenomenology of it, you realize that we don't think up our thoughts the way we execute a plan in the physical world. That is, no one can have an idea or a feeling *before* they think it or feel it. So, in a way, all our thoughts occur to us, come to us as if from somewhere else. But most people, if they notice this at all, assume that the "somewhere else" in question is an unconscious part of their own minds, and therefore as likely to be fallible as anything else associated with them.

Not so the visionaries. In case you are contemplating a career as a visionary, here is the formula (workshops available). Jerry Falwell has learned to believe that when ideas come to him in a certain, very special, syrupy way, with a very specific, flowing-honey feeling—that means they come from God. Larry Ellison has exactly the same experiences, but he doesn't think they come from God—he knows they come from Larry Ellison. But he's *Larry Ellison*, so it's almost as good.

After a while, for these visionaries, authorization doesn't just derive from the fact that ideas come to them. It derives from the fact that they come to *them.* Especially when sycophantic choirs have been assembled to greet their every utterance with appropriate expressions of awe for lo these many years. After a while, well—you just *are* a visionary.

But it's not all their fault. The expectation that they know what's going on and what to do about it is built into the situation—and pressures run both ways.

When I talk publicly about mediation, I get predictable objections that I can usually satisfy, one by one—when time permits. After people catch on—when they start to understand that this isn't so much about media per se, but about being a mediated person, about existing, in the Heideggerian sense, in a world that is made up of a flattering field of represented options—then they usually switch from making objections to saying one of two things: "Okay, I see what you mean, but isn't that a good thing?" or "Okay, I see what you mean, but what's the solution?"

The Justin's Helmet Principle takes care of the first question, but people with the second response are harder to reach. They speak with a very particular tone of voice, the tone of one who holds a trump—namely, in this case, the settled assumption that a critical analysis that doesn't provide a solution is a waste of time.

That's why almost every book of social criticism, every article, even every little op-ed piece, must conclude with some solution, however lame.

Which came first? Audience expectation or visionary bogosity? With cultural forms like this it's hard to tell. What is clear is that this genre requirement is a vestige of modernity's faith in the technological fix—with "technological" meant broadly, to include political and social and even psychological programs and reforms. I say "vestige" because I think a lot of people who consume social criticism and futurist tracts don't fully believe in these solutions anymore either. Not all, but a lot. Like the visionaries, they are trapped in the genre. I think what's going on now, especially since

9/11, in Bush's America, is that more and more people are realizing, at a gut level, that we are all in that car fishtailing around on a snowy road, that so far we haven't gone over the edge—but that doesn't mean that anybody or anything is in control. It just means that, so far, we've been lucky (some of us, anyway).

I think more and more people understand that events are beyond our comprehension, let alone our management capacities. We can sense the flop sweat behind the stern masks of jut-jawed leadership, especially now that terror by WMD is starting to feel inevitable, just a matter of when, not whether.

Which *was* totally predictable all along, by the way; it's one of the few things that you could have known would happen some-day. But the jut-jawed leaders of yore were too busy with whatever immediate crisis they had created back then to bother about the *totally obvious* long-run consequences of making these lethal technologies in the first place, not to mention pursuing policies bound to get us hated by most of the people on the planet.

Realizing that things have gotten out of hand isn't just irrational intuition. The premise upon which modernity's faith in the fix is based is logically flawed. "If people cause X, people can cure X" just isn't true. A man who jumps off a bridge can't arrest his descent in midair. At a certain point, if we keep pumping junk into the environment, we will pass a point of no return. Maybe we already have.

So if my suspicions on this score are justified, why do we keep producing and consuming these lame predictions and solutions? Could it just be, as I'm trying to get up the nerve to assert, because it's a condition of employment and entertainment in this genre? Do we conclude with solutions and predictions because that gives us the closure we need before moving on to the next thing we want to produce or consume? An aesthetic convention, in other words, that panders to a niche of people who identify as engaged and knowledgeable, people hooked on insights into megatrends, people who crave the rush of righteous resolve that comes with knowing what needs to be done on the world historical stage.

After all, even if everyone understands, on some unconscious level, that things are pretty much out of control, who wants to hear *that* over and over again? I mean, you get one book, max, out of that insight, and then what? Everybody stops pontificating?

Not a chance.

Evidence of hidden skepticism is rampant, though, once you begin to look for it. It lends a particular hue, for example, to the National Public Radio talk show host's voice, coming out of the final break, addressing the expert guest. It's a stepping-back tone as the host says something like, "Well, okay, so how do we as a society begin to deal with . . ."—whatever it is. Once, when I was discussing the numbing effects of relentless mediation, emphasizing the way it teaches us to move on, and the host started doing this wrap up shtick, I impulsively interrupted to ask if he really expected me to say anything useful in the two remaining minutes of air time. He laughed—right away, enjoying himself. He had been intelligently attentive and he got the connection between my question and the topic we had been discussing. So he said, in spontaneous self-parody, something like, "I guess not, but it's that time in the show! I have to get ready for the next segment! We have to move on!"

Maybe prediction/solution conclusions persist because they are like that rising tide of music at the end of the movie, the surge of strings that elevates the camera as the expanding horizon shot opens up around the protagonists and gives you that tied-up-in-a-bow feeling to take home with you.

Even though, actually—I hate to be a drag, but, have you

noticed? Movie endings are getting lamer and lamer lately, especially in the action/sci-fi/scary area. There's this very specific phase in so many of these films, a phase that's so marked I bet there's some insider lingo for it. It's when the suspenseful set-up phase—which is often pretty good, very atmospheric, intriguing character foibles—ends and the resolution phase begins. At that point, everything seems to go on automatic, and the rest of the movie spins out flat and formulaic, but really loud and fast, as if hoping to distract you from the vacuity. It's like the writer and director just give up. They somehow manage to make their endings old hat and over the top at the same time. A weird combination.

That's how they came up with those phony-relief endings in scary movies, you know the ones I mean? The first time they did that it must have been way cool, because the relief ending in a scary movie up to that time was *so* entrenched. The monstrous thing subsided beneath the surface, the music slowed, and the camera irised gently out as Whit Bissell and Barbara Bel Geddes embraced. Fade. The End. Then somebody started playing games with this convention, and turned it into the Monstrous Thing subsiding beneath the surface, and etc., as the couple embraces— when suddenly (cut to disgusting close-up and a crash of atonal shrilling) the Thing thrusts up again, more ferocious than ever, and grabs her ankle.

But then, after a while, of course, it got so you *expected* the apparent ending to be interrupted with a renewal of horror.

The Sixth Sense offered a breakthrough, a genuine surprise ending, when you realized that Bruce Willis had been dead, been a ghost, the whole time. But that just served to underline, by contrast, how unsatisfying most endings have become, riddled with twists though they be.

We have achieved predictable surprise.

Oh, the paradoxes of mediation, how they multiply in the wake of the Blob's procession.

Somebody, please—*stop it!*

The Fate of Originality

But there's another side to the bogosity issue. We've touched on the fate of heroes and the rise of performers as an aspect of the general cultural situation in which mediated people learn to star in their own lives. Something along those lines applies here as well. Most people don't slavishly adopt the views of this or that visionary leader peddling his wares in the marketplace of ideas. Most people sit in judgment. Most people pick and choose. The flattery of being perpetually addressed, of being solicited—quite shamelessly when you think about the herds of authors shuffling between the green rooms and bookstores, hawking their visions, recycling anecdotes and catchphrases, improvising their way through a string of set pieces like politicians on the stump, craving every vote. So undignified, at some level, isn't it? The neediness, I mean. It's actually a bit embarrassing, all that flaunting, so apparent beneath the guises of gravitas and artistry, once you learn to look for it.

Anyway, the cumulative effect of it all is that you, in your specialness, are authorized to create your own vision and philosophy, to cobble one together out of whatever notions strike your fancy as you browse through those endless aisles, in those bookstores vast as oceans. And the result? You know how it is. Name a topic and, presto, everyone has an opinion, everyone can speculate, everyone has a "take," as we say nowadays—implicitly acknowledging that no one has time for much more than that—so, what the heck, mine could be as good as the next one.

To each his own worldview.

Once again it is all about you. The reader, the viewer, the customer is the ultimate center of the represented universe. Those in the limelight come and go in accordance with the dictates of your attention. They need you much more than you need them. The very structure of, let's say, a really big Barnes & Noble bookstore, the layout of the sections, in recognition of your tastes, the jackets on display, so lovingly designed to arrest your sovereign gaze, and the names of the famous asking you to trust them, yet again promising to provide you with more of the same thing you liked so much the last time. The whole ensemble amounts to this: you are being treated as if you were, or soon will be, Master of your Destiny and Judge of The World, as if The Crisis in the Middle East, The Global Economy, The Starvation of Millions, The Rise of This Huge Thing, The Decline of That Huge Thing, it's all— this is implicit, built into the format—for you, for your attention, for your approval, for your judicious consideration, there to assist you in matters emotional and financial, addressing anything and everything you could possibly be interested in for any reason whatsoever.

So, if you want predictions and solutions—well, them too, you're gonna get 'em. If that's what you need to feel on top of things, say no more. They will be forthcoming. Predictions and solutions adapted to every suite of prejudices. And more in the making as we speak, you may be sure. Because—as one of those book titles once put it—this is all about the "Next New Thing." Or was it the "New New Thing"?

But it can get to be a problem, this new new thing thing. More and more so, for reasons that are so obvious, once you consider them, that it makes me wonder if we aren't just in denial.

Consider the mood that sometimes comes over us—the feeling

that it's all been done. Maybe that's not just a mood. Maybe it has. Not in the digi-bio-techie department, of course; there, the prospects for novelty seem unlimited. I mean in those areas occupied by what platform proprietors call "content providers."

What a phrase! Could any expression register devastation of the human spirit more completely than that casual little generic? Could meaning suffer a more complete evacuation? Not since we landed on the moon and found nothing has our cultural unconscious encountered so traumatic a void.

Maybe the postmodern taste for retro and pastiche is more than a cultural phase? Maybe it's necessity. Maybe—as with nature, so with culture—there's a limit. Maybe more or less everything that can be done in the plastic arts, say, has been done? How many different ways can a finite set of shapes and colors be arranged in a finite space, after all? Maybe there just isn't room left in the frame for anything different. After all, we aren't talking infinitely divisible Platonic geometry here. Maybe there just isn't any really new way to put X shapes and Y colors into Z permutations. Maybe someday it will be obvious that the characteristic gestures of twentieth-century art were all flailing out against this simple fact. Cézanne's planes, Magritte's pipe, Pollack's swirls, Warhol's soup can, Christo's vast draperies, Serrano's piss, all the installations— so many desperate efforts to elude the end of originality?

Likewise, with music? How many distinguishable sounds can be made in how many patterns? There has to be some limit. After you've integrated techno and Brazilian-Afro and Tibetan monko and humpbacked whalo, at some point, surely, there's going to be nothing left but play it again, Sam. Maybe that's why it's the age of the mix. And characters and plots, in stories and shows? I mean what's the raw material? Sex, cool outlaws, illness, death, master villains, the fall of giants, fate, just desserts, the dark side, redemption by the little things, a few other themes—we all know the repertoire. Maybe it's just impossible to think of anything to present in a dramatic or literary context that couldn't be described, after the fashion of all contemporary pitches, as "It's *To the Lighthouse* meets *Sex and the City*" or "It's Hannibal Lecter meets Orphan Annie."

Imagine the Wayans brothers pitching *White Chicks*. Let's see, *Mean Girls I* meets *Bad Boys II* meets *As You Like It* meets Adam Sandler meets . . .

More, mixes, more fusion. The Blob's metabolism actually becomes visible in mixes and fusion.

This would account for so many cultural trends, wouldn't it? For revivals and remakes and period pieces, obviously, and for cable reruns and video stores and all the referencing and citing, and also the flow of parody and irony, and media covering media and memoirs and reality shows too. And for pushing the violence and sex envelopes in all directions, and for the profusion of special effects in every presentational format. Also for the proliferation of niches; because one way to produce original content is to make it for a very small number of people. (There is now a magazine for city folk who grow herbs in window boxes. Just kidding. I think.) Or even just for yourself and whomever you happen to bump into, as in everyperson's Web page in the galaxy of bloggers.

And if you're sitting in the middle of a network of Friendsters and Pretendsters—or maybe in the middle of several networks you've created for your avatars—well, talk about being what you want to be! There you have a perfect fusion of the satisfactions that accrue to the anonymous voyeur and the celebrity in the limelight.

So no wonder you are inclined (if you have time) to make forays into all sorts of creative enterprises in order to express your self or selves. Sometimes it feels as if absolutely everyone is in a band or doing art or writing a screenplay or something like that, doesn't it? At least at some stage in their lives—I bet everyone you know was doing something creative and thinking about committing to it, or did commit to it, at least for a while.

But all this creative activity—while indubitably mostly a good thing—has to reach a certain point of mass meaninglessness; it has to, doesn't it? Even the apparently limitless flexibility that a digitally enhanced everyperson enjoys in the creation of whatever they want—there has to be a limit, doesn't there? Doesn't it get to be like that old thing about if a million monkeys type at random on a million keyboards for infinity, one of them will eventually write *Hamlet*?

Except this is sort of the opposite, I guess.

Does that make sense?

Anyway, for example, think about how hard it has become to think up a logo. It's no mystery why. There are so many institutions and enterprises, large and small, and they all know that if they want to succeed they have to have a communications department, be a brand, have a logo. But the laws of Euclidean geometry remain unchanged—I think, but who knows, maybe the guys who stopped light can do something in this area. But, whatever, the point is like before with painting: there's only so much space you can put a design in. I mean, you have the Mercedes-Benz star and Traveler's umbrella and Nike's swoosh, and you keep going like that and pretty soon you are at a loss for how to create a little design that will be both simple *and* distinctive—which is the whole point of a logo.

That's why logo design has entered what you might call a baroque period. Just look around and you'll see what I mean, if you haven't noticed already.

And what about car names. For some reason, this is my favorite example, even more than medication names, though they're good too. I mean, Advanta, Alanta, Altima, Bravada, Celica, Cimera, Impreza, Maxima, Previa, Serena, Sonata, Supra, Vectra, Volanta, Xantia—and that's just a tiny sample of the ones that take some connotative syllable and tack on the concluding *a* to signify thrust. At some point, surely, you just have to shrug and say—you know what's coming, all together now:

Whatever!

The prospect of the end of originality would also account for the turn to sensation. It's as if intensity of presentation could make up for repetition. Of course, as we've seen, sensation is also a response to clutter on the screen, the way to grab the most possible attention in the least amount of time. But that also accounts for why everything's already been done, and so it cycles on—fill the pages, fill the time slots, fill the channels, the Web sites, the roadsides, the building façades, the fronts and backs of shirts and caps, everything, everything must be saying something, every minute. But what? What's left to say? It doesn't matter. Cut to the response.

Zap. Whimper. Flinch. Cringe. Melt. Assert! Exult! Weep. Subside. Ahhh . . .

Eventually we can just wire our glands directly to a console of sensation buttons, platform to platform, and be done with this tiresome content altogether. Call it P2P communication. Talk about interactive. Thus will the human soul be compensated for the despair of finitude.

Maybe some day "sensationalism" will occupy the same semantic space as "socialism" or "liberalism"—it will name a social philosophy and a way of life.

Closure for You; Jedermensch ein Übermensch

Okay, you want closure? Wrap yourself in this:

What would Nietzsche have to say about cloning if he were alive today? It's hard to know, but one thing's for sure; he would *not* be noodling around on the practical margins; he would *not* allow the experts to reduce this fabulous eventuality to mere policy. He would plunge straight to the metaphysical heart of the matter, to the delicious and terrible dilemmas that cluster around the possibility of self-replication.

And so will we, because one way to interpret the account of mediation I have offered is to say that we have now realized—but democratically—the concept of the Overman, the Übermensch. That Olympian figure was to earn his standing by dint of self-overcoming, you may recall. That meant self-creation. Nietzsche thought of this as the most demanding of all projects, to be undertaken only by the rarest and greatest spirits in history. But the enterprise of self-construction turned out to belong to everybody.

Nietzsche thought a lot about how the herd was flattered by its shepherds, but even he couldn't foresee the extent of that flattery's effects or the technological modalities of its expression. The possibility of cloning yourself is the ultimate representational achievement, the very archetype of simulation, the final form of flattery.

That's the context for thinking about the possibility of cloning. And let's not forget that the Human Genome Project is coming to fruition at the same time, as if scheduled by Sophocles. The information technology we call genetic engineering is opening up fabulous new options for the single parent of tomorrow.

How conveniently the term stands ready to assume its full meaning!

Nietzsche might have helped us understand cloning as the ecstatic realization of a destiny. Maybe we should welcome this as the defining triumph of the mediated self. "God is dead" would sum it up just right if you considered the whole sweep of the enterprise of self-construction culminating in literal self-(re)con-struction through cloning and genetic engineering. Self-help on a divine scale. If I hadn't already said I didn't trust the idea of huge unfolding historical patterns anymore, I'd be mighty tempted to see this as a logical outcome, the climactic fulfilment of moder-nity's essential aim: replacing God with Me.

You want a monster vision? Here.

The aim of modernity fulfilled means this: humanly created options that endow ordinary people with entitlements no mortal in history, no matter how exalted, could ever have assumed before. While these entitlements are now limited to a relative and privileged few, this cohort already comprises many millions, shows every indication of expanding, and is, in any case, the source of the global zeitgeist. Members of this cohort either have, or can realistically anticipate, the obliteration of all barriers of time and space, instant access to every text and image ever made, the free exercise of any lifestyle or belief system that does not infringe on the choices of others, custom-made environments, commodities, and experiences in every department of activity, multiple enhancements of mind and body, the eradication of disease, the postponement of death, and the manufacture of their progeny in their own image.

Plus improvements.

How could we not think of divinity in the presence of such powers? If we refuse the description because God does not seem to us secular humanists to be playing a prominent role at this climactic moment, aren't we collaborating with a repression of the obvious? If our usurpation of God's role is in fact the climax of the modern story, is it surprising that we would want to keep it quiet? We resist religious literalisms for obvious reasons, but their resurgence among us, all over the world, is certainly a response to the situation as I am describing it—and we ignore that at our peril. God, in His various forms, has been obliged by our silence to make a last stand among fundamentalist refuseniks clinging to anchors no longer grounded in anything but willful blindness, compulsive ritual, and totalitarian discipline. But where else could God go after He was—not expelled, but counseled out, shall we say? The whole transaction had to be discreetly handled, a manifold of dissimulations crafted to disguise our assumption of His responsibilities—you know, creating life, creating human beings, stuff like that. The trick has been to leave that whole topic off the table and concentrate on practical issues, health and environment issues, instead of *the* "issue," in the original sense of the word, instead of what it *means* for us to be creating life-forms like goats that give milk that turns to spinnable silk because they've had spider genes implanted in them.

It helps if the only people talking about this development— modernity in general, cloning in particular—in terms of displacing or replacing God are those fundamentalists. That could be why you might not want to think about things in these terms. Nietzsche did, though, and that's good enough for me. He understood that you don't have to believe in God in order to recognize Him as a major historical player. Unmasking power, exposing its various guises, especially the humble ones—that was Nietzsche's mission. And the power of the flattered self at the center of the field of representations in this mediated age has been very effectively disguised. Look, we could always say, I don't have power, it's them, the rich and famous ones, those corporations, those prime ministers and presidents, look over there, don't look at me.

If you're wondering why no one has exposed you before, it's because everybody who addresses you wants to please you. They want you reclining there, on the anonymous side of the screen, while they parade before you, purveyors of every conceivable blandishment, every form of pleasure, every kind of comfort and consolation, every kind of thrill, every kind of provocation—anything you want. You're the customer, after all, you're the voter, you're the reader, you're the viewer—you're the boss.

So, naturally, everyone who addresses you is kissing your ass. Except me.

But let's consult some other established big thinkers on this issue, besides Nietzsche. Here's a little gem from the one who first gave us the modern self, in its purest form:

> Now, if I were independent of all other existence, and were myself the author of my being . . . I should have given myself all those perfections of which I have some idea, and I should thus be God.
>
> —Descartes

Now Descartes was highlighting his imperfections in this passage. He was denying himself divinity. His deficiencies were to be the premise for a logical proof of God's existence. But—like Locke with his fantasies about adjustable eyeballs—Descartes was flirting with a possibility. After all, he had just called the existence of his own consciousness the only thing of which he could be absolutely certain, the one thing he couldn't doubt. He had discovered that his mind continued to exist in the very effort to doubt it. That's what "I think, therefore I am" means.

And he was about to show that everything outside his mind, outside his subjective experience, trees and tables, other people, his own body—even God—had to be *derived* by argument from his own mental existence.

So, right off the bat, we've got the human self in a pretty central position.

And, in other contexts, when God wasn't immediately on his mind, Descartes was eager to promote a standing for humanity that resonates like a call to arms. For example, when he called for

a practical philosophy . . . by which, knowing the power and the effects of fire, water, air, the stars, the heavens, and all the other bodies which surround us, as distinctly as we know the various trades of our craftsmen, we might put them in the same way to all the uses for which they are appropriate, and thereby make ourselves, as it were, masters and possessors of nature.

"As it were?"

Please.

Or there's the concluding paragraph of *Discourse on Method*, the prototype of modern self-help books. Descartes there commits himself to the exclusive study of medicine, on the basis of his method, and hints at finding a cure for death.

Stuff like that. Lots of it. Right from the beginning of the modern adventure. Like Locke, Descartes could not explicitly countenance the implication, but it was definitely there. He had to know at some level.

When educated people think of modernity, they think of technology, first of all, and then of individualism (human rights, free enterprise), and also of secularization—the separation of church and state, the decline of medieval institutions. And they are right to do so. But these features of modernity worked together, as aspects of a single historical development. Cloning and genetic engineering, regarded as the crowning synthesis of that development, reveal the underlying unity. They constitute the ultimate in mediation—life-forms express a code, after all, and, with genetic engineering, living creatures become the screens that display our designs.

Let's coin a term. "Proprietorial humanism"—to contrast with Renaissance humanism, the kind they introduce in high school history, Erasmus and da Vinci and so on. Renaissance humanism took classical antiquity as a model in order to leverage itself out of the Middle Ages. That's the basic story line there. What I'm calling proprietorial humanism emerged later, in the seventeenth century, as moderns decided they had surpassed the ancients by dint of achievements in what they called the "useful arts"—that is, technology and all its systematic applications.

Effects of technology on material nature have always been obvious. Some metaphorical extensions are also obvious—the machinery of government, things like that. But other influences were subtler. They shaped the way the rising middle classes, the historical agents of modernity, conceived of themselves. They called themselves the "productive classes," to sharpen the political contrast with aristocracies. They were thinking of products of industry in the usual sense, but the term can be revealingly extended—modern persons and societies were also products. That's the essential point to grasp.

Here's the beginning of a list: the French Republic, the Ford Motor Company, Teddy Roosevelt. Here's the beginning of another: the New Britain, Google, Governor Arnold. You could extend the lists indefinitely. Your grandparents probably belong on the first list. You probably belong on the second. And what a

difference between the lists. Those hoary old industrial-age constructs feel as solid as the Rocky Mountains compared to the
hyper-fabrications of our time.

This book has mostly been about the difference between the
two lists.

But notice that the entities on both lists were consciously
designed. Compared to medieval or tribal institutions and persons,
they have this in common: they are all fabrications. Products.

These products vary enormously, of course. The French Republic of 1792 was not the Weimar Republic of 1921. The
bohemian aesthete of the late nineteenth century was not a captain
of industry. But he might have been his brother.

What makes all the variants modern (and, later, postmodern)
is this: using raw materials of nature and historical circumstance,
people undertook to construct themselves in accordance with
their own designs—through politics and education, fashion,
manners, psychology, through enterprises of all kinds. People
began to make themselves as they remade the world. And these
self-made people and their projects flourished, succeeded—they
just took over.

That is the essence of proprietorial humanism. The reflexivity
and self-construction we have been talking about throughout this
book begins here. Popular expressions that reflect that origin have
always shaped our public culture—make something of yourself,
the American dream, the better tomorrow.

But we can get a deeper grip on why the word "proprietorial" is
so apt a description, and on why cloning and genetic engineering
realize the concept.

Let's return to John Locke, this time to consider some ideas he is
known for. Brief excerpts only, but every word counts:

The mind as it left the "hand of nature," is a tabula rasa, a blank slate or "white paper" or "empty cabinet."

All the Straw, Bran, Bread . . . is worth . . . is the Effect of Labor . . . Nature and Earth furnished only the almost worthless materials.

He that is nourished by the Acorns he pickt up . . . when did they begin to be his? When he digested? . . . Or when he boiled? . . . if the first gathering made them not his, nothing else could.

For Men being all the Workmanship of one Omnipotent, and infinitely wise Maker . . . they are his Property, whose Workmanship they are.

The first three claims were Locke's most influential. Founders of modern institutions from Sieyès to Jefferson had them specifically in mind when they did their constituting work. Anyone who takes a survey course on Western thought is exposed to them. The blank-slate doctrine (empiricism) justified scientific method and progressive education. The labor theory of value made property a natural right—not something kings and lords could claim by hereditary right, but something the productive classes earned.

The fourth selection only matters today to specialists interested in Locke's religious beliefs. But it was the foundation of the whole enterprise for Locke.

In his attack on absolute monarchy, Locke depended upon this premise: human beings have a natural (God-given) right to preserve themselves. They are free to do whatever serves that purpose as long as the same right is respected in others. Most substantially, their human labor, which gives value to the almost worthless raw materials of nature as it transforms them into useful goods, *also gives title to those goods*.

Thus were a parasitic monarchy and nobility disenfranchised, and the productive classes given their due.

See how the fourth selection provides the foundational analogy? The human right to property mirrors God's ownership of His human creatures, who were His Workmanship.

Everything follows from that. All the rights and duties Locke attributed to persons he discovered in them *as products of the Maker*. He figured out how God intended human beings to live the way you might figure out how some gadget works. There was undeniable evidence of functional design in our physical nature, after all—from the eyeball, to the hand, to the physiognomy of the sexes. Don't forget, Locke had no concept of evolution or natural selection to account for that. The Maker's designs were evident in the human products of His Workmanship, in his human properties—and Locke took it from the physical to the political and ethical on that basis. He says murder is wrong because it is robbery of God; likewise, suicide and slavery. The right to life and liberty, the right to make laws and elect representatives—all the rights and duties that defined the modern political landscape were derived, in Locke's mind, from our obligation to preserve the Maker's human creatures. Politicians would hold such truths to be self-evident because inalienable rights were given to us the way hearts and feet and teeth were given to us. By our Maker.

That's the core of Locke's political philosophy. And it was accepted—more than accepted, it was taken for granted by educated early moderns.

But, in another classic text, focusing on abstruse epistemological matters, Locke declared that the human mind, the defining characteristic of the human being, left the hand of nature—as a tabula rasa.

Oh, fateful seed.

Do you see what's coming?

Locke never let himself see the consequences of combining his political and epistemological premises. But think about it in light of the four little quotes just cited. Locke was opening up the most fabulous investment and development opportunity of all time. The tabula rasa of human nature was an uncultivated and unimproved piece of raw material of an entirely new order, and the human analogs of the divine Maker were quick to seize upon it. The improvement of humanity itself, the labor of civilization, would become the first aim of modern progress.

Moderns pursued the project of progress into every natural space and cultural arena. And the more extensively and elaborately they labored, the more everything in the world became manmade. It just did. That's just a fact. And what was not—the forests, the heavens, the depths of the sea—was frontier, molded in the aspiration of the map. And similarly for one's own potential, and for children, and for the lower orders, and for savages—these were also raw materials for the project. Whatever was not yet consciously designed and governed was marked for improvement, or simply for using. The process of modernizing, in all its detail and variety, over the whole course of those astounding centuries, was a process of fabrication through which moderns took over the Maker's role.

And title to ownership was accordingly transferred.

By the mid-nineteenth century, in the shadow of Malthus and Darwin, the implicit aim was made explicit. Modernity's hidden agenda surfaced.

For Marx, "the whole of what is called world history is nothing more than the creation of man through human labor, and the development of nature for man," which provides "a palpable and incontrovertible proof of his self-mediated [Marx's usage] birth" and renders "an alien being, a being above nature and man . . . impossible in practice."

The founder of positivism was even more explicit. Comte went beyond exposing God's irrelevance. He established a religion, with ritual and liturgy, an active church, the Church of Positivism— whose members worshipped Humanity, the "only true Great Being."

With Nietzsche, the death of God was formally announced and the figure of the Overman—*the one who makes himself*—appears on the horizon, hailed in terms that leave no doubt as to his standing.

God died slowly. He was not executed on a given horrific day. As the status of Maker fell more and more to those who actually made the settings that constituted people's lives, God simply evaporated. He could not sustain Himself as the subject of a world that no longer displayed His designs. At the most comprehensive level, this giant phenomenological fact is what accounts for the retreat of religion to the realm of private belief and practice under the regime of modernity.

What applies to the settings in which we live applies also, and more essentially, to our selves. As we become authors of our being, the proprietorial entitlement follows. Across the whole spectrum of the means and ends by which moderns have practiced self-government, socially and individually, since the seventeenth century, they have been *realizing* (as in "making real") the connection between secularization, the rise of technology, and the emergence of the modern individual—the self-maker, the self-owner. This book has focused on how much more extensive, various, and malleable self-ownership becomes as representations and options multiplied with the rise of mediation—but such are the roots.

With just that much perspective, genetic engineering and cloning appear as the fulfillment of a destiny. Literal human self-making is obviously continuous with the whole process of modern fabrication, but, with the focus on the theme of God, it looks more than continuous—it looks climactic. And this holds no matter how you evaluate it, no matter how secular your convictions are. You might see it, with Lee Silver, as a triumph, a breakthrough in our noble quest to liberate humanity from accidents of nature. You might welcome it, in the manner of Donna Haraway, because it liberates us from categories like "natural" and "human." Or you might see it, as Husserl or Heidegger would have, surely—as the ultimate technological abomination.

The story I just outlined accommodates all these evaluations, and more besides.

You decide.

Obviously, a clone of you, improved or not, wouldn't literally be you, wouldn't have the same consciousness, experiences, memories. People realize this, but that doesn't smother the frisson of taboo evoked by the idea of self-replication, the rapture and horror of a narcissism intensified to the point of incestuous implosion. For the questions that hover at the edge of every mind that even glances toward a future populated by our virtual progeny living in virtual worlds, the questions that haunt this prospect at its moral limits, the questions Nietzsche would have seized upon immediately, are these:

What would it be like to gaze into your own eyes? What would it be like to caress and comfort, to love and care for, a clone of yourself? To kiss a person who looks exactly like you did thirty years ago?

It would be as if the impossible solipsism of Descartes's original meditations were being acted out in the flesh. And then there's the whole question of giving yourself "all those perfections" Descartes mentioned, and so becoming the "author" of your being.

What would it be like to endow a clone of yourself with a few extras—an ear for music, an eye for color, a talent for languages, not to mention those few extra inches that make all the difference.

And then, having given yourself what you were missing, what would it be like to raise and educate yourself as you deserve?

Well, some of us are going to find out. Bank on it. It's a destiny.

Parental pride at school concerts will take on a whole new dimension. And imagine those soccer games.

CODA: TERROR

WELL, WHERE I was when the World Trade Center was hit was in a little park by the East River, on the Brooklyn side, right next to the famous bridge, a favorite haunt of mine—until recently, when they began to "restore" the neighborhood, which had been so wonderful just as it was. The view of Manhattan from that park is glorious and—until 9/11 obviously—dominated by the twin towers. I couldn't actually see them from where I was sitting, curled up on the grass with coffee and the newspaper, because the great arc of the bridge and its buttresses came between. I must have been very absorbed in somebody's reporting because, although I heard a huge explosion in the distance, I didn't stop reading. I vaguely thought "gas main," though I'm not even sure what a gas main is. I just have the impression that a big explosion ensues when one ignites.

A few minutes later I became aware of a lot of sirens from a lot of vehicles, all over the place, going down the FDR Drive, over the bridge above me—way more than I had ever heard or seen before. I looked around and saw a little cluster of people on a knoll in the park, all of them looking up and out across the river, and something about the way they were standing got to me, so I rose and walked over to them, turning as I went. And then I saw it. The first tower, standing there like always, but with a great circle of flame erupting from around it, about three fourths of the way up, like some mammoth hellish collar. I couldn't believe what I was seeing.

I either realized that this might be terrorism, and that it might not be over, or someone said something to that effect, I can't remember which, but I thought immediately of my daughter who was teaching in a nearby school, thought of her well-being, thought also of others I love, but they were not nearby—and so I went to her, joined her, and her little students, and all the others too, in the basement of the school, very crowded, chaotic, verging on hysteria, one nearly desperate father, I particularly remember, thrusting through the crowd to retrieve his weeping child. I thought "I bet the mother works there," but I didn't say anything.

We were in that basement when the second tower got hit. A radio informed us.

A few hours after that—the news from D.C. and Pennsylvania was in, my daughter calm, tending her flock—I started getting restless. I wanted to go over there—maybe to help, if I could, or just to see—but she guessed my mind as I was leaving and made me swear to stay in Brooklyn, so I did. For the next few days, I followed things from there, in the media and on the streets, on the promenade overlooking Manhattan. When I went over at last, I looked for ways to help at first, but so many people were helping, more than were needed—unless you had real skills, which I didn't, being barely able to screw in a lightbulb. But I do have some gift for observation, so I did that.

Like a movie, people said. And so many more have since remarked how people said that—and therein lies our tale, of course. Surreal, people said, people who never heard of André Breton were saying that for weeks and months. And so many more remarked how people were saying that—and therein lies our tale as well.

This surreality was most intense in New York and Washington, and that says a lot about what the word was intended to express.

People in those cities felt the most fear, first of all, obviously. They felt directly attacked. And that jolt set them up for the aftermath, for the task of integrating the two channels of information open to them at a moment when the difference between them, between reality and representation, was more sharply and extensively drawn than ever before in the history of the media age. An unprecedented array of images and sensations from both sources, flowing and fusing and fragmenting, and all that mongrel input blending with memory and fantasy by way of the same primordial associative processes that produce myths and dreams, and all of this happening automatically, randomly—just as the original surrealists prescribed. The familiar was defamiliarized on the grandest scale, and by some alchemy of cultural history the repositories of high culture supplied the vernacular with just the right word. *Surreal.*

So, if you lived in New York, you saw (and heard and smelled) the flesh and stone of events, and you recalled (you could not help it) imagery from some movie, and you saw TV footage of flesh and stone events you had seen in reality, and maybe you heard a friend who worked downtown describe the ash people walking like refugees across the Brooklyn Bridge, which was also shown on CNN, by the way, and maybe you went later to the bridge itself and saw the ghastly footprints, and then you woke up at 3 A.M., afterimaging it all—and so on, round and round, on and on, as those eerie, early days drifted by.

It came down to this. The ever-present absence of media representation framed the real scene, when you were in it, visiting the perimeter, standing by the barricades, going to work by unfamiliar routes, avoiding Grand Central. Why the frame? How could an absence of representation frame a reality? Because we have been so conditioned by representations and their characteristics, the ones we usually take for granted, the ones we have been concerned with in this book. They have a focus by their very nature. They are about something, and they are for something, for you, they make you the subject of everything that happens.

But the real scene, when you were in it, wasn't about or for anything or anybody. It was chaos, a gigantic instantiation of necessity and accident. Suddenly, your point of view had no special claim. This is what visitors to the site were trying to say when they talked about how the real scene had such depth and size, how it surrounded you, and so on—as compared to the pictures on TV, they meant, they all said that. But even before you got to the site, you were made aware of the pointlessness of reality, the absence of a center. Murmuring pigeons round a Dumpster in the alley you happened to glance down, as you made your way toward ground zero, each pigeon full of its particular need, each brick, chipped just so, each scrap of trash and greasy puddle, unique in the universe, insisting on its right to be, asserting the equivalence of all things under the blind sky. Or, from a distance, from uptown or across the rivers, the plume of smoke that rose into that sky, for all to see, for miles around, for days on end, rose from a hole in the skyline—another absence, for the hole only gaped in virtue of superimposed memory of a presence in that space, a space which (you couldn't help but notice) took up so tiny a fraction of the vastness of the wide horizon and the great bowl of the heavens above, so tiny a fraction of that vastness across which you cast your eyes whenever you looked away, a vastness into which that smoke was rising, so tenderly, until it dispersed at last into the brilliant blue.

Which brings me to the sheer beauty of those early days, the perfect September weather, the marvelous light, constant reminders, they were, of the utter indifference of nature to us and all our arrangements, all our roiling and striving, the stands we take, our murderous sanctimony, things of beauty, fields of gore. Those torn girders, thrusting up at angles from the pit—at first glance they expressed so powerfully the anguish they seemed to stand for. But on second thought, you knew that steel cares nothing for its shape.

But, unlike the absence of representation framing the real scene, the absence of the towers themselves was tangible, as tangible as an absence can be anyway. The place was marked. By the ruin, first of all, a ruin that most New Yorkers made a point of approaching, glimpsing at least—the long view down Church Street from the corner of Chambers, the yawning threshold at the end of Liberty. Even without those glimpses, there was location to this absence. From Central Park, from the ferry dock at Hoboken or Staten Island, from a Park Slope rooftop; you knew more or less exactly where the towers used to stand. You used to see them just there, when you were sitting on this bench.

Compared to the possibility of another attack, compared to the invisible ubiquity of that possibility, the absence of the towers was specific and contained.

Especially compared to germs.

The classic distinction between fear and angst originally fell along this axis. Freud thought he was diagnosing a neurotic condition, Heidegger thought he was revealing to consciousness the mood of its own freedom—but they both held a threatening nothing-in-particular, anything-and-everything to be the proper object of angst. The surreality of everyday life in a bubble of privilege pierced by terror was nourished in the early days by a mood very like angst, but not quite, because this possibility was real. The object of this mood was miasmic, lurking in the mail, the water, the food, the air. The very ground was suspended in possibility. The mighty bridges, the highways and tunnels, the mountainous buildings—all the landmarks, as they are so aptly called, these orienting monuments that were once as settled as north and south or up and down; their necessity was drained away. Once apparent only to artists and metaphysicians, the contingency of all things became apparent to everyone. It was as if the world were saturated with some new color, some spiritual hue, visible only to the eye of the mind in this mood.

But what about the much remarked kindness and coming-togetherness that people noticed in the early days and weeks? We do not associate surreality with that atmosphere. Surreality belongs to an isolated and alienated consciousness. What about that sense of heightened trust and easy sociality between strangers, across divides of class and race, surely that was the antithesis of surreality?

Well, yes and no. In the very first days, the first week, say, that sociality was only to be found where there was a focus. It arose where people came together to feed the rescue workers, to sign the book at a firehouse, to bear witness in the candlelight. The atmosphere in the streets in general was very different, very strange; it *was* isolating and alienating. The cops and firefighters were everywhere, and all the other workers and vehicles, decked out in their functional gear. We were not yet used to them, so many of them, and they were just that much more intent than usual, marked by a special gravity to which we were not entitled. The nuances in the manner of their office, denoting significance in this hour of confusion, served to underscore our irrelevance. They were as rocks in the stream, stabilized by purpose. We were the water, aimless around them.

And there was a corresponding array of subtle changes in our bearing too, in those very early days. People with nothing to contribute found their basic habits slightly skewed, hard to pinpoint exactly how, impossible to list the ways—but, taken together, enough to transfigure the classic New York scene, the scene of crowds in motion, eddying through the streets and stations. Some people walked a bit more briskly, as if to convince themselves that they still had business that mattered. Others seemed to drift, like boats making leeway, navigating across sidewalks they no longer quite recognized. Everyone's rhythms were a hair off; people yielding passage to the next person a shade more readily, eyes searching other eyes without meaning to, then glancing away too quickly, as if to make up for the intrusion. Every once in a while, not all the time, but often enough, an utterly stricken or deranged face swam into view, then fell away, swept along with the current of the crowd. Most disconcerting of all, so many faces in which sympathy or zeal or shock was exaggerated, dramatized, so inflected by self-consciousness that you knew you wouldn't want to hear this person's story, that it wouldn't ring true, even if it was.

That was the atmosphere in the very beginning. The mood of enhanced solidarity emerged from it, almost by way of response to that aimless strangeness, the discordances of a multifarious habituality that wasn't quite holding up. People began to reach out, as they say, to repair the fabric of the automatic with threads of conscious consideration.

That's when you heard the old bromide about how people naturally come together in a crisis. This vague gesture in the direction of nature, presumably invoking a genetic basis for the response, actually functions as a distancing mechanism for people who fasten on to it. It reassures them of their independence and agency, even as they take comfort in the syndrome. The explanation packages the experience. But of course the lived reality of this mysterious union of strangers is entirely beyond our ken. It comes over us not out of us. We are not its agents, but its patients, as Durkheim noticed long ago.

It is something like the way people unite in song or laughter. But not so focused, not so directed. There was no identifiable single thing—the song, the joke—that brought people together in this case. And the reason is obvious, as just described. The generality of the possibility of terror was matched by a generality of response, by a mood of generalized care for all the things and people in our world, now residing together in suspense. Hence the diffuse and improvisational, almost holiday-spirit quality to the extra courtesies we extended, the banter across the deli counter that went on a little longer than before, the door held open more patiently, the comfort of a chat with an accidental neighbor at the bus stop.

And the official atmosphere, the effect of the performances of those others, the famous ones in government and media? They contributed their dollop to the mood in the beginning, by way of inadequacies they could not hide, moments when they verged on hysteria, others in which they seemed bent on self-parody. For once, mirabilu dictu, they were working against virtualization, though quite unwittingly. They helped to sustain the suspension of our world in existential possibility by saying the only thing that could truly be said in the first few weeks and months, namely, "Go back to normal, but be alert, because death could strike at any moment."

People anxious to believe in a semblance of normality got very annoyed at the authorities for saying this. After all, they had come to rely upon them for every sort of assistance in creating and sustaining façades and rationalizations, for stories that help them feel good about themselves. Suddenly (for self-interested reasons, but never mind), these same authorities were communicating a profound truth. No wonder complaints followed, in which the whine of inconvenienced privilege was unmistakable, for people were much discomfited by this unseemly transgression of a social compact that had always aimed at the *summa bonum* of their own comfort level. People protested, "What's the point of telling us that; it's impossible! You can't go back to normal and be alert for terrorists at the same time!" And so those in charge, abandoning the profundity they had touched upon, took up the stern-but-loving parent role, one of their favorites, and proceeded to lecture us about "A different world now . . . Londoners during the Blitz . . . strike a balance . . ."

And so on. And on and on, and that's what will do it in the end, if it can be done at all, that's what will grind it all down to a simulation of emergency, the on-and-on part. How, for example—if you were in the USA—did you feel when the Department of Homeland Security raised the threat level to "Orange Alert" (almost Red!) during the Christmas season in 2003? Were you cringing, afraid you would see carnage every time you turned on the TV? Or were you one of those who barely noticed?

There was a range of reactions, a range of possibilities even. Optionality was approached, if not achieved.

For as long as nothing major happens on American soil, the cumulative effect of coverage will be to diminish the surreality—diminish, muffle, but not completely exorcise, not for a long time, maybe not ever. The moods of particular individuals will vary, of course—but, on the whole, the virtualizing effect of coverage will work as a natural antidote to the surrealizing effect of the possibility of terror, but, for as long as that possibility is real, it will not entirely succeed.

Always just beyond the reach of what can be shown or said, the possibility of terror, the haunting effect that now surrounds, for example, the Christmas tree in Rockefeller Center—that effect eludes virtualization, which is also a haunting, though of a very different kind, the kind that turns Mt. Everest into "Mt. Everest," remember? Like surreality, virtuality is a hue that's visible only to the eye of the mind, but in another mood. And these two hues are like Platonic opposites, like heat and cold. Where the one enters, the other recedes. To the extent that Rockefeller Center is haunted by the surrealizing possibility of terror, it won't feel like a theme park mock-up of Rockefeller Center, a simulation of itself, which was the way it had come to feel in recent decades.

But what will have happened by the time you read these words— some horror? Maybe tens of thousands of people retching, con- vulsing, dying like roaches in the subways of New York or London, maybe half of Los Angeles flattened, the other half radioactive, hundreds of thousands of people seared to the bone, incinerated, burnt meat.

Or maybe nothing.

I hope nothing.

But if a major WMD event has happened, by the time you read this, what will life be like, what will have become of us? What will the USA and Britain and Europe be doing in foreign lands, by way of retaliation and defense? What will become of Iraq? North Korea and Iran?

A book like this one—one that aims to "zap the zeitgeist," as one prospective editor described it—has somehow to reckon with the possibilities, all of them, including the possibility of nothing happening at all, or of just a suicide bomber now and then, in a theater or a mall, or of bigger things, truck-bombed hotels, but overseas, in Asian places where, you know, it's gotten to seem almost like par for the course.

From here, I mean.

There is no limit, no definition, you see, to this range of possibilities, and no reliable way to calibrate likelihoods—because any one of them becomes inevitable as soon as it has happened. All I can do is conjure up examples and ask them to stand for all the possibilities. But the possibility itself can't be represented, even though you can definitely feel it, oh yes, you can feel it as surely as you can feel the nose on your face. It's real.

The possibility is real.

The same is true of more prosaic fatalities, of course. You might get run over, you might get mugged, you might choke on your own vomit and die in the night. Most people manage to ignore these possibilities, most of the time. Others are inclined to obsess—but, either way, they accompany us through our lives. The possibility of death, at any moment, is the anticipation of a convergence of the particular accidents and necessities that will—inevitably, and in exactly *this* way—be your death someday. You can imagine scenarios, if you want to, but the state of being dead—like pure possibility—cannot be represented.

Your end is real. It is always there.

The *possibility* of your end is always here.

Neither can be represented.

But the possibility of mass terror doesn't just haunt *you*. People who try to cope by reducing it to a personal when-your-number's-up fatalism can't even convince themselves; you can see it in their eyes, during the interview, explaining why they aren't changing their travel plans, the callow bravado to which they cling, like children determined to have fun with their toys in spite of the hate they can hear in their parents' voices from behind the bedroom door. The possibility of mass terror haunts the world. It's a different order of reality. And, no matter how exhaustively the agents of mediation cover terror, they cannot "cover" its possibility. They can represent what happened after it happens, they can represent what might happen in this or that case—that is, they can depict specific possibilities endlessly—but they can't depict the sheer possibility they nevertheless evoke.

They can't represent that reality. It is beyond mediation.

Some people try to convince themselves that, okay, there is a special intensity about the possibility of mass terror that you don't get from the possibility of everyday accident and death. But you can still "learn to live with it," they say—look how people in certain places live with the possibility, even the inevitability, of huge earthquakes?

Nice try.

Nobody *aims* earthquakes.

The haunting that is the possibility of terror is also a hunting.

The *New York Times* ran a piece recently—December 28, 2003—that was pretty typical. The first paragraph purported, rhetorically, to express relief over Libya's sudden decision to dismantle its WMD programs with full transparency for U.N. inspectors—and, surely, this was cause for celebration? But the second paragraph relayed some speculation from within the "intelligence community" (don't you love that one?). Why would Qadaffi suddenly do that, wondered an anonymous expert source—maybe it's because he *knows* that al-Qaeda already has a nuclear device and a definite plan to use it soon, and he wants to be fully in the clear afterwards, when the United States gets around to punishing rogue states.

Makes sense.

Almost anything you can think of makes sense these days. That's part of the unrepresentable mood that eludes mediation at the dawn of the age of terror.

But they can try anyway, and they will, and, for as long as nothing else happens, they will come close enough to satisfy most of us—accustomed as we are to semblances. A New America is on the drawing boards for the twenty-first century. Various versions are being designed and promoted, and the great assembly of flattered selves is shopping again, shopping for a representation of the world that will distract us most convincingly from the reality of unrepresentable possibility. As the chosen versions, whatever they turn out to be, take hold of the way everything gets represented, and therefore, eventually, of the way everything gets constituted, the surreal atmosphere will dissipate and virtuality will fuse with reality again, to create a good-enough semblance of normality. Masses of people who found themselves and their world projected into the existential nothing after 9/11, will find relief from that state of suspense, and great industries will be devoted to providing it, and profiting from that provision. That state is one in which world-transforming questions can be raised, but it is the very opposite of comfortable. It is the state that existentialists and surrealists once prescribed for the sensibility of an avant-garde adjusting to mechanized madness and slaughter in the early twentieth century. We saw that sensibility democratized, for a while, at the beginning of the twenty first. But it will not last, for it is vulnerable to unbearable truths. The bubble of self-regarding self-representation that has insulated us for so long from the suffering of millions in a world dominated by our interests and institutions—that bubble will reform around us, and cradle us again.

Until the next time.

Digby, Nova Scotia
August 2004

A NOTE ON THE AUTHOR

Thomas de Zengotita is a contributing editor at
Harper's Magazine and holds a Ph.D. in anthropology
from Columbia University. He teaches at the
Dalton School and at the Draper Graduate Program
at New York University.

A NOTE ON THE TYPE

This old-style face is named after the Frenchman
Robert Granjon, a sixteenth-century letter cutter
whose italic types have often been used with the
romans of Claude Garamond. The origins of this face,
like those of Garamond, lie in the late-fifteenth-
century types used by Aldus Manutius in Italy.